AF905039

Competition Law in China

Competition Law in China

Third Edition

Xiaoye Wang
Jessica Su
Wei Han

This book was originally published as a monograph in the International Encyclopaedia of Laws/Competition Law.

Founding Editor: Roger Blanpain
General Editor: Frank Hendrickx
Volume Editors: Francesco Denozza & Alberto Toffoletto

Wolters Kluwer

Published by:
Kluwer Law International B.V.
PO Box 316
2400 AH Alphen aan den Rijn
The Netherlands
E-mail: international-sales@wolterskluwer.com
Website: lrus.wolterskluwer.com

Sold and distributed in North, Central and South America by:
Wolters Kluwer Legal & Regulatory U.S.
7201 McKinney Circle
Frederick, MD 21704
United States of America
Email: customer.service@wolterskluwer.com

Sold and distributed in all other countries by:
Air Business Subscriptions
Rockwood House
Haywards Heath
West Sussex
RH16 3DH
United Kingdom
Email: international-customerservice@wolterskluwer.com

Printed on acid-free paper

ISBN 978-90-411-9590-6

e-Book: ISBN 978-90-411-9591-3
web-PDF: ISBN 978-90-411-9593-7

Printed in the United Kingdom.

The Authors

Xiaoye Wang is a Distinguished Professor of Law at Hunan University, China and a Professor of Law at the Chinese Academy of Social Sciences, China. Professor Wang works in the areas of economic law, international economic law, and focuses on competition law. She holds an LLM from Renmin University, China and a Doctor Juris from the University of Hamburg, Germany. She is the author and the editor of 20 books and over 300 articles published in Chinese, German, and English including ‘Monopole und Wettbewerb in der chinesischen Wirtschaft’(J.C.B. Mohr1993) and (The Evolution of China’s Antimonopoly Law) (Edward Elgar 2014). As the leading expert in the field of competition law in China, she was advisor of the Drafting Committee of China’s Anti-Monopoly Law under the State Council and the National People’s Congress, and the Head of the Consultant Committee for WTO Trade and Competition Policy of the Ministry of Commerce and lectured twice in the Standing Committee of National People’s Congress. She serves now as Vice President of National Economic Law Research Association of China, and consultant expert for the Anti-Monopoly Commission under the State Council of the People’s Republic of China.
In international academic activities, Professor Wang is a founding member of the Academic Society for Competition Law (ASCOLA) and the Asia Competition Forum (ACF), and member of the International Advisory Board of CUTS C-CIER and American Antitrust Institute (AAI). During 2005 and 2006, she spent one year at Chicago-Kent College of Law, USA as Fulbright Scholar. She has lectured on Chinese competition law at American Bar Association, International Bar Association, Inter-Pacific Bar Association, ACF, Harvard University, Columbia University, Washington University (St. Louis), New York University, Korea Fair Trade Commission, Chatham House, International League of Competition Law, Max-Planck Institutes, and many other institutions.

The Authors

Dr Jessica Su is an Associate Professor at the Institute of American Studies (USA), Chinese Academy of Social Sciences (China) (CASS). Dr Su's research focuses on comparative competition policy and governance, and investment and trade policy. She provides consulting services to regulators and the businesses and is a research consultant to Professor Allan Fels AO, the Australia and New Zealand School of Government. She has worked with Professor Xiaoye Wang and Professor Allan Fels to edit the *China Competition Bulletin*, which reports the latest developments of competition and regulatory policy in China. Prior to her current positions, Dr Su was a postdoctoral fellow at the Institute of Law, CASS, China from 2010 to 2013, a consultant at the law firm Freshfields Bruckhaus Deringer LLP in Beijing from 2007 to 2010 and a consultant at the Competition Division of the Organisation for Economic Co-operation and Development (OECD) in Paris in 2007.
Dr Su has worked on a variety of projects including cross-border mergers and acquisitions, cartel investigations and litigation, distribution practices, abuse of dominance, and the interface between antitrust and intellectual property matters. She has been involved in the drafting of the implementing regulations and capacity building projects of China's Anti-Monopoly Law and enforcement. Dr Su holds an LLB from Zhengzhou University, China, an LLM with distinction from University College Dublin, Ireland, and a PhD in law from Queen Mary, University of London, London. She was admitted to practice law in the People's Republic of China in 1999.

The Authors

Dr Wei Han is a Lecturer, University of Chinese Academy of Social Sciences, China. In the past few years, he has published one monograph on merger remedies (Study of Merger Remedies, China Law Press, 2013), four books as editor-in-chief (Competition Policy of OECD, New Antitrust Rules of US and EU, Competition Policy of WIPO, and Competition Policy in Digital Market, all by China Law Press), and more than fifty papers related to various competition law issues. He is also the chief expert of some competition law research programs funded by Chinese national foundations. Dr Han worked temporarily as an expert in the antimonopoly bureaus of the National Development and Reform Commission (NDRC), the Ministry of Commerce (MOFCOM), and the Sate Administration for Industry and Commerce (SAIC), where he participated in important legislations and policy research projects, in particular the MOFCOM regulation on merger remedies and the SAIC IPR Regulation.

Dr Han received his Bachelor of Law and Master of Law degrees from Southwest University of Political Science and Law, China and his PhD degree from the Graduate School of Chinese Academy of Social Sciences, China. Dr Han was a postdoctoral fellow of the University of Chinese Academy of Sciences, China.

Table of Contents

Table of Contents

List of Abbreviations

AAI	American Antitrust Institute
ACCC	Australian Competition and Consumer Commission
ACF	Asian Competition Forum
AIC	Administration for Industry and Commerce
AMC	Anti-Monopoly Commission, PRC
AMEA	Anti-Monopoly Enforcement Agency, PRC
ASCOLA	Academic Society for Competition Law
CASS	Chinese Academy of Social Sciences
CBRC	China Banking Regulatory Commission
CIRC	China Insurance Regulatory Commission
CNY	Yuan Renminbi (Chinese currency)
CPC	Communist Party of China
CSRC	China Securities Regulatory Commission
EU	European Union
GDP	Gross Domestic Product
HHI	Herfindhal-Hirschman Index
ICN	International Competition Network
IPR	Intellectual Property Right
MIIT	Ministry of Industry and Information Technology, PRC
MOFCOM	Ministry of Commerce, PRC
MOFTEC	Ministry of Foreign Trade and Economic Cooperation, PRC
NDRC	National Development and Reform Commission, PRC
NPC	National People's Congress, PRC
OECD	Organisation for Economic Co-operation and Development
PBC	People's Bank of China
RPM	Resale Price Maintenance
PRC	People's Republic of China
SAFE	State Administration of Foreign Exchange, PRC
SAIC	State Administration for Industry and Commerce, PRC

SASAC	State-Owned Assets Supervision and Administration Commission, PRC
SAT	State Administration of Taxation, PRC
SERC	State Electricity Regulatory Commission, PRC
SETC	State Economy and Trade Commission, PRC
SIPO	State Intellectual Property Office, PRC
SOE	State-Owned enterprise
SSNIP	Small but Significant and Non-transitory Increase in Price
WTO	World Trade Organization

List of References of Legislative Documents of China

Laws

Administrative Litigation Law	Administrative Litigation Law 1989
Administrative Penalty Law	Administrative Penalty Law 1996 (amended 2009)
Administrative Reconsideration Law	Administrative Reconsideration Law 1999 (amended 2009)
AML	Anti-Monopoly Law 2007
AUCL	Anti-Unfair Competition Law 1993
Bidding Law	Law on Bid Invitation and Bidding 1999
Civil Law Principles	General Principles of Civil Law 1986
Civil Procedure Law	Civil Procedure Law 1991 (amended 2007 and 2012)
Commercial Banking Law	Commercial Banking Law 1995 (amended 2003)
Constitution	Constitution 1982 (amended 1988, 1983, 1999, and 2004)
Contract Law	Contract Law 1999
Copyright Law	Copyright Law 1990 (amended 2001 and 2010)
Criminal Law	Criminal Law 1997 (amended 1999, 2001, 2002, 2005, 2006, 2009, and 2011)
Criminal Procedure Law	Criminal Procedure Law 1979 (amended 1996 and 2012)
Foreign Trade Law	Foreign Trade Law 1994 (amended 2004)
Insurance Law	Insurance Law 1995 (amended 2002 and 2009)
Legislation Law	Legislation Law 2000
Patent Law	Patent Law 1984 (amended 1992, 2000 and 2008)
Postal Law	Postal Law 1986 (amended 2009 and 2012)
Price Law	Price Law 1997

List of References of Legislative Documents of China

Trademark Law	Trademark Law 1982 (amended 1993, 2001, and 2013)

Secondary Legislation (Regulations, Measures, Guidelines, etc.) and Judicial Interpretations

AML Judicial Interpretations	Provisions on Several Issues Concerning the Application of Law in the Trail of Civil Dispute Cases Arising from Monopoly Conduct 2012
Circular on National Security Review	Circular on Establishing a Mechanism of Security Review of Mergers and Acquisitions of Domestic Enterprises by Foreign Investors 2011
Divestiture Measures	Interim Measures on Implementing Assets or Business Divestitures by Concentrations of Undertakings 2010
Draft Intellectual Property Guidelines	Guidelines on Anti-Monopoly Enforcement in Relation to Intellectual Property Rights (the 5th draft)
Draft Measures on Simple Merger Cases	Interim Measures on the Applicable Standards in Simple Cases of Concentrations of Undertakings (Consultation Draft)
Draft Measures on the Definition of Undertakings	Measures on the Definition of Undertakings Participating in Concentrations (2010 draft)
Draft Measures on Non-notifiable Concentrations	Interim Measures on Evidence Collection for Concentrations of Undertakings that Do Not Meet the Notification Thresholds but Are Suspected of Monopoly (2009 draft)
Draft Merger Remedy Measures	Measures on Restrictive Conditions Imposed on Concentrations of Undertakings (Consultation Draft)
Franchising Measures	Administrative Measures on Commercial Franchising 2004
Franchising Regulations	Regulations on the Administration of Commercial Franchising 2007
Information Requirement Guidance	Guidance for Notification Documents and Materials for Concentrations of Undertakings 2009

List of References of Legislative Documents of China

Interim M&A Rules	Interim Provisions on Mergers and Acquisitions of Domestic Enterprise by Foreign Investors 2003
Interim Provisions on Price Monopoly	Interim Provisions on the Prohibition of Monopolistic Pricing Behaviour 2003 (repealed 2011)
IPR Regulation	Provisions on the Prohibition of the Abuse of Intellectual Property Rights to Exclude or Restrict Competition 2015
Judicial Interpretations on Technology Contracts	Supreme People's Court Interpretations on Certain Issues on the Application of Law for the Trial of Disputes on Technology Contracts 2004
M&A Rules	Provisions on Mergers and Acquisitions of Domestic Enterprises by Foreign Investors 2006 (amended 2009)
Market Definition Guidelines	Guidelines on the Definition of the Relevant Market 2009
Measures on the Prohibition of Abuse of Dominance	Measures on the Prohibition of Abuse of Dominant Market Position 2011
Measures on the Prohibition of Monopoly Agreements	Measures on the Prohibition of Monopoly Agreements 2011
Measures on the Prohibition of Price Monopoly	Measures on the Prohibition of Price Monopoly 2011
Merger Assessment Measures	Interim Measures on the Assessment of Competitive Effects of Concentrations of Undertakings 2011
Notification Measures	Measures on the Notification of Concentrations of Undertakings 2009
Notification Thresholds Rules	Rules on Notification Thresholds for Concentrations of Undertakings 2008
Procedural Measures on Monopoly Agreements and Abuse of Dominance Cases	Measures on Procedures for Investigating and Handling Cases of Monopoly Agreements and Abuse of Market Dominance 2009
Procedural Measures on Price Monopoly Cases	Measures on the Administrative Enforcement Procedures of the Prohibition of Price Monopoly 2011
Provisions on Regional Blockades	Provisions on the Prohibition of Regional Blockades in Market Economy Activities 2001
Provisional Regulation on Simple Cases	Provisional Regulation on the Standards Applicable to Simple Cases of Concentrations between Business Operators 2014

List of References of Legislative Documents of China

Retailers and Suppliers Measures	Administrative Measures on Fair Trading between Retailers and Suppliers 2006
Review Measures	Measures on the Review of Concentrations of Undertakings 2009
Rules on Failure to Notify Mergers	Interim Measures on the Investigation and Handling of Concentrations of Undertakings That Failed to Notify in Accordance with Laws 2011
Regulation on Merger Remedies	Regulation on the Imposition of Restrictive Conditions on Concentrations between Business Operators (for Trial Implementation) 2014
Technology Import and Export Regulations	Regulations on the Administration of Technology Import and Export 2001
Telecom Regulations	Telecommunications Regulations 2000
Turnover Calculation Measures for Financial Institutions	Measures on the Calculation of Turnover for Concentrations of Financial Institutions 2009

General Introduction

1. This book aims to provide an outline of competition law in the People's Republic of China (PRC) and is intended for readers who are generally familiar with basic competition law concepts, norms, and methodology.[1] The book focuses on China's *Anti-Monopoly Law 2007* (AML) and refers to the related laws and regulations wherever necessary.[2] It reviews and analyses China's competition law rules on restrictive agreements, abuse of dominance, merger control, and administrative monopoly, but does not cover unfair trading practices.[3]

2. The remaining paragraphs of this chapter aim to provide the readers with an overview of the background context of China and the competition law developments in China.

§1. General Background of the Country

3. China has a long and rich written history dating back to the Xia Dynasty (2100–1600 BC). In 221 BC, Emperor Qin Shi Huang created an imperial bureaucracy that constituted the basic institutional framework of a centralised political system. Feudalist China established an authoritarian governance tradition, supported by the bureaucratic elite and rationalised by the Confucian philosophy of harmony, loyalty, benevolence, and piety. For centuries China stood as one of the most advanced societies,

1. The Law is stated as at 30 Sep. 2013. The laws and regulations of the People's Republic of China (PRC) cited in this book are authentic in Chinese. Sources of English translation are provided for reference only. All websites cited in this book were last visited on 30 Jul. 2017.
2. For the purpose of this book only and unless otherwise indicated, 'China' refers to the mainland of the PRC, excluding the Hong Kong Special Administrative Region, the Macao Special Administrative Region and the Taiwan region. The AML was promulgated by the Standing Committee of the National People's Congress (NPC) on 30 Aug. 2007 and effective on 1 Aug. 2008, English translation available at www.npc.gov.cn/englishnpc/Law/2009-02/20/content_1471587.htm. Another source of unofficial English translation is available as an appendix to Nathan Bush, 'The PRC Antimonopoly Law: Unanswered Questions and Challenges Ahead', *Antitrust Source* (October 2007), available at http://apps.americanbar.org/antitrust/at-committees/at-ic/pdf/spring/08/03-26-08-Bush.pdf.
3. In China, unfair trading practices (including passing off, commercial bribery, misleading advertising, commercial secret infringement, illegal prize-attached sales, and defamation) are prohibited by the *Anti-Unfair Competition Law 1993* (AUCL); *see* AUCL, Arts 5, 8–10, 13–14, 20–22, and 24–26. In addition to unfair trading practices, the AUCL also prohibits certain types of anticompetitive behaviour and is deemed as another major pillar of China's competition law system; *see* para. 19 below for more information of the AUCL. The AUCL was promulgated by the Standing Committee of the NPC on 2 Sep. 1993 and effective on 1 Dec. 1993, English translation available at www.npc.gov.cn/englishnpc/Law/2007-12/12/content_1383803.htm.

economies, and civilisations in the world but the country was beset by internal weakness, civil war, and foreign occupation during the nineteenth and the early twentieth centuries. Feudalist China lasted over 2,000 years until the collapse of the Qing Dynasty and the subsequent establishment of the Republic of China in 1911. Founded in 1949, the PRC covers an area of 9.6 million square kilometres and, in 2010, had a population of 1.3 billion, and that figure is expected to reach 1.42 billion by the end of 2020.[4]

4. The Communist Party of China (CPC). Founded in 1921, the CPC is China's ruling party and the leading political power.[5] At the end of 2011, the CPC had a membership of approximately 82.6 million.[6] Ranging from the legislature, the executive, and the judiciary to the military, many important positions are held by CPC members. The CPC Central Committee holds the final decision-making power of the party and has substantial influence over China's legislative, executive, and judicial processes. There are eight registered democratic parties in China. Multiparty cooperation and political consultation under the leadership of the CPC is a basic political system in China.[7]

5. The central and local government. The State Council is China's highest executive organ and is composed of a premier, the vice premiers, the State councillors, the ministers in charge of ministries and commissions, an auditor-general, and a secretary general. The work of the State Council is presided over by executive meetings composed of the premier, the vice premiers, the State councillors, and the secretary general. At the provincial level, China consists of four centrally administered municipalities, twenty-three provinces (including Taiwan), five autonomous regions, and two special administrative regions.[8]

---

4. National Health and Family Planning Commission of the PRC, http://www.renkou.org.cn/china/beijing/2017/6157.html; For official information of China, including background, politics, economy, and finance and banking, *see* 'China Factfile' published by China's central government at http://english. gov. cn/about. htm; for a general introduction of China, *see* Central Intelligence Agency (CIA), *World Factbook: China*, www.cia.gov/library/publications/the-world-factbook; for further reading on China's history, *see* Ray Huang, *China: A Macro History* (New York: M. E. Sharpe, 1990).
5. China's Constitution is based on the 'Four Fundamental Principles', one of which is the CPC's leadership. The 'Four Foundational Principles' refer to 'the socialist road, the people's democratic dictatorship, the leadership of the CCP, and the Marxism-Leninism and Mao Zedong Thought'; *see Constitution 1982* (amended in 1988, 1993, 1999, and 2004) (hereinafter 'Constitution'), Preamble, para. 7; The Constitution was promulgated by the NPC on 4 Dec. 1982, effective on the same day, and amended in 1988, 1993, 1999, and 2004, English translation available at http://english. gov. cn/2005-08/05/content_20813. htm.
6. Communist Party of China News, *Communist Party of China Memoir 2012* (in Chinese), http://cpc.people.com.cn/n/2012/1031/c64164-19454317.html.
7. Constitution, Preamble, para. 9.
8. For more information about China's State Council and local governments, *see* http://english. gov. cn/2008-03/16/content_921792. htm and http://english. gov. cn/2007-10/29/content_30395. htm.

§2. The Economic System

6. A command economy based on the Soviet pattern prevailed in China from 1949–1978.[9] During those three decades, virtually every industry was planned and output proportioned. The scope of the tight control was extended to every aspect of daily life, including food, clothing, shelter, transportation, and health care. Since the late 1970s, China has been in transition from a centrally planned economy to a more market-oriented economy. Economic reform has accelerated since 1992 following the Fourteenth National Congress of the CPC. In 1993, the Second Amendment to the *Constitution 1982* (hereinafter 'Constitution') declared that 'the State implements socialist market economy'.[10]

7. The concept of socialist market economy. It was Deng Xiaoping who devised the concept of 'socialist market economy' and brought the idea of 'socialism with Chinese characteristics' into China.[11] When answering the question of whether there is a latent contradiction between a market economy and the socialist system, Deng stated that:

> There is no fundamental contradiction between socialism and a market economy. The problem is how to develop the productive forces more effectively. We used to have a planned economy, but our experience over the years has proved that having a totally planned economy hampers the development of the productive forces. If we combine a planned economy with a market economy, we shall be in a better position to liberate the productive forces and speed up economic growth.[12]

8. In a speech delivered during his famous 'southern tour' in 1992, Deng noted that:

> We should be bolder than before in conducting reform and opening to the outside and have the courage to experiment...The proportion of planning to market forces is not the essential difference between socialism and capitalism. A planned economy is not equivalent to socialism, because there is planning under capitalism too; a market economy is not capitalism, because there are markets under socialism

9. For a detailed analysis of China's economic performance over the past centuries and an assessment of China's prospects for the next quarter century, *see* Angus Maddison, *Chinese Economic Performance in the Long Run, Revised and Updated: 960-2030 AD*(2nd ed., Paris: Organisation for Economic Co-operation and Development (OECD), 2007).
10. *See* Constitution, Art. 15.
11. For background information about Deng Xiaoping, *see* http://english. peopledaily. com. cn/ data/people/dengxiaoping. shtml.
12. *See* excerpts from an interview on 23 Oct. 1985 between Deng Xiaoping and a delegation consisting of senior journalists and entrepreneurs, organised by the Time Inc., available at www. china.org.cn/english/features/dengxiaoping/103358.htm.

too. Planning and market forces are both means of controlling economic activity... We shall push ahead along the road to Chinese-style socialism.[13]

9. State ownership remains significant in China. However, through pursuing pragmatic reforms, opening up the market, recognising private wealth, and allowing competition under the socialist political structure, China has become one of the world's most promising emerging economies. Between 1978 and 2008, China achieved an average annual growth rate of Gross Domestic Product (GDP) of approximately 10%.[14] China has demonstrated its capacity to weather the global financial crisis better than many other countries and its GDP rose by 8.7% in 2009, which was beyond the target set by the Chinese government.[15] Measured on a purchasing power parity basis that adjusts for price differences, China replaced Japan in 2009 to be the second-largest economy in the world. Although China's per capita GDP in 2009 stood at USD 3,687 a year, ranking 103rd worldwide, living standards have improved significantly for most Chinese citizens.[16] The estimated growth in total real household consumption has been among the most rapid worldwide, at 9.6% annually from 2004–2008.[17] Although China was faced with downward economic pressure in 2016, the GDP had increased by 6.7% compared to 2015.[18] This economic growth also facilitates the development of a civil society in which individuals have more opportunities to pursue personal choices.

10. Although China has a vigorous growth record, this remarkable economic progress has been made against a backdrop of limited political reforms. The robust performance of the Chinese economy has surprised observers and many are watching carefully to see if China can stay on the fast-growth track. A number of salient policy problems challenge China's economic system and sustainable development.[19] Among other things, China is making efforts to restore long-term growth following from the global economic crisis, restructure the economy away from heavily relying on exports, reduce the high national saving rate, foster higher domestic consumption, resolve regional and urban-rural imbalances, and build a resource-efficient and eco-friendly

13. Deng Xiaoping, *Excerpts from Talks Given in Wuchang, Shenzhen, Zhuhai and Shanghai (18 Jan.–21 Feb. 1992)*, in *Selected Works of Deng Xiaoping*, vol. 3, 360, 361 & 370 (1982–1992) (Beijing: Foreign Languages Press, 1994).

14. World Bank, *Data: GDP Growth*, http://data. worldbank. org/indicator/NY. GDP. MKTP. KD. ZG.

15. Xinhua News Agency, *Facts and Figures: key Indicators of China's Economic Performance in 2009 and Previous Years*, http://news.xinhuanet. com/english2010/database/2010-01/21/c_13145387. htm, 21 Jan. 2010.

16. Xinhua News Agency, *China's Developing-Country Identity Remains Unchanged*, http://news. xinhuanet. com/english2010/indepth/2010-08/13/c_13443881. htm, 13 Aug. 2010; CIA, *World Factbook: China*, https://www.cia.gov/library/publications/the-world-factbook/index.html.

17. OECD, *China in the 2010s: Rebalancing Growth and Strengthening Social Safety Net*, www. oecd.org/dataoecd/4/21/44878634.pdf, 9.

18. . Financial Times, http://www.ftchinese.com/story/001071081.

19. OECD, *China in the 2010s*, 1 and 3; Angus Maddison, *Chinese Economic Performance*, 20–22.

society.[20] It is noted that, going forward, 'the centre of gravity of the global economy is on course to continue to shift towards China'.[21]

§3. The Legal System

11. The traditional Chinese concept of law was very different from that which is familiar to most in the modern world. Manifested mainly as criminal rules, Chinese law until the 1890s was primarily a tool for dominance and its principal purpose was to deter potential wrongdoing. Relationships based on family and social classes were at the core of civil society, corresponding with Confucian doctrines, which consider that family and social status were the essential themes of ethical codes and the backbone of the social order; as a result, social norms based on morality governed Chinese society. The law was not perceived to protect individual rights but was deemed as an instrument of last resort. The modernisation of China's legal system started in the final two decades of the Qing Dynasty between 1890 and 1911. Through drawing inspiration from the civil law system and borrowing from westernised Japanese law, continental European law and later from Soviet law, the modern Chinese legal system has witnessed a radical disconnection with the past.[22]

12. After an initial attempt to establish a new socialist legal order in the early to mid-1950s, China's legal system was paralysed during two decades of legal nihilism beginning in 1957 with the Anti-Rightist Movement and ending in 1976 with the end of the Cultural Revolution. Chinese lawmaking resumed in the late 1970s with the enactment of the Constitution in 1978 and a small number of generally worded statutes. By 2010, after three decades of legal construction, lawmaking, and institution building in China have reached impressive levels.

13. The legislature.[23] The National People's Congress (NPC) is China's highest legislative body that has the authority to, among other matters, appoint and remove leaders of State organs at the central level, decide national development plans and State budgets, and interpret and supervise the implementation of Chinese constitutional law.[24] The NPC has a large number of delegates and meets once per year to exercise its power.[25] The NPC elects a Standing Committee to act on its behalf when it is not in session. Because of its smaller size, the NPC Standing Committee is able to hold regular meetings every two months.[26] Pursuant to the *Legislation Law 2000* (hereinafter 'Legislation Law'), the legislative procedure of national laws involves four stages, namely, the submission of bills, deliberation (reading), voting, and approval and

20. Official information on China's economic system and development strategies is available at http://english. gov. cn/about/economy. htm.
21. OECD, *China in the 2010s*, 3.
22. For a brief historical review of China's legal system, *see* Wang Kui Hua, *Chinese Commercial Law*, 1–49 (South Melbourne: Oxford University Press, 2000).
23. Official information on China's legislature is available at www.china.org.cn/english/features/legislative/75857.htm.
24. Official information on China's NPC is available at www.npc.gov.cn.
25. For example, the Eleventh NPC has 2,987 delegates in total.
26. The NPC Standing Committee has approximately 150 members.

promulgation. Legislative procedure for administrative regulations, ministerial rules, and local regulations and rules are varied.[27]

14. Since the late 1970s, the role of the NPC in making laws, supervising law enforcement and the work of administrative organs, and making decisions about State affairs have all been strengthened. As at March 2008, the number of effective laws promulgated by the NPC and its Standing Committee reached 229, the number of administrative regulations promulgated by the State Council reached 600, and the number of local regulations issued by local people's congresses and local governments reached 7,000.[28]

15. On 10 March 2011, Mr Wu Bangguo, the Chairman of the Standing Committee of the NPC, in his delivery of a work report of the Standing Committee of the Eleventh NPC at a plenary meeting of the NPC's annual session, stated that a socialist system of laws with Chinese characteristics has been established 'on schedule' in China. According to Wu, China now has a complete set of types of laws covering all areas of social relations, with basic and major laws of each type already in place, together with comprehensive corresponding administrative regulations and local statutes. The goal of establishing a socialist system of laws with Chinese characteristics by 2010 was set at the Fifteenth National Congress of the CPC in 1997.[29]

16. The judiciary.[30] China's court system is divided into four levels: the basic people's court (at the district level or county level), the intermediate people's court (at the prefecture level or at capital cities of provinces), the higher people's court (at the provinces, autonomous regions, or centrally administered municipalities), and the Supreme People's Court (the highest court in China). Usually, a civil case is heard at two levels (the first-instance trial and the appellate trial), but if any party is dissatisfied with the appellate judgment, the party may apply to invoke a trial supervision procedure.[31] In addition, there are special courts, including military courts, maritime courts, and railway transportation courts. Echoing China government's emphasis on the rule of law in all respects, the Supreme People's Court (hereinafter referred to as 'SPC') has since 2014 started to establish pilot circuit courts, namely cross-jurisdictional People's Courts and the People's Procuratorates. On the one hand, People's Courts and People's Procuratorates being part of the local administrative system gives rise to concerns of 'judiciary localisation'. The introduction of circuit courts helps avoid or at least decrease the interference of so-called local protectionism, which is of assistance in optimising the allocation of judicial resources and achieving a separation of powers between judiciary and executive. On the other hand, circuit courts can be effective in providing adjudication guidance to local courts and directly hear difficult cases from the local

27. *See* Legislation Law, Arts 12–41. The Legislation Law was promulgated by the NPC on 15 Mar. 2000 and effective on 1 Jul. 2000, English translation available at www.gov.cn/english/laws/2005-08/20/content_29724.htm.

28. Li Lin, *China's Legislative Experience in the Past Three-Decade Reform and Opening Up* (in Chinese), http://news. xinhuanet. com/theory/2008-08/16/content_9371663. htm, 16 Aug. 2008.

29. Xinhua News Agency, *Socialist System of Laws Established in China*, www.china.org.cn/china/NPC_CPPCC_2011/2011-03/10/content_22099470.htm, 10 Mar. 2011.

30. Official information on China's judiciary is available at http://english. gov. cn/2005-08/29/content_27294. htm.

31. Further information on civil procedures in China's courts is available at paras 183–223 below.

level, which is helpful to promote justice and professionalism in the adjudication of those cases. By the end of 2016, the SPC has set up six circuit courts respectively at Shenzhen, Shenyang, Nanjing, Zhengzhou, Chongqing, and Xi'an (in chronological order), covering twenty-six provinces/municipalities/districts in China. As dispatch agencies of the SPC, circuit courts are conferred with judicial authority equivalent to that of the SPC, and, therefore, their judgments are regarded as made by the SPC and final as well.

17. During the first two decades of reforms, the CPC exercised direct control over personnel appointments to the court system and over important court decisions. The situation undermined the capacity of the judicial organs to carry out their functions properly. As a commentator noted, the Chinese judiciary 'suffers from shortcomings with respect to decisional independence, external independence, internal independence, collective independence, and personal independence'.[32] The situation has changed gradually, and the Chinese judicial system now plays an increasingly important role in law enforcement, has become more independent, and has been more open to the public and the media.[33]

§4. Historical Background of Antitrust Law

18. Chinese competition law was conceived in the 1980s, soon after China adopted its reform and opening-up policy.[34] Prior to the entry into force of the AML, China dealt with competition-related issues through a series of laws and regulations. The *Interim Provisions on Promoting and Protecting Socialist Competition 1980* was the first normative document to protect competition and regulate government monopolies in China.[35] The Interim Provisions stipulated that, 'in economic activities, with the exception of products exclusively managed by State-designated departments and organisations, monopolisation or exclusive dealing is not allowed'.[36]

19. The enactment of the *Anti-Unfair Competition Law 1993* (AUCL) was the first major step in establishing China's competition law system. The AUCL prohibits unfair trading practices and incorporates provisions that address certain types of restrictive behaviour, including designated transactions by public utilities and other

32. Randall Peerenboom, *China's Long March toward Rule of Law*, 298–316. (New York: Cambridge University Press, 2002).
33. Chris X. Lin, *A Quiet Revolution: An Overview of China's Judicial Reform*, 4 Asian-P. L. & Policy J. 293 et seq (2003).
34. For a comprehensive review of the AML, *see* Xiaoye Wang, *Highlights of China's New Anti-Monopoly Law*, 75 Antitrust L. J. 133–150 (2008) and *The New Chinese Anti-Monopoly Law: A Survey of a Work in Progress*, 54 The Antitrust Bull. 579–619 (2009); for further reading on competition law development in China, *see* Xiaoye Wang, *Issues Surrounding the Drafting of China's Anti-Monopoly Law*, 3 Wash. U. Global Stud. L. Rev. 285–296 (2004); Xiaoye Wang, *The Prospect of Antimonopoly Legislation in China*, 1 Wash. U. Global Stud. L. Rev. 201–231 (2002).
35. The Interim Provisions on Promoting and Protecting Socialist Competition were promulgated by the State Council on 17 Oct. 1980 and repealed on 6 Oct. 2001, official Chinese text available at the official Gazette of the State Council, No. 487.
36. *Ibid.*

statutory monopolists, administrative monopoly, below-cost sales, tying, and bid rigging.[37] The *Price Law 1997* (hereinafter 'Price Law') is principally a price control law enforced by the National Development and Reform Commission (NDRC) and the corresponding local price authorities. The Price Law also prohibits certain unfair pricing activities. These include collusion to control market price, selling products below-cost in order to eliminate competitors or monopolise the market, offering the same products or services at discriminatory prices, and seeking excessive profits.[38]

20. In 2003, a merger control regime was introduced as part of the *Interim Provisions on Mergers and Acquisitions of Domestic Enterprises by Foreign Investors* (hereinafter 'Interim M&A Rules').[39] The *Provisions on Mergers and Acquisitions of Domestic Enterprises by Foreign Investors 2006* (amended 2009) (hereinafter 'M&A Rules') were issued in 2006 and replaced the Interim M&A Rules.[40] Before the 2009 amendment, the M&A Rules provided a basic regulatory framework for mergers and acquisitions of domestic enterprises by foreign investors and included a chapter that contained four articles devoted to anti-monopoly review, under which the Ministry of Commerce (MOFCOM) and the State Administration for Industry and Commerce (SAIC) were jointly responsible for accepting, reviewing, and approving mergers and acquisitions.[41]

21. Nevertheless, the gradual and piecemeal competition-legislation regime resulted in fragmented and discriminatory provisions, ill-designed procedures and remedies, and insufficient enforcement power. For example, the AUCL prohibits designated transactions by public utilities or any other business operators occupying statutory monopoly status, but also prohibits below-cost sales and tying arrangements

37. *See* AUCL, Arts 6 and 23 regarding designated transactions by public utilities and other statutory monopolists; Arts 7 and 30 regarding administrative monopoly; Art. 11 regarding below-cost sales; Art. 12 regarding tying; and Arts 15 and 27 regarding bid rigging.

38. *See* Price Law, Art. 14 (1), (2), (5) & (7). The Price Law was promulgated by the Standing Committee of the NPC on 29 Dec. 1997 and effective on 1 May 1998, English translation available at www.fdi.gov.cn/pub/FDI_EN/Laws/law_en_info.jsp?docid=50956.

39. The Interim M&A Rules were jointly issued by the former Ministry of Foreign Trade and Economic Cooperation (MOFTEC), the State Administration of Taxation (SAT), the State Administration for Industry and Commerce (SAIC), and the State Administration of Foreign Exchange (SAFE) on 7 Mar. 2003 and effective on 12 Apr. 2003, English translation available at www.fdi.gov.cn/pub/FDI_EN/Laws/law_en_info.jsp?docid=51173. The MOFTEC was subsequently reorganised to integrate the former State Economy and Trade Commission (SETC) and renamed the Ministry of Commerce (MOFCOM) on 25 Mar. 2003.

40. The M&A Rules were jointly issued by the MOFCOM, the SASAC, the SAT, the SAIC, the China Securities Regulatory Commission (CSRC), and the SAFE on 8 Aug. 2006 and effective on 8 Sep. 2006, English translation available at www.fdi.gov.cn/pub/FDI_EN/Laws/law_en_info.jsp?docid=66925.

41. To be consistent with the AML, the M&A Rules were amended on 22 Jun. 2009 by the MOFCOM. The 2009 amendment repealed the anti-monopoly review provisions, expressly referred the anti-monopoly review of mergers to the AML, and transformed the M&A Rules to a pure instrument of investment law governing takeovers of domestic enterprises by foreign companies. English translation of the amended M&A Rules is available at www.fdi.gov.cn/pub/FDI_EN/Laws/law_en_info.jsp?docid=108906.

without considering whether dominance should be a threshold.[42] The M&A Rules only regulate mergers and acquisitions of domestic enterprises by foreign investors and thus raises concerns of discrimination against foreign investors. As regards sanctions and remedies, for example, the maximum administrative fine for abusive behaviour by public utilities is only CNY 200,000, which does not provide the AUCL with effective and sufficient deterrent force.[43] In addition, without a centralised and independent competition authority, a number of agencies and their corresponding local bureaus have shared enforcement powers and the situation has caused fragmented and unaccountable enforcement activities.[44]

22. Following the promulgation of the AUCL in 1993, the drafting of the AML bill started in 1994 and the AML, envisaged as a principal pillar of Chinese competition law, was placed on the legislative agendas of the Eighth, the Ninth, and the Tenth NPC. As noted by a Chinese official, the AML is perhaps the law with the longest drafting time in China.[45] The legislative history of the AML had witnessed intense debates on the necessity and the suitability of the law, fighting between agencies to gain enforcement powers, warnings about the potential damage the law on the State-owned economy and foreign investment, and complaints of foreign control and anticompetitive behaviour, real or perceived, of multinational corporations in the Chinese market. Globalisation and China's accession to the WTO have been two of the main driving forces behind the enactment of the AML.[46] In 2004, the MOFCOM, as the agency responsible for drafting the AML, submitted a bill to the Legislative Affairs Office of the State Council. After another two years of consideration and consultation, the State Council submitted a bill to the Standing Committee of the Tenth NPC in June 2006. The bill was then reviewed and revised three times in June 2006, June 2007, and August 2007. The AML was finally enacted on 30 August 2007 at the Twenty-Ninth Session of the Standing Committee of the Tenth NPC and became effective on 1 August 2008.

23. Similar to other major competition law regimes, the AML covers three main areas: anticompetitive agreements, abuse of dominance, and merger control. The AML also covers a fourth area, which is the abuse of administrative powers to eliminate or restrict competition, widely referred to as 'administrative monopoly'. Most AML provisions broadly conform to international norms and are comparable to competition laws in the European Union (EU), the US, and elsewhere, although some of the provisions have notable Chinese characteristics. Focusing on business operators' competitive behaviour in the marketplace and based on the rationale that competition delivers lower prices, better quality, and more choices, the AML is expected to improve consumer and social welfare in China. Furthermore, the AML affects government agencies at all levels through the prohibition of administrative monopoly. Therefore,

42. *See* AUCL, Arts 6 and 23 regarding designated transactions by public utilities, Art. 11 regarding below-cost sales, and Art. 12 regarding tying.
43. AUCL, Art. 23.
44. Bruce M. Owen, Su Sun & Wentong Zheng, *China's Competition Policy Reforms: The Anti-Monopoly Law and Beyond*, 75 Antitrust L. J. 233–236 (2008).
45. Wu Zhenguo, *Perspectives on the Chinese Anti-Monopoly Law*, 75 Antitrust L. J. 76 (2008).
46. For comments on how globalisation and the World Trade Organization accession have driven China's competition law development, *see* David Gerber, *Global Competition: Law, Markets, and Globalization*, 223–227 (Oxford: Oxford University Press, 2010).

as a milestone in China's legal history, the promulgation of the AML reflects the immense success of three decades of economic and political reform and promotes the establishment and development of a competition culture in China.[47]

24. The design of the AML enforcement mechanism was one of the most heavily debated issues in the AML legislative process. A single enforcement authority was considered or perceived to be politically impossible.[48] The NDRC, the SAIC, and the MOFCOM had enforced the various competition-related laws in existence prior to the enactment of the AML. Those same three agencies enforce the AML because the three agencies were designated as the Anti-Monopoly Enforcement Agencies (AMEAs) with respect to their particular functions.[49]

25. Minor adjustments to the competition enforcement structure occurred in 2008 when the AML entered into force. Headed by the Vice Prime Minister and comprised of senior officials from fifteen ministries, a high-level Anti-Monopoly Commission (AMC) was established in August 2008. Pursuant to the AML, the AMC is in charge of developing general policy and policy guidelines, assessing overall market conditions and coordinating AML enforcement by the AMEAs. The AMC established a working office within the MOFCOM. The AMEAs, mandated with concrete enforcement functions, have a triumvirate structure that consists of three departments under each of the MOFCOM, the SAIC, and the NDRC. Based on the three agencies' pre-existing competition-related enforcement authority, the MOFCOM Anti-Monopoly Bureau is solely in charge of merger control, the SAIC Competition Enforcement Bureau is responsible for non-price-related anti-monopoly agreements, abuse of dominance and administrative monopoly, and the NDRC Price Supervision and Anti-Monopoly Bureau is responsible for price-related anti-monopoly agreements, abuse of dominance and administrative monopoly.[50]

26. In June 2011, the MOFCOM announced that the State Council had formally approved the official establishment of the Office of the State Council Anti-Monopoly Commission (AMC Office) under the MOFCOM. Mr Yao Jian, spokesperson for the MOFCOM, said that the AMC Office has been situated within the MOFCOM since the establishment of the Anti-Monopoly Commission in August 2008. The formal establishment of the AMC Office within the MOFCOM will improve the effectiveness

47. *See* para. 18 above, n. 1; Xiaoye Wang, *Highlights of China's New Anti-Monopoly Law*, 144–45; *The New Chinese Anti-Monopoly Law*, 584–598, 618–619.

48. *See* para. 22 above, n. 1, Wu, 103–105; Wang, *The New Chinese Anti-Monopoly Law*, 587–592.

49. *See* the State Council Circular on the Composition of Departments under the State Council, 2008 No. 11, promulgated on 24 Apr. 2008, official Chinese text available at http://news. xinhuanet. com/politics/2008-04/24/content_8044595. htm; People's Daily Online, *Three Agencies Designated with the Authorities to Enforce the Anti-Monopoly Law* (in Chinese), http://politics. people. com. cn/GB/1025/7751741. html, 1 Sep. 2008.

50. The authorities of the SAIC, the NDRC, and the MOFCOM were established by the AUCL, the Price Law, and the M&A Rules respectively. Based on these laws and regulations, the SAIC, the NDRC, and the MOFCOM played separate, but sometimes overlapping, roles in regulating competition-related matters.

of AML enforcement, enhance the coordination among the various ministries of which the AMC is comprised, and more effectively promote economic development.[51]

27. Since the AML entered into force, a series of implementing regulations and guidance were issued or are currently under consideration.[52] The MOFCOM has become an active merger control enforcer and has rendered twenty-nine conditional clearance decisions, and the most recent conditional case is the merger between Dow Chemical and Dupont[53]and two prohibition decisions to date,[54] and the recent forbidden case is Maersk A/S ('Maersk'), MSC Mediterranean Shipping Company S.A. ('MSC'), and CMA CGM S.A. ('CMA CGM') establishing a network centre.[55] Starting from early 2010, the NDRC and the SAIC as well as their local bureaus began to take official enforcement actions, testing the boundaries of the AML.[56] Private enforcement has stood at the frontier from day one and has indicated how far China's antitrust jurisprudence has progressed in the nine years since the AML came into effect on 1 August 2008.[57]

51. *See* the MOFCOM's news release at http://www.mofcom.gov.cn/aarticle/ae/ai/201106/20110607592332.html, and the MOFCOM monthly press conference at http://www.mofcom.gov.cn/xwfbh/20110615.shtml.
52. *See* paras 40–42 and 43–46 below for lists of the AML implementing regulations and guidelines promulgated to date and those are under consideration.
53. *See* MOFCOM's Announcement at http://fldj.mofcom.gov.cn/article/ztxx/201705/20170502568075.shtml.
54. *See* discussions at paras 351–426 below. Official Chinese text of the MOFCOM's announcements of these decisions is available at http://fldj.mofcom.gov.cn/article/ztxx/.
55. *See* MOFCOM's Announcement at http://fldj.mofcom.gov.cn/article/ztxx/201406/20140600628586.shtml.
56. *See* discussions at paras 233–346 below.
57. *See* discussions at paras 183–223 below.

Part I. The Structure of Antitrust Law and Its Enforcement

Chapter 1. Sources of Antitrust Law

28. This chapter briefly reviews the sources of China's competition law. Analyses of provisions of the relevant laws and regulations are provided in greater detail in later chapters.

§1. National Sources

29. China's competition law is mainly derived from national sources. The national sources of China's competition legislation are: (1) the AML, which is the key competition legislation in China; (2) the competition-related provisions in the relevant economy-wide legislation enacted prior to the AML; and (3) the competition-related provisions in the relevant sector-specific legislation.

30. The economy-wide legislation enacted prior to the AML that contains competition-related provisions primarily include:

(1) AUCL.
(2) Price Law.
(3) Law on Bid Invitation and Bidding 1999 (hereinafter 'Bidding Law').[58]
(4) Contract Law 1999 (hereinafter 'Contract Law').[59]

58. *See* Bidding Law, Arts 32 and 53. The Bidding Law was promulgated by the Standing Committee of the NPC on 30 Aug. 1999 and effective on 1 Jan. 2000, English translation available at www.fdi.gov.cn/pub/FDI_EN/Laws/law_en_info.jsp?docid=50918.
59. *See* Contract Law, Arts 52(2), (3), (5), and 329. The Contract Law was promulgated by the NPC on 15 Mar. 1999 and effective on 1 Oct. 1999, English translation available at www.fdi.gov.cn/pub/FDI_EN/Laws/law_en_info.jsp?docid=50943.

(5) Supreme People's Court Interpretations on Certain Issues on the Application of Law for the Trial of Disputes on Technology Contracts 2004 (hereinafter 'Judicial Interpretations on Technology Contracts').[60]
(6) Criminal Law 1997 (amended 1999, 2001, 2002, 2005, 2006, 2009, and 2011) (hereinafter 'Criminal Law').[61]
(7) Foreign Trade Law 1994 (amended 2004) (hereinafter 'Foreign Trade Law').[62]
(8) Patent Law 1984 (amended 1992, 2000, and 2008) (hereinafter 'Patent Law').[63]
(9) Regulations on the Administration of Technology Import and Export 2001 (hereinafter 'Technology Import and Export Regulations').[64]
(10) Administrative Measures on Fair Trading between Retailers and Suppliers 2006 (hereinafter 'Retailers and Suppliers Measures').[65]
(11) Provisions on the Prohibition of Regional Blockades in Market Economy Activities 2001 (hereinafter 'Provisions on Regional Blockades').[66]

60. *See* Judicial Interpretations on Technology Contracts, Art. 10. The Judicial Interpretations on Technology Contracts were promulgated by the Supreme People's Court on 30 Nov. 2004 and effective on 1 Jan. 2005, official Chinese text available at http://law. chinalawinfo. com/ newlaw2002/SLC/slc. asp?db=chl&gid=56393, English translation available by subscription at www.lawinfochina.com.

61. *See* Criminal Law, Art. 223 on the bid rigging offence. The Criminal Law was promulgated by the NPC on 4 Mar. 1997, effective on 1 Oct. 1997 and amended in 1999, 2001 (twice), 2002, 2005, 2006, 2009, and 2011, English translation available at www.npc.gov.cn/englishnpc/ Law/2007-12/13/content_1384075.htm. English translation of the Amendments I, II, III, VI, V, and VI of the Criminal Law is available at www.npc.gov.cn/englishnpc/Law/Frameset-page6. html; English translation of the Amendments VII and VIII of the Criminal Law is available by subscription at www.lawinfochina.com.

62. *See* Foreign Trade Law, Arts 30, 32–33. The Foreign Trade Law was promulgated by the Standing Committee of the NPC on 12 May 1994, effective on 1 Jul. 1994 and amended in 2004, English translation available at www.fdi.gov.cn/pub/FDI_EN/Laws/law_en_info. jsp?docid=50900.

63. *See* Patent Law, Art. 48. The Patent Law was promulgated by the Standing Committee of the NPC on 12 Mar. 1984, effective on 1 Apr. 1985 and amended in 1992, 2000, and 2008, English translation available at www.fdi.gov.cn/pub/FDI_EN/Laws/law_en_info.jsp?docid=125096.

64. *See* Technology Import and Export Regulations, Art. 29. The Technology Import and Export Regulations were promulgated by the State Council on 30 Oct. 2001 and effective on 1 Jan. 2002, English translation available at www.wipo.int/clea/docs_new/pdf/en/cn/cn125en.pdf.

65. *See* Retailers and Suppliers Measures, Arts 4, 7, and 18. The Retailers and Suppliers Measures were promulgated by the MOFCOM, the NDRC, the Ministry of Public Security, the SAT, and the SAIC on 12 Oct. 2006 and effective on 15 Nov. 2006, English translation available at www. fdi.gov.cn/pub/FDI_EN/Laws/law_en_info.jsp?docid=74959.

66. The Measures on Regional Blockades were promulgated by the State Council on 21 Apr. 2001 and effective on the same day, official Chinese text of the Provisions on Regional Blockades available at www.gov.cn/gongbao/content/2001/content_60843.htm, English translation available by subscription at www.lawinfochina.com.

(12) Interpretation of the Supreme People's Court on Several Issues Concerning the Application of Law in the Trial of Disputes over Infringement of Patent Rights (II).[67]

31. The sector-specific legislation that contains competition-related provisions primarily include:

(1) *Postal Law 1986* (amended 2009 and 2012, 2015) (hereinafter 'Postal Law').[68]
(2) *Commercial Banking Law 1995 (amended 2003, 2015) (hereinafter 'Commercial Banking Law').*[69]
(3) *Telecommunications Regulations 2000 (amended 2016, hereinafter 'Telecom Regulations').*[70]
(4) *Insurance Law 1995 (amended 2002 and 2009, 2015) (hereinafter 'Insurance Law').*[71]
(5) *Regulations of International Ocean Shipping 2001 (amended 2013, 2016) (hereinafter 'International Shipping Regulations').*[72]
(6) *Regulation on the Administration of Domestic Water Transport 2012 (amended 2016, hereinafter 'Domestic Shipping Regulations').*[73]

67. The Interpretation of the Supreme People's Court on Several Issues Concerning the Application of Law in the Trial of Disputes over Infringement of Patent Rights (II) were promulgated by SPC on 21 Mar. 2016 and effective on 1 Apr. 2016, official Chinese text available at http://www.court.gov.cn/fabu-xiangqing-18482.html , English translation available by subscription at www.lawinfochina.com.

68. *See* the Postal Law, Arts 4 and 18. The Postal Law was promulgated by the Standing Committee of the NPC on 2 Dec. 1986, effective on 1 Jan. 1987 and amended in 2009 and 2012, English translation available by subscription at www.lawinfochina.com.

69. *See* Commercial Banking Law, Art. 9. The Commercial Banking Law was promulgated by the Standing Committee of the NPC on 10 May 1995, effective on 1 Jul. 1995 and amended in 2003, English translation available at www.npc.gov.cn/englishnpc/Law/2007-12/12/content_1383716.htm.

70. *See* Telecom Regulations, Arts 4, 7, 8, 12, 17–22, 31, 41–42, and further discussion at para. 60 below. The Telecom Regulations were promulgated by the State Council on 25 Sep. 2000 and effective on the same day, English translation available at www.fdi.gov.cn/pub/FDI_EN/Laws/law_en_info.jsp?docid=87900.

71. *See* Insurance Law, Arts 67 and 115. The Insurance Law was promulgated by the Standing Committee of the NPC on 30 Jun. 1995, effective on 1 Oct. 1995 and amended in 2002 and 2009, official Chinese text available at www.gov.cn/flfg/2009-02/28/content_1246444.htm, English translation available by subscription at www.lawinfochina.com.

72. *See* International Shipping Regulations, Arts 3, 27(1), (3), (4), 35–41. The International Shipping Regulations were promulgated by the State Council on 11 Dec. 2001, effective on 1 Jan. 2002, and amended in 18 Jul. 2013, English translation available by subscription at www.lawinfochina.com.

73. *See* Domestic Shipping Regulations, Art. 3. The Domestic Shipping Regulations were promulgated by the State Council on 13 Oct. 2012 and effective on 1 Jan. 2013, English translation available by subscription at www.lawinfochina.com.

§2. International Sources

32. To date, China has not reached any multilateral or bilateral cooperation agreements in relation to competition law. Thus, international sources of competition law currently do not exist in China. However, China's accession to WTO in December 2001 is relevant in this context. It is noted that competition law could manifest China's willingness to take its WTO obligations to reduce trade barriers and support market principles, although WTO membership does not create an obligation on members to enact a competition law.[74] The drafting of the AML had been accelerated after China became the 143rd member of the WTO and China's legislature noted that the enactment of a WTO-consistent AML would be necessary for China to implement its WTO commitments.[75]

33. In the soft law area, China is not yet a member of the International Competition Network (ICN). It should be noted that China has been increasingly involved in international competition enforcement discussions. In 2003, China and the EU established a structured Competition Dialogue (hereinafter 'Dialogue') to establish a permanent mechanism of consultation and transparency between China and the EU. The Dialogue is also aimed at enhancing the EU's technical and capacity assistance to China in the area of competition policy. The contact points of the Dialogue are the Anti-Monopoly Bureau (formerly the Treaty and Law Department) of the MOFCOM and the Directorate for Policy Development and Coordination of the European Commission Directorate-General for Competition.[76] China is reportedly keen to continue the contact it has established with Brussels and to develop a more formal bilateral cooperation mechanism.[77]

34. The EU-China Competition Weeks. In addition to the EU-China Competition Dialogue, the 'EU-China Competition Weeks' (hereinafter 'Competition Weeks') were launched in 2009 that is a twice-yearly week series of forums for discussion and cooperation on competition policy between the EU and China. Currently the Competition Weeks are held under the auspices of the EU-China Trade Project II (EUCTP II). The EUCTP II organises the Competition Week mainly through dedicated workshops and seminars with the MOFCOM, the NDRC, and the SAIC, focusing on topical issues and the needs identified during the AML enforcement activities. The Competition Weeks also holds conferences for the Chinese business community to raise awareness of competition law and policy, which have generated positive feedback from the

74. David Gerber, *Global Competition: Law, Market, and Globalization*, 226–227 (Oxford: Oxford University Press, 2010).

75. *See* 'Spokesperson Zeng Jianhui Answers Questions at the First Press Conference of the 5th Session of the 9th NPC', Chinese version of the script available at http://news. eastday.com/epublish/gb/paper200/1/class020000001/hwz612380.htm, 4 Mar. 2002. Legal documents of China's accession to the WTO (in Chinese and English) are available at www.mofcom.gov.cn/aarticle/zhongyts/ar/200207/20020700032358. html.

76. European Commission, *Declaration on the Start of a Dialogue on Competition by the EU and China* and *Term of Reference of the EU-China Competition Policy Dialogue*, http://ec. europa.eu/competition/international/legislation/china.pdf.

77. SAIC, *Minister Mr Zhou Bohua's Meeting with Ms Meglena Kuneva and Ms Neelie Kroes* (in Chinese), www.saic.gov.cn/ywdt/gjjl/200909/t20090911_70418.html, 10 Sep. 2009.

participants.[78] The Competition Weeks are a model of the ongoing cooperation between China and the EU in competition policy. The cooperation recognises that the development of competition law and policy in China is in its early stages and faces a variety of challenges. China can learn from the experiences and, in particular, the mistakes of more experienced jurisdictions.[79]

35. The EU-China Competition Policy Mini-site. Funded by the EU, the 'EU-China Competition Policy Mini-site' (www.euchinacomp.org) (hereinafter 'Mini-site') was launched in June 2012. The Mini-site provides, among other things, English and Chinese versions of a collection of key texts of the European competition law and presentation materials at the Competition Weeks.[80] The Mini-site has become one of the main sources for China's competition community to follow-up with the developments of the European counterpart.

36. The AMEAs' MOUs with the Russian, Romanian, UK, and US competition authorities. The SAIC signed a memorandum of understanding (MOU) in 2009 with the Russian Federal Anti-Monopoly Service to facilitate cross-border cooperation in investigations for 2010–2011.[81] In 2010, the SAIC signed another MOU with the Romanian Competition Council to exchange information on competition legislation and to share experiences in investigation procedures and in establishing relationships with other government agencies, especially sector regulators.[82]

37. In November 2010 and January 2011 respectively, the SAIC and the NDRC each signed an MOU with the UK's Office of Fair Trading, aiming to establish and develop cooperation in the enforcement of competition policy and related matters. The scope of cooperation includes: (1) the exchange of information on the policies, laws, and rules regarding competition policy, as well as the progress of legislation and enforcement; (2) the exchange of information on each country's competition regimes and respective 'agency effectiveness' experiences; (3) sharing best practice, knowledge,

78. Reports on the EU-China Competition Week are available at www.euctp.org and the relevant editions of the China Competition Bulletin; conference materials of the 'EU-China Competition Week' are available at www.euchinacomp.org/index.php/competition-weeks.
79. For an updated review on technical assistance in capacity building provided to the AMEAs, *see* Stanley Wong, *Effectiveness of Technical Assistance in Capacity Building on Competition Law and Policy: the Case of China*, in *China's Anti-Monopoly Law: The First Five Years*, 357–374 (Adrian Emch & David Stallibrass eds, Alphen aan den Rijn: Kluwer Law International, 2013).
80. *See* more information at www.euchinacomp.org.
81. SAIC, *Minister Mr Zhou Bohua Led a Mission to the BRIC Competition Conference and Delivered Keynote Speech* (in Chinese), www.saic.gov.cn/ywdt/gjjl/200909/t20090911_70417.html, 1 Sep. 2009.
82. SAIC, *Minister Mr Zhou Bohua Led a Mission to the Romania Competition Council and Signed Memorandum of Undertaking for Cooperation* (in Chinese), www.saic.gov.cn/ywdt/gjjl/201004/t20100415_82270.html, 15 Apr. 2010.

and expertise in tackling market problems and encouraging compliance; and (4) specific projects for cooperative working.[83]

38. In July 2011, the MOFCOM, the NDRC, and the SAIC signed an MOU with the US Department of Justice and the Federal Trade Commission. The MOU is expected to enhance cooperation on competition enforcement between the US and Chinese antitrust agencies through (1) keeping each other informed of significant competition policy and enforcement developments; (2) enhancing each agency's capabilities with appropriate activities related to competition policy and law such as training programmes, workshops, study missions, and internships; (3) exchanging experiences on competition law enforcement, when appropriate; (4) seeking information or advice from one another regarding matters of competition law enforcement and policy; (5) providing comments on proposed changes to competition laws, regulations, rules, and guidelines; (6) exchanging views with respect to multilateral competition law and policy; and (7) exchanging experiences in raising companies', other government agencies', and the public's awareness of competition policy and law.[84]

39. Efforts of the BRICS countries. During the 1st BRIC International Competition Conference, which was held in Russia, the heads of the BRIC countries' competition authorities signed a joint communiqué in 2009, according to which Brazil, Russia, India, and China intend to broaden cooperation, reinforce bilateral or multilateral dialogues, and coordinate enforcement activities in order to enforce competition law vigorously and effectively.[85] In September 2011, heads of the Brazilian, Russian, Indian, Chinese, and South African competition authorities signed the 'Beijing Consensus' during the 2nd BRICS International Competition Conference in Beijing. The Beijing Consensus states that the BRICS countries pay great attention to new developments in global competition laws and policies and are willing to share ideas on this issue. The Beijing Consensus called on all countries and regions to adopt effective competition policies and encouraged them to communicate and reach a consensus with each other.[86] In 2013 and 2015, BRIC International Competition Conference was held in India and South Africa respectively.

83. Office of Fair Trading of the United Kingdom, *Memorandum of Understanding on Cooperation between the Office of Fair Trading of the United Kingdom of Great Britain and Northern Ireland and National Development and Reform Commission of the People's Republic of China*, www.oft.gov.uk/shared_oft/about_oft/international/China.pdf, 10 Jan. 2011; Global Competition Review (GCR), *UK and China Sign Competition Memorandum*, www.globalcompetitionreview.com/news/article/29303/uk-china-sign-competition-memorandum/, 12 Nov. 2010; GCR, *China and UK Agencies Form Cooperation Agreement* www.globalcompetitionreview.com/news/article/29571/china-uk-agencies-form-cooperation-agreement-/, 12 Jan. 2011.

84. *See* the relevant reports at www.gov.cn/gzdt/2011-07/27/content_1914969.htm (in Chinese), www.justice.gov/atr/public/press_releases/2011/273306.htm, and www.ftc.gov/opa/2011/07/chinamou.shtm.

85. *See* SAIC, *Minister Mr Zhou Bohua Led a Mission to the BRIC Competition Conference and Delivered Keynote Speech* (in Chinese), www.saic.gov.cn/ywdt/gjjl/200909/t20090911_70417.html, 1 Sep. 2009.

86. *See* the relevant reports at www.brics2011.org.cn//english/.

§3. Secondary Sources

40. Lists of the major secondary sources of China's competition law, including the relevant regulations, measures, and guidelines, are provided in this section and their contents are discussed in the relevant chapters of Part II below. The secondary sources codify the AMEAs' practices, incorporate suggestions from public comments, and provide clarifications on various key issues. Further implementing regulations and guidelines on various aspects of the AML are expected to be published in the future, and may clarify a number of substantive and procedural issues, such as the availability of the expedited review of concentrations, the rules on leniency application, access to files, and confidentiality.

I. Regulations

41. The AML implementing regulations and measures. The AML contains the objectives, principles, and general legal framework of the Chinese competition law regime, but the delineation and interpretation of the AML provisions have been left to secondary legislation, including regulations, measures, and guidelines. The State Council and the AMEAs have conducted intensive public consultation on secondary legislation. To date, the following AML implementing regulations and measures (collectively 'AML implementing regulations') have been issued:

(1) State Council *Rules on Notification Thresholds for Concentrations of Undertakings* 2008 (hereinafter 'Notification Thresholds Rules').[87]
(2) MOFCOM, People's Bank of China (PBC), China Banking Regulatory Commission (CBRC), SCRC, and China Insurance Regulatory Commission (CIRC) Measures on the Calculation of Turnover for Concentrations of Financial Institutions 2009 (hereinafter 'Turnover Calculation Measures for Financial Institutions').[88]
(3) MOFCOM Measures on the Notification of Concentrations of Undertakings 2009 (hereinafter 'Notification Measures').[89]

87. The Notification Thresholds Rules were promulgated by the State Council on 3 Aug. 2008 and effective on the same day, official Chinese text available at http://fldj.mofcom.gov.cn/aarticle/c/200811/20081105917434.html, English translation available at http://fldj. mofcom. gov. cn/aarticle/c/200903/20090306071501.html.
88. The Turnover Calculation Measures for Financial Institutions were promulgated on 15 Jul. 2009 and effective on 15 Aug. 2009, official Chinese text available at http://fldj.mofcom.gov.cn/aarticle/c/200907/20090706411691.html, English translation available by subscription at www.lawinfochina.com.
89. The Notification Measures were promulgated by the MOFCOM on 21 Nov. 2009 and effective on 1 Jan. 2010, official Chinese text available at http://fldj.mofcom.gov.cn/aarticle/c/200911/20091106639149.html, English translation available at www.fdi.gov.cn/pub/FDI_EN/Laws/law_en_info.jsp?docid=115877.

(4) MOFCOM Measures on the Review of Concentrations of Undertakings 2009 (hereinafter 'Review Measures').[90]
(5) MOFCOM Interim Measures on Implementing Assets or Business Divestitures by Concentrations of Undertakings 2010 (hereinafter 'Divestiture Measures').[91]
(6) MOFCOM Interim Measures on the Assessment of Competitive Effects of Concentrations of Undertakings 2011 (hereinafter 'Merger Assessment Measures').[92]
(7) MOFCOM Interim Measures on the Investigation and Handling of Concentrations of Undertakings That Failed to Notify in Accordance with Laws 2011 (hereinafter 'Rules on Failure to Notify Mergers').[93]
(8) MOFCOM Provisional Regulation on the Standards Applicable to Simple Cases of Concentrations between Business Operators 2014(hereinafter 'Provisional Regulation on Simple Cases').[94]
(9) MOFCOM Regulation on the Imposition of Restrictive Conditions on Concentrations between Business Operators (for Trial Implementation) 2014(hereinafter 'Regulation on Merger Remedies').[95]
(10) MOFCOM Remedy Trustee Agreement Template for Merger Review 2015(hereinafter 'Merger Remedy Trustee Template').[96]

90. The Review Measures were promulgated by the MOFCOM on 24 Nov. 2009 and effective on 1 Jan. 2010, official Chinese text available at http://fldj.mofcom.gov.cn/aarticle/c/200911/20091106639145.html, English translation available at www.fdi.gov.cn/pub/FDI_EN/Laws/law_en_info.jsp?docid=115886.
91. The Divestiture Measures were promulgated by the MOFCOM on 8 Jul. 2010 and effective on the same day, official Chinese text available at http://fldj.mofcom.gov.cn/aarticle/c/201007/20100707012000.html, English translation available by subscription at www.lawinfochina.com.
92. The Merger Assessment Measures were promulgated by the MOFCOM on 29 Aug. 2011 and effective on 5 Sept. 2011, official Chinese text available at http://fldj.mofcom.gov.cn/article/c/201109/20110907723357.shtml, English translation available by subscription at www.lawinfochina.com.
93. The Measures on Failure to Notify Mergers were promulgated by the MOFCOM on 30 Dec. 2011 and effective on 1 Feb. 2011, official Chinese text available at http://fldj.mofcom.gov.cn/article/c/201201/20120107921682.shtml, English translation available by subscription at www.lawinfochina.com.
94. Provisional Regulation on the Standards Applicable to Simple Cases of Concentrations between Business Operators were promulgated by the MOFCOM on 11 Feb. 2014, official Chinese text available at http://fldj.mofcom.gov.cn/article/c/201409/20140900743277.shtml.
95. Regulation on the Imposition of Restrictive Conditions on Concentrations between Business Operators (for Trial Implementation) were promulgated by the MOFCOM on 4 Dec. 2014, official Chinese text available at http://www.mofcom.gov.cn/article/b/c/201412/20141200835207.shtml .
96. Remedy Trustee Agreement Template for Merger Review were promulgated by the MOFCOM on 27 Nov. 2015, official Chinese text available at http://fldj.mofcom.gov.cn/article/c/201511/20151101196166.shtml .

(11) SAIC Measures on Procedures for Investigating and Handling Cases of Monopoly Agreements and Abuse of Market Dominance 2009 (hereinafter 'Procedural Measures on Monopoly Agreements and Abuse of Dominance Cases').[97]
(12) SAIC Measures on Procedures for the Prohibition of Abuse of Administrative Powers to Eliminate or Restrict Competition 2009.[98]
(13) SAIC *Measures on the Prohibition of Monopoly Agreements 2011* (hereinafter 'Measures on the Prohibition of Monopoly Agreements').[99]
(14) SAIC *Measures on the Prohibition of Abuse of Dominant Market Position 2011* (hereinafter 'Measures on the Prohibition of Abuse of Dominance').[100]
(15) SAIC Measures on the Prohibition of Abuse of Administrative Powers to Eliminate or Restrict Competition 2011.[101]
(16) SAIC Provisions on the Prohibition of the Abuse of Intellectual Property Rights to Exclude or Restrict Competition 2015(hereinafter 'IPR Regulation').[102]
(17) NDRC *Measures on the Prohibition of Price Monopoly 2011* (hereinafter 'Measures on the Prohibition of Price Monopoly').[103]

97. The Procedural Measures on Monopoly Agreements and Abuse of Dominance Cases were promulgated by the SAIC on 10 Jun. 2009 and effective on 1 Jul. 2009, official Chinese text available at www.saic.gov.cn/fldyfbzdjz/zcfg/zcfg/200910/t20091013_71551.html, English translation available by subscription at www.lawinfochina.com.
98. The Measures on Procedures for the Prohibition of Abuse of Administrative Powers to Eliminate or Restrict Competition 2009 were promulgated by the SAIC on 10 Jun. 2009 and effective on 1 Jul. 2009, official Chinese text available at www.saic.gov.cn/fldyfbzdjz/zcfg/zcfg/200909/t20090928_71372.html.
99. The Measures on the Prohibition of Monopoly Agreements were promulgated by the SAIC on 31 Dec. 2010 and effective on 1 Feb. 2011, official Chinese text available at www.saic.gov.cn/fldyfbzdjz/zcfg/zcfg/201101/t20110107_103378.html, English translation available by subscription at www.lawinfochina.com.
100. The Measures on the Prohibition of Abuse of Dominance were promulgated by the SAIC on 31 Dec. 2010 and effective on 1 Feb. 2011, official text in Chinese available at www.saic.gov.cn/fldyfbzdjz/zcfg/zcfg/201101/t20110107_103379.html, English translation available by subscription at www.lawinfochina.com.
101. The Measures on the Prohibition of Abuse of Administrative Powers to Eliminate or Restrict Competition 2011 were promulgated by the SAIC on 31 Dec. 2010 and effective on 1 Feb. 2011, official text in Chinese available at www.saic.gov.cn/fldyfbzdjz/zcfg/zcfg/201101/t20110107_103380.html.
102. Provisions on the Prohibition of the Abuse of Intellectual Property Rights to Exclude or Restrict Competition were promulgated by the SAIC on 7 Apr. 2015, official Chinese text available at http://www.saic.gov.cn/fldyfbzdjz/zcfg/xzgz/201507/t20150724_233535.html.
103. The Measures on the Prohibition of Price Monopoly (also translated as 'Measures on Anti-Price Monopoly') were promulgated by the NDRC on 29 Dec. 2010 and effective on 1 Feb. 2011, official Chinese text available at http://jjs. ndrc. gov. cn/zcfg/t20110104_389399. htm, English translation available by subscription at www.lawinfochina.com.

(18) NDRC Measures on the Administrative Enforcement Procedures of the Prohibition of Price Monopoly 2011 (hereinafter 'Procedural Measures on Price Monopoly Cases').[104]

42. The regulations accompanying the AUCL, the Price Law, and the Bidding Law. The key regulations and measures issued, or currently under consideration and/ or public consultation, to implement the AUCL, the Price Law, and the Bidding Law are the following:

(1) NDRC *Provisions on the Administrative Penalties for Price Violations 1999* (amended 2006, 2008 and 2010) (hereinafter 'Provisions on Administrative Penalties for Price Violations').[105]
(2) NDRC Provisions on the Prohibition of Below-Cost Dumping Conduct 1999.[106]
(3) SAIC Provisions on the Prohibition of Restrictive Conduct of Public Utilities 1993 (hereinafter 'Provisions on Public Utilities').[107]
(4) SAIC Interim Provisions on the Prohibition of Bid Rigging 1998.[108]
(5) Implementing Regulations of the Bidding Law (hereinafter 'Bidding Law Implementing Regulations').[109]

104. The Procedural Measures on Price Monopoly Cases were promulgated by the NDRC on 29 Dec. 2010 and effective on 1 Feb. 2011, official Chinese text available at http://jjs. ndrc. gov. cn/zcfg/t20110104_389401. htm, English translation available by subscription at www. lawinfochina.com.

105. The Provisions on Administrative Penalties for Price Violations were promulgated by the former State Development and Planning Commission (predecessor of the NDRC) on 1 Aug. 1999 and amended in 2006, 2008 and 2010, official Chinese text available at www.gov.cn/zwgk/2010-12/10/content_1762672.htm, English translation available by subscription at www.lawinfochina.com.

106. The Provisions on the Prohibition of Below-Cost Dumping Conduct 1999 were promulgated by the former National Development and Planning Commission on 3 Aug. 1999 and effective on the same day, official Chinese text available at www.ndrc.gov.cn/zcfb/zcfbl/zcfbl2003pro/t20050707_27844.htm.

107. The Provisions on Public Utilities were promulgated by the SAIC on 24 Dec. 1993 and effective on the same day, official Chinese text available at www.saic.gov.cn/fldyfbzdjz/zcfg/200705/t20070523_57730.html, English translation available by subscription at www.lawinfochina.com.

108. The Interim Provisions on the Prohibition of Bid Rigging 1998 were promulgated by the SAIC on 6 Jan. 1998 and effective on the same day, official Chinese text available at www.saic.gov.cn/fldyfbzdjz/zcfg/200705/t20070523_58208.html.

109. The Bidding Law Implementing Regulations were promulgated by the State Council on 20 Dec. 2011 effective on 1 Feb. 2012, English translation available by subscription atwww.lawinfochina.com. The Bidding Law Implementing Regulations at Arts 39, 40, and 41 detail the situations where collusion between bidders and between tenderee and bidders is deemed as bid rigging. *See* discussion on the Bidding Law Implementing Regulation at para. 256 below.

II. Guidelines

43. To provide administrative guidance to interested parties, the AMC has issued the *Guidelines on the Definition of the Relevant Market 2009* (hereinafter 'Market Definition Guidelines').[110] The contents of the Market Definition Guidelines are outlined in paragraphs 117–125 below.

44. In addition to the Market Definition Guidelines, the AMC has entrusted the AMEAs to draft the *Guidelines on Anti-Monopoly Enforcement in Relation to Intellectual Property Rights* (hereinafter 'Draft Intellectual Property Guidelines'). The Draft Intellectual Property Guidelines were published by the General Office of AMC on 23 March 2017 for public comments.[111] Additionally, NDRC drafted the Guideline on Determining Illegal Income and the Amount of Fine,[112] Guidelines on General Terms and Procedures for Exemptions from Monopoly Agreements,[113] Antitrust Guidelines for Automotive Industry,[114] Draft Guidelines for the application of Leniency Rules in Horizontal Monopoly Agreement,[115] and Draft Guidelines on Commitments by Undertakings in Monopoly Cases.[116]

45. In the merger control area, the MOFCOM issued a series of guidance in January 2009 that provided details on the information a notifying party is required to submit and clarified key procedural issues regarding how the MOFCOM will conduct merger control reviews under the AML, including:

(1) Guidance for Notification of Concentrations of Undertakings 2009.[117]
(2) *Guidance for Notification Documents and Materials for Concentrations of Undertakings 2009* (hereinafter 'Information Requirement Guidance'), including a sample Notification Form and a flowchart outlining the merger control review process of the MOFCOM.[118]
(3) Working Guidance on Anti-Monopoly Review of Concentrations of Undertakings 2009 (amended 2010).[119]

---

110. The Market Definition Guidelines were issued by the AMC on 24 May 2009, official Chinese text available at http://fldj.mofcom.gov.cn/aarticle/j/200907/20090706384131.html, English translation available by subscription at www.lawinfochina.com.
111. *See* http://fldj.mofcom.gov.cn/article/zcfb/201703/20170302539418.shtmlfor the Chinese text.
112. *See* http://jjs.ndrc.gov.cn/fjgld/201606/t20160617_807541.html for the Chinese text.
113. *See* http://jjs.ndrc.gov.cn/fjgld/201605/t20160512_801559.html for the Chinese text.
114. *See* http://jjs.ndrc.gov.cn/fjgld/201603/t20160323_795740.html for the Chinese text.
115. *See* http://jjs.ndrc.gov.cn/fjgld/201602/t20160203_774287.html for the Chinese text.
116. *See* http://jjs.ndrc.gov.cn/fjgld/201602/t20160203_774286.html for the Chinese text.
117. The Guidance for Notification of Concentrations of Undertakings was issued by the MOFCOM in January 2009, official Chinese text available at http://fldj.mofcom.gov.cn/aarticle/xgxz/200901/20090105993824.html, English translation available by subscription atwww.lawinfochina.com.
118. The Information Requirement Guidance was issued by the MOFCOM in January 2009, official Chinese text available at http://fldj.mofcom.gov.cn/aarticle/xgxz/200901/20090105993841.html, English translation available by subscription atwww.lawinfochina.com.
119. The Working Guidance was issued by the MOFCOM in January 2009 and revised in March 2010, official Chinese text available at http://fldj.mofcom.gov.cn/aarticle/xgxz/200902/20090206034057.html.

46. On 6 June 2012, the MOFCOM issued a revised sample Notification Form (hereinafter 'Notification Form 2012') and instructions for completing the form pursuant to the AML and the relevant AML implementing regulations. The Notification Form 2012, replacing the previous sample form that had been used since January 2009 following the issue of the Information Requirement Guidance, should be used for notifications of mergers and acquisitions on or after 7 July 2012. The Information Requirement Guidance continues to be effective. If there are conflicts between the Information Requirement Guidance and the Notification Form 2012 together with the accompanying instructions, the latter should prevail.[120]

§4. Sources' Relation and Hierarchy

47. The AML overlaps with some competition-related provisions in other legislations such as the AUCL and the Price Law. In addition, sectors such as telecommunications and banking are subject both to sector-specific legislation and to the AML. The AML does not explicitly repeal competition-related provisions existing in other laws and regulations and, therefore, coexists with many pertinent provisions in other legislations. It should be noted that the M&A Rules were amended in 2009 to be consistent with the AML, and the SAIC is responsible for drafting the amendments of the AUCL to align the AUCL with the AML.

48. Based on the hierarchy of laws pursuant to the Legislation Law, in the case of contradictions, laws prevail over regulations and new laws prevail over old laws.[121] Therefore, in case of conflict, the AML, as the more recent general legislation, should take precedence over previous general laws and regulations. To the extent that they do not contradict the AML, prior legislation also applies.

49. Pursuant to the Legislation Law, with regards to laws and regulations, a special provision shall prevail over a general provision if there is inconsistency and if the provisions are formulated by one and the same organ.[122] The Legislation Law provides that where an inconsistency exists between the new general provisions and the old special provisions in different laws governing one and the same subject matter and it is difficult to decide which provision shall prevail, a ruling shall be made by the Standing Committee of the NPC.[123] However, such ruling rarely happens in practice. In particular, the relationship between the AML and the sector-specific laws and regulations can be problematic and inconsistencies do exist.

120. The revised sample Notification Form and instructions were issued by the MOFCOM on 6 Jun. 2012 and effective on 7 Jul. 2012, official Chinese text available at http://fldj.mofcom.gov.cn/article/zcfb/201206/20120608166903.shtml.

121. *See* Legislation Law, Arts 79 & 83.

122. *See* Legislation Law, Art. 83.

123. *Ibid.*, Art. 85.

§5. Role and Authority of Precedents

50. China is a civil law country so it does not adopt the doctrine of stare decisis. Therefore, precedents are not binding as case law. The power to interpret laws, especially the Constitution, is solely vested in the legislature.[124] With the notable exception of the Supreme People's Court, Chinese courts have only a limited role in the interpretation of laws. It should be noted that, in practice, the Supreme People's Court rarely hears cases and its main function is to issue comments on decided cases and interpretations on the application of particular laws and conduct trial supervisions.

51. There is currently no general mechanism to ensure consistency in the interpretation and the application of laws in China. However, it is noteworthy that there have been discussions among Chinese scholars and judges on whether Chinese courts should adopt the doctrine of stare decisis and/or the extent to which the doctrine could be adopted.[125] A leading Chinese jurist has argued that China should not adopt the doctrine because it is unsuited to the current Chinese political and legal regimes. In addition, it is noted that Chinese judges are not familiar with the methodologies required to apply stare decisis.[126] However, other commentators have argued that, in practice, decided cases complement statute law by filling the gaps in the legislation and thus should serve as precedents for Chinese courts and judges for reference purposes.[127] In general, although China lacks a system of precedential case law, the role of precedents should not be ignored, especially those well-informed judgments and model cases published by the Supreme People's Court. These precedents inform interested parties of the substantive and procedural aspects of the law, as well as educate the public about relevant legal developments in China.

---

124. *See* Constitution, Art. 67 (1) & (4); Legislation Law, Art. 42.
125. Wang Jiancheng, *Some Ideas about Precedent Law* (in Chinese), 13 J. of Yantian U. (2001), available at www.chinalawinfo.com.
126. Li Guanghu, *On the Precedent System* (in Chinese), *The People's Court Daily*, 20 Sep. 2002.
127. Shen Zongling, *Revisit Precedents of Contemporary China* (in Chinese), *Precedents and Research* (2005), available at www.chinalawinfo.com; Chris X. Lin, *A Quiet Revolution: An Overview of China's Judicial Reform*, 4 Asian-P. L. & Policy J. 293 et seq (2003).

Chapter 2. Scope of Application

52. The principal subject matter of the AML is monopoly conduct, which is defined as 'monopoly agreements, abuse of dominant market position and anticompetitive concentrations of undertakings'.[128]

53. The AML is a piece of economy-wide legislation and thus is in principle applicable to all undertakings, industry associations as well as public authorities.[129] The AML primarily applies to undertakings, and an undertaking is defined as 'a natural person, legal person, or other organisation that engages in manufacturing or operating commodities or providing services'.[130] Industry associations are required to 'strengthen the self-discipline of industries, guide undertakings towards lawful competition and maintain the order of market competition' and are prohibited from organising undertakings to engage in monopoly agreements.[131] Additionally, the AML applies to public authorities (including administrative agencies and organisations empowered by laws or regulations to administer public affairs) that abuse their administrative powers to eliminate or restrict competition, a type of behaviour often referred to as administrative monopoly.[132]

§1. Territorial Reach

54. The AML governs monopoly conduct in economic activities within and outside of China's territory that has the effect of eliminating or restricting competition in China's domestic market.[133]

55. Similar to other major competition regimes, China's competition law and policy is facing increasing challenges caused by globalisation. The AML appears to rely on the effects of doctrine as a basis to assert jurisdiction over anticompetitive conduct occurring outside of China's territory.[134] However, the extraterritorial application of competition law is challenging since it 'lies in the crossroads between law and politics and the conflicts triggered by it involve important political questions'.[135] It is noted that '[u]nilateral national regulation tends to create a global market divided by different policy regimes', and '[t]he extraterritorial application of law can have serious

128. AML, Art. 3.
129. *See* paras 58–74 below for information of the application of the AML on special sectors, State-owned enterprise and public utilities.
130. AML, Arts 12 & 16.
131. *Ibid.*, Art. 11.
132. *Ibid.*, Arts 32–37.
133. AML, Art. 2.
134. Judge Learned Hand laid down in the *Alcoa* case in 1945 what is known as the effects doctrine by pronounced that the Sherman Act applies to agreements concluded outside the United States which were intended to affect US imports and did actually affect them. *See United States v. Aluminium Co of America*, 148 F. 2d 416 (2d Cir. 1945).
135. Maher Dabbah, *The Internationalization of Antitrust Policy*, 167 (Cambridge: Cambridge University Press, 2003).

political effects'.[136] Case law and statutes developed in the US and the EU have demonstrated an increasingly cautious approach toward the extraterritorial application of competition law. For example, the US *Foreign Trade Antitrust Improvements Act 1982* stipulates that the antitrust laws will not apply unless the conduct has a 'direct, substantial and reasonably foreseeable effect...on trade or export commerce with foreign nations...'.[137]

56. The extraterritoriality established by the AML appears expansive because the statutory language does not establish any minimum requirement of national nexus under public international law. A strict textual reading of the AML does not require directness, substantiality or foreseeability as a condition to extend the law's extraterritorial application. This characteristic of the AML has raised concerns over the potential scope and the intrusiveness of the implementation of the AML, and how it will affect anticompetitive conduct that does not have a substantial connection with China.[138]

57. Having said that, it should be noted that, in relation to the AML merger control regime, a sufficient nexus to China is established if at least two undertakings to the concentration each have a minimum turnover in China of CNY 400 million, as required by the Notification Thresholds Rules.[139]

§2. Special Sectors

58. The AML provides a statutory exclusion for agricultural producers by declaring that the law will not apply to alliances or concerted practices among agricultural producers and rural economic organisations in operational activities such as the production, processing, sales, transportation, and storage of agricultural products.[140] It is noteworthy that this is not a general exception for the entire agricultural sector. For example, in July 2010 the NDRC announced that several local price authorities had made three decisions in relation to price collusion and manipulation in the green beans and garlic industries, and fines and warnings were imposed on a number of agricultural trade associations and trading companies.[141] Except for alliances or concerted practices among agricultural producers, the AML is a piece of general legislation applying to all economic sectors.

59. However, as illustrated in the discussion at paragraph 31 above, sector-specific competition provisions exist in prior legislation for certain industries, in

136. Peter Muchlinski, *Multinational Enterprises and the Law*, 114 & 116(2nd ed., Oxford: Oxford University Press, 2007).
137. 15 USC § 6a.
138. Michael Han & Jessica Su, *China's Antimonopoly Law: Status Quo and Outlook*, Global Competition Policy, www.competitionpolicyinternational.com/chinas-antimonopoly-law-status-quo-and-outlook/, August 2008.
139. *See* a discussion on the AML merger notification thresholds at para. 460 below.
140. AML, Art. 56.
141. NDRC, 'NDRC, MOFCOM and SAIC Announced the Investigation against and Penalties Imposed on Hoarding and Price Collusion of Agricultural Products' (in Chinese), http://jjs.ndrc.gov.cn/gzdt/t20100702_358457.htm, 2 Jul. 2010.

particular the regulated industries. These sectors include, among others, telecommunications, post, banking and insurance, and shipping.

60. Telecom. The Telecom Regulations stipulate that the supervision and administration of the telecommunications industry shall be based on the principles of separating government functions from enterprise management, prohibiting monopoly, encouraging competition, and facilitating development, openness, equality, and fairness.[142] A licensing system is established based on the recognition of differences between basic telecommunications services and value-added telecommunications services.[143] Dominant telecommunications enterprises are prohibited from refusing the requests to access their telecommunication networks.[144] Customers have the rights to choose service suppliers and designated transactions are prohibited.[145] Furthermore, restrictive practices such as exclusive dealing, predatory pricing, and irrational cross-subsidies are prohibited.[146] However, compared with the AML, the Telecom Regulations stipulate different legal liabilities and are enforced by the Ministry of Industry and Information Technology (MIIT) and its local bureaus at the provincial level.[147] Although the AML has a higher level of legal hierarchy than the Telecom Regulations, which one will be applicable in practice still remains to be seen. Sectoral laws and regulations for the post, banking and insurance, and shipping industries raise similar problems of concurrent jurisdictions between the AMEAs and the relevant sectoral regulators, and of inconsistency legal liabilities.

61. Post. The Postal Law stipulates that universal postal services and competitive postal services should be separately operated.[148] Pursuant to the Postal Law, the postal administrative department under the State Council (i.e., the State Post Bureau) shall supervise and administer the national postal market based on the principles of openness, fairness, justness, encouraging competition, and promoting development.[149]

62. Banking and Insurance. The Commercial Banking Law stipulates that commercial banks shall carry out businesses based on the principle of fair competition and shall not engage in unfair competitive behaviour.[150] The Insurance Law also stipulates that insurance companies shall operate businesses based on the principle of fair competition and shall not engage in unfair competitive behaviour.[151] The insurance regulatory body under the State Council (i.e., the China Insurance Regulatory Commission) is required, when examining an application for the establishment of an insurance company, to consider the needs of development of the insurance sector and fair competition.[152]

---

142. Telecom Regulations, Art. 4.
143. *Ibid.*, Arts 7, 8 & 12.
144. *Ibid.*, Arts 17–22.
145. *Ibid.*, Arts 31 & 41 (1)–(2).
146. *Ibid.*, Art. 42.
147. *Ibid.*, Art. 3 & Ch. VI.
148. Postal Law, Art. 18.
149. *Ibid.*, Art. 4.
150. Commercial Banking Law, Art. 9.
151. Insurance Law, Art. 115.
152. *Ibid.*, Art. 67.

63. Shipping. The Domestic Shipping Regulations stipulate that the State shall encourage and protect fair competition of the water transport market and prohibit monopoly and unfair competition.[153] Moreover, the International Shipping Regulations prohibit the use of advantageous positions by international shipping service providers to impose prejudicial pricing or other restrictive conditions to harm transaction counterparties.[154] The Implementation Rules of the International Shipping Regulations prohibit international shippers or their agents, warehouse storage service providers for international shipping, and international shipping containers and storage providers from providing services at abnormal and unreasonable rates and thus impeding fair competition as well as abusing advantageous positions to restrict the right of the transaction counterparties to freely select providers of ancillary services to international shipping, and from using their dominant positions in the relevant industries to entice parties to enter the transaction and thus harming competition in the industry.[155]

64. The prospect of convergence and harmonization between the AML and the sector-specific laws and regulations is questionable because the issue of which law or regulation will prevail in the event of conflict has not yet been resolved. Thus, conflicts in statutory hierarchy may happen in practice and may cause legal uncertainty.[156] In practice, while there has been no case where industry regulators impose penalties against anticompetitive activities in the industry, the AMEAs have been enforcing the AML against anticompetitive activities in various regulated industries. In 2011, the NDRC investigated alleged anticompetitive activities by China Telecom and China Unicom in the broadband licensing market.[157] The NDRC and the SAIC have both handled collusion cases in insurance industry. For example, in 2013, NDRC imposed administrative fines on twenty-three insurance companies in Zhejiang Province for collusion. [158]

§3. State-Owned Enterprises and Public Utilities

65. Since the beginning of China's economic reforms in 1978 and especially since 1997, China has privatised a large number of State-owned Enterprises (SOEs) but SOEs remain significant in public utilities, including telecommunications, post, water, energy, and railroads, as well as other sectors such as banking and aviation. It has been noted that the most dominant SOEs in China are those in the public utilities

153. *Domestic Shipping Regulations*, Art. 3.
154. International Shipping Regulations, Art. 27(3).
155. *See* Implementation Rules of the International Shipping Regulations (promulgated by the Ministry of Transport in 2003 and amended in 2013), Art. 37, English translation available by subscription at www.lawinfochina.com.
156. *See* a discussion on sources' relation and hierarchy at paras 47–49 above. For a detail analysis on the relationship between the AML and the regulated industries and statutory monopoly, *see* Yong Huang, *Pursuing the Second Best: The History, Momentum, and Remaining Issues of China's Anti-Monopoly Law*, 75 Antitrust L. J. 126–128 (2008).
157. *See* Jinrongjie, The Anti-Monopoly Investigation on China Telecom and China Unicom, http://news.xinhuanet.com/english2010/database/2010-01/21/c_13145387.htm, 12 Dec. 2011.
158. *See* NDRC, Decision of Administrative Penalty, http://www.sdpc.gov.cn/gzdt/201409/t20140902_624550.html, 31 Dec. 2013.

and other strategic sectors that remain under the close supervision and the tight control of the government.[159]

66. As a piece of economy-wide legislation, the AML, by providing a broad definition of undertaking, in principle applies to all undertakings irrespective of their ownership or sector. However, Article 7 of the AML provides that the State shall protect the legitimate operating activities of industries dominated by the State-owned economy that are vital to the Chinese national economy or national security or both.[160] The legislative language of Article 7 is vague. This article has led some to believe that, with respect to the operation of the AML, special treatment will be given to large SOEs that operate effectively as monopolies in industries such as telecommunications and energy.[161]

67. It is noteworthy that Article 7 is in fact consistent with the Constitution, which provides that 'the state-owned economy, that is, the socialist economy under the ownership of the whole people, is the leading force in the national economy. The State ensures the strength and development of the state-owned economy'.[162] In addition, the AML provides that 'the State formulates and implements competition rules compatible with the socialist economy, improves macro regulation and control, and strengthens a unified, open, competitive and orderly market system'.[163]

68. Merger review as an example. Currently many of China's largest companies are SOEs whose merger and acquisition transactions are likely to qualify for merger review under the AML. Although Article 7 of the AML may be read to allow special treatment to SOEs operating in key industrial sectors, the MOFCOM has indicated that this will not be the case with respect to the AML merger control regime.[164] However, whether or not these SOEs will actually be subject to the AML merger control regime is doubtful, as some SOEs appear to be reluctant to comply with the AML merger control regime. This is illustrated by the China Unicom/China Netcom merger in October 2008.

159. Eleanor Fox, *An Anti-Monopoly Law for China – Scaling the Walls of Government Restraints*, Antitrust L. J. 173 (2008).

160. Article 7 of the AML states: Undertakings in industries controlled by the State-owned economy and relied upon by national economy and national security, as well as industries that conduct exclusive and monopolistic sales in accordance with law shall be protected by the state to conduct their legitimate business activities. The state shall implement supervision, adjustment and control of business operations and pricing activities of these undertakings in accordance with law, and safeguard legitimate interests of consumers and promote technological progress. The undertakings mentioned in the preceding paragraph shall conduct their business in accordance with law in an honest and trustworthy manner, impose strict self-discipline, and accept supervision from the public. These undertakings shall not harm the interests of consumers by taking advantage of their controlling or exclusive position.

161. Bruce M Owen, Su Sun & Wentong Zheng, *China's Competition Policy Reforms: The Anti-Monopoly Law and Beyond*, 75 Antitrust L. J. 231, 244–247 (2008).

162. Constitution, Art. 7.

163. AML, Art. 4.

164. People's Daily, *Four Main Points of the Anti-Monopoly Law: An Interview with Shang Ming* (in Chinese), http://news. xinhuanet. com/politics/2007-08/31/content_6635548. htm, 31 Aug. 2007.

69. The China Unicom/China Netcom merger. A number of articles published by leading Chinese newspapers in April and May 2009 alleged that the acquisition of China Netcom Group Corporation (Hong Kong) Limited (hereinafter 'China Netcom') by China Unicom Limited (hereinafter 'China Unicom'), both leading telecommunications companies in China, in October 2008 violated the AML as the parties failed to notify the transaction to the MOFCOM.[165] According to these newspaper articles, the transaction qualified as a concentration of undertaking under the AML. Given the huge turnover of the parties in China (approximately CNY 100.47 billion and CNY 86.92 billion in 2007 for China Netcom and China Unicom respectively), the transaction should have triggered the mandatory prior notification obligation pursuant to the AML. It was reported that the MOFCOM had confirmed that a filing should have been made but that the parties defended their actions on the basis that the transaction was both consistent with the broad reform plan of China's telecommunications industry led by the MIIT and approved by the central government. However, the parties themselves contemplated obtaining AML merger clearance prior to the closing of the transaction, as one of the conditions precedent to closing was that the transaction shall have obtained all necessary registrations, notices, and exemptions from the relevant regulators and all waiting periods prescribed by law such as the AML, if applicable, had expired.[166]

70. It was also reported that China's State-owned Assets Supervision and Administration Commission (SASAC) had confirmed that a number of mergers and acquisitions involving central-level, large SOEs neither complied with the AML merger control rules nor go through the MOFCOM's anti-monopoly review procedure. It is believed that, among central-level SOEs, it is common for mergers and acquisitions to close without having first obtained AML merger clearance. This practice may be attributed to a misunderstanding by these SOEs that Article 7 of the AML exempts enterprises that are important to the national economy and people's livelihood from the operation of the AML. It was hoped that the MOFCOM and the SASAC would respond to China Unicom and China Netcom's alleged AML violation as it would shed light on the government's position on how Article 7 should be interpreted and whether the MOFCOM can assert its AML jurisdiction over the operations of SOEs. However, no official statement on this matter has been made by the MOFCOM or other relevant government agencies to date. Legal practitioners have observed that, as long as sector regulators at a similar hierarchical level to the MOFCOM believe that their regulation and management of sector businesses should not be subject to AML merger review by the MOFCOM, the practice of closing mergers and acquisitions without first obtaining AML merger clearance is likely to continue in relation to other mergers and acquisitions involving China's SOEs.[167]

71. In this context, there are concerns that the MOFCOM may struggle to obtain sufficient support from high levels within China's central government to challenge domestic deals that, while raising competition concerns, also align with China's

165. Economic Observer, *The China Unicom/China Netcom Merger may Infringe the Anti-Monopoly Law* (in Chinese), www.eeo.com.cn/industry/it_telecomm/2009/05/01/136645. shtml.
166. Economic Observer, *The Arrogant Big State-owned Enterprises and the Weak Anti-Monopoly Law* (in Chinese), www.eeo.com.cn/observer/pop_commentary/2009/05/01/136656.shtml.
167. Economic Observer, *The Arrogant Big State-owned Enterprises and the Weak Anti-Monopoly Law* (in Chinese), www.eeo.com.cn/observer/pop_commentary/2009/05/01/136656.shtml.

industrial policy of encouraging consolidation in domestic markets and the building of national champions.[168] However, as a system of rules to protect free and fair competition and a tool to increase consumer's welfare, the AML should apply equally to enterprises regardless of their ownership and nationality. If the MOFCOM has no authority to review or challenge transactions promoted by China's industrial policy or those involving the large SOEs, it would compromise the establishment of a competition culture in the Chinese market and undermine the public's confidence in the AML.

72. In the past few years, as China's economic structure changes, mega mergers and acquisitions between giant enterprises have emerged. For example, two railway equipment manufacturers, namely China South Railway and China North Railway, merged in 2015 to become China Railway Rolling Stock Corporation, which is the only enterprise in the sector and hence with monopolistic power. [169]In 2016, Baosteel Group and Wuhan Iron and Steel (Group) Corporation's merger resulted in the genesis of China Baowu Steel Group, China's largest and the world's second largest iron and steel company. [170]While merger filings were submitted with MOFCOM for both transactions, because the State Council and the SASAC had already approved both transactions before the merger filing process commenced, the aforesaid merger filings were of little substantive meaning.

73. The NDRC's investigation on abusive behaviour of China Telecom and China Unicom.[171] China Telecom and China Unicom own broadband networks and provide broadband services in Mainland China. On 9 November 2011, Ms Li Qing, Deputy Director of the Price Supervision and Anti-Monopoly Bureau of the NDRC, confirmed that the NDRC opened an investigation on the alleged abusive behaviour of China Telecom and China Unicom in charging Internet service providers discriminatory network access fees in order to squeeze out competitors. On 2 December 2011, the NDRC confirmed that it had received an application for the suspension of investigation from China Telecom and China Unicom, respectively. China Telecom also submitted a plan to adjust and rectify its current practices. China Telecom stated that it plans to expand interconnection capacity, achieve interoperability with other backbone telecom operators, standardise network access fees charged to Internet service providers and reduce that fee to 'a proper level', and reduce end user broadband access charges by around 35% per bandwidth unit within five years. It was reported that the NDRC has requested that China Telecom should submit a revised proposal that is more detailed and specific as its initial plan was too vague and would be difficult to monitor.

74. The conduct of the NDRC's investigation and the level of public discourse it has generated demonstrate that the AMEAs are improving their enforcement

168. Hannah C. L. Ha, John M. Hickin & Gerry P. O'Brien, *China's Anti-Monopoly Law Merger Control Regime – 10 Key Questions Answered (Part I)*, www.mondaq.com, 11 Mar. 2010.
169. *See* http://www.chinanews.com/cj/2015/08-06/7451268.shtml.
170. *See* http://finance.qq.com/a/20160923/005424.htm.
171. Qing Ping, *Anti-Monopoly Investigation on China Telecom and China Unicom: Law or Technology?* (in Chinese), Legal Daily, 18 Nov. 2011, page 7, available at http://epaper.legaldaily.com.cn/fzrb/content/20111118/Articel07001GN.htm; also *see* Xinhua, *China Telecom, China Unicom pledge to mend errors after anti-monopoly probe*, http://news.xinhuanet.com/english2010/business/2011-12/02/c_131285213.htm, 2 Dec. 2011.

capabilities and that a general awareness of competition law is quickly developing in China. Unfortunately, China Telecom's proposal failed to adequately address the alleged abusive behaviour and had instead diverted attention away from the focus of the NDRC's investigation. This case will be a litmus test on how the AML will be applied to SOEs and will play its role in China's regulatory reform. The NDRC's investigation looks like it is ongoing and no decision has been publicly made to date.

§4. Sensible Effect and De Minimis

75. There are no clear rules in this regard. The AML, the AML implementing regulations, and other competition-related laws and regulations do not contain *de minimis* rules or provide any safe harbour rules. In addition, no block exemption regulations implementing the AML have been promulgated to date.

Chapter 3. Overview of Substantive Provisions

76. The AML, similar to other major competition law regimes, addresses three main areas: restrictive agreements, abuse of dominant market positions and merger control.[172] The AML also covers a fourth area, the abuse of administrative powers to eliminate or restrict competition, which is widely referred to as an administrative monopoly. Most AML substantive provisions broadly conform to international norms and are comparable to competition laws in the EU and the US, although some of the provisions have distinct Chinese characteristics. This chapter provides an overview of the AML substantive provisions.

77. Other relevant laws and regulations, such as the AUCL, the Price Law, the Bidding Law, and their implementing regulations also address certain types of restrictive agreements and abuse of dominance. To some extent, there are inconsistencies between these provisions and their counterparts under the AML. These provisions are discussed in this chapter, wherever appropriate.

§1. Restrictive Agreements

78. The AML adopts the term 'monopoly agreements' and defines it as 'agreements, decisions or other concerted practices that eliminate or restrict competition'.[173] This definition broadly accords with the concept of restrictive agreements under EU competition law.[174] The AML provides an illustrative list of prohibited horizontal monopoly agreements, according to which competing undertakings are prohibited from engaging in price-fixing, output restriction, market sharing, certain restrictions on products or technology developments, joint boycotts, and other horizontal monopoly agreements as determined by the AMEAs.[175] The AML further prohibits non-competing undertakings from fixing the resale price, setting a minimum resale price, and other vertical monopoly agreements as determined by the AMEAs.[176] Industry associations are specifically prohibited from organising undertakings to engage in monopoly agreements.[177]

79. The AML establishes a general exemption mechanism that provides that the prohibition on horizontal and vertical monopoly agreements shall not apply if the undertakings involved can prove that the agreement in question meets three criteria. An agreement, except for that for the purpose of safeguarding the legitimate interests in foreign trade and economic cooperation or falling with other circumstances as stipulated by law and the State Council, will be exempted from the application of the AML if the undertakings can prove that the agreement: (1) aims to realise objectives

172. AML, Art. 3.
173. AML, Art. 13.
174. *See* Treaty on the Functioning of the European Union [2008] OJ C115/47, Art. 101.
175. AML, Art. 13.
176. *Ibid.*, Art. 14.
177. *Ibid.*, Art. 16.

specified by the AML; (2) does not substantially eliminate competition in the relevant market; and (3) enables consumers to share the interests derived from the agreement.[178]

80. Infringement of the AML prohibition on monopoly agreements may lead to the investigation and the imposition of penalties by the AMEAs.[179] In addition, the AMEAs have a general power to determine and penalise other monopoly agreements that are not explicitly prohibited by the AML.[180] Penalties for infringement include orders to cease the conduct, confiscation of illegal gains, and fines between 1%–10% of the annual turnover in the preceding accounting year. For monopoly agreements that are not implemented, a fine of up to CNY 500,000 may be imposed. The AMEAs may reduce or exempt sanctions for undertakings that voluntarily report important information and provide evidence concerning monopoly agreements.[181] Moreover, offenders are liable for damages to those injured by the monopoly agreements.[182] Unsatisfied parties may apply for administrative reconsideration of decisions made by the AMEAs, and then bring administrative litigation to challenge the result of the administrative reconsideration. Parties are also allowed to bring administrative litigation without seeking administrative reconsideration in the first instance.[183]

81. Prohibition of restrictive agreements by other laws and regulations. The Price Law prohibits price collusion and fabrication and dissemination of information on price increases.[184] An infringing undertaking will be ordered to rectify the conduct and be confiscated of the illegal gains, and it may also be subject to a fine of less than five times the illegal gains. Warnings will be given and fines may be imposed if there are no illegal gains. Where the circumstances are serious, the infringing undertaking will be ordered to suspend business operations or have its business licence revoked.[185]

82. The AUCL and the Bidding Law explicitly prohibit bid rigging.[186] Under the AUCL, an undertaking engaging in bid rigging is subject to a fine between CNY 10,000 and CNY 200,000 and the collusive bid is void. Under the Bidding Law, an undertaking engaging in bid rigging is subject to a fine between 0.5%–1% of the total value of the bidding project, illegal gains will be confiscated, and if the circumstances are serious, the undertaking will be disqualified from participating in bidding for one to two years or have its business licence revoked. The person in charge or any other person directly responsible is subject to a fine between 5%–10% of the total amount of fine imposed on the undertaking. In addition, the Bidding Law states that if the bid rigging constitutes a criminal offence, the undertaking will be prosecuted pursuant to the Criminal Law.

178. *See* discussion on the AML general exemption at para. 104 below.
179. AML, Arts 38–46.
180. *Ibid.*, Arts 13(6) & 14(3).
181. *Ibid.*, Art. 46.
182. *Ibid.*, Art. 50.
183. *Ibid.*, Art. 53, para. 1.
184. Price Law, Art. 14(1) & (3).
185. *Ibid.*, Art. 40.
186. *See* AUCL, Arts 15 & 27 and Bidding Law, Arts 32 & 53.

83. The Price Law, the AUCL, and the Bidding Law do not provide exemptions for restrictive agreements. Under these laws, offenders are liable for damages to injured parties.[187]

§2. Dominant Undertakings

84. Pursuant to the AML, a dominant undertaking is defined as an undertaking having a dominant market position that enables the undertaking to control prices, product quantities, or other trading conditions in the relevant market, or to restrict or affect market entry.[188] In addition to market share, the AML provides a list of factors to be considered when determining whether a dominant market position exists, including competitive conditions in the relevant market, the financial status and technical capabilities of the undertakings, and entry barriers.[189] The AML also provides that an undertaking is assumed to have a dominant market position if it, or together with other undertakings, accounts for a certain proportion of the relevant market. This assumption can be rebutted.[190]

85. Dominant undertakings are prohibited from abusing their positions to eliminate or restrict competition.[191] It should be noted that the AML does not prohibit attempts to acquire a dominant position; only the actual abuse of a dominant position is prohibited. The AML does not define the concept of abuse, but provides an illustrative list of types of behaviour considered to be abusive, plus a catch-all provision. The list of prohibited behaviour includes both exploitative and exclusionary conduct, and dominant undertakings are prohibited, without valid justification, from engaging in excessive pricing, below-cost sales, refusal to deal, exclusive or forced dealing, tying or imposing other unreasonable transactional terms and discriminatory dealing.[192] In addition, the AMEAs have a general power to determine and penalise other abuses of dominant market position that are not explicitly prohibited by the AML.[193]

86. Infringement of the AML prohibition on the abuse of dominant market position may lead to an investigation and the imposition of penalties by the AMEAs.[194]Penalties for infringement include orders to cease the conduct, confiscations of illegal gains, and fines of between 1%–10% of annual turnover in the preceding accounting year.[195] In addition, offenders are liable for damages to those injured by the abusive behaviour.[196] Unsatisfied parties may apply for administrative reconsideration of decisions made by the AMEAs, and then bring administrative litigation to challenge the result of the

187. *See* Price Law, Art. 41; AUCL, Art. 20; Bidding Law, Art. 53.
188. AML, Art. 17, para. 2; also *see* a discussion on 'Market Power/Dominant Position' at paras 127–132 below.
189. AML, Art. 18.
190. AML, Art. 19; also *see* a discussion on the finding of a dominant position at paras 130–132 below.
191. AML, Art. 6.
192. *Ibid.*, Art. 17(1)–(6).
193. *Ibid.*, Art. 17(7).
194. AML, Arts 38–45; 47.
195. *Ibid.*, Art. 47.
196. *Ibid.*, Art. 50.

administrative reconsideration. Parties are also allowed to bring administrative litigation without seeking administrative reconsideration in the first instance.[197]

87. Prohibition of dominant undertakings' abusive behaviour by other laws and regulations. The AUCL prohibits public utilities and other undertakings with statutory monopolies from forcing others to buy goods from designated business operators so as to exclude other operators from fair competition.[198] An infringing undertaking will be ordered to make a rectification and may be imposed a fine between CNY 50,000 and CNY 200,000.[199]

88. In addition, the Retailers and Suppliers Measures provide that retailers with an advantageous position are prohibited from: (1) refusing to accept goods from suppliers (unless due to the suppliers' fault or as otherwise agreed) after signing contracts with those suppliers; (2) demanding that suppliers take losses from damaged goods without prior agreement; (3) taking suppliers' goods from the shelves without prior agreement (unless as required by relevant laws, regulations or administrative orders); (4) forcing suppliers to participate in sales rebate programmes unconditionally or, having previously set a certain sales target as the condition of a sales rebate, forcing suppliers give sales rebates even if those sales targets have not been met; and (5) forcing suppliers to purchase designated goods or designated services.[200] The Retailers and Suppliers Measures do not clarify what would constitute an advantageous position. Thus, it remains to be seen how the Retailers and Suppliers Measures will interact with the AML.

89. Prohibition of abusive behaviour regardless of the presence of a dominant position by other laws and regulations. Except for the prohibitions on designated transactions by public utilities and statutory monopolists and on administrative monopoly, the AUCL prohibitions on two other types of abusive conduct apply to undertakings in general, without attempting to draw a distinction between dominant and non-dominant undertakings. These include below-cost sales (with a few exceptions) for the purpose of forcing out competitors, and tying or imposing other unreasonable conditions against the purchaser's wishes.[201] The AUCL does not provide for administrative liabilities for below-cost sales and tying or imposing other unreasonable conditions. However, infringing undertakings are liable to injured parties for civil liabilities.[202]

90. The Price Law prohibits the sale of goods at a price below-cost to drive competitors out of the market or to monopolise the market, price discrimination, and obtaining excessive profits in violation of the laws and regulations, and these prohibitions apply regardless of the existence of dominance.[203] An infringing undertaking will be ordered to rectify the conduct and be confiscated of the illegal gains, and it may also be subject to a fine of less than five times the illegal gains. Warnings will be given and fines may be imposed if there are no illegal gains. Where the circumstances are serious,

197. *Ibid.*, Art. 53, para. 1.
198. AUCL, Art. 6.
199. *Ibid.*, Art. 23.
200. Retailers and Suppliers Measures, Art. 6.
201. AUCL, Arts 11 & 12.
202. *Ibid.*, Art. 20.
203. Price Law, Art. 14 (2), (5) & (7).

the infringing undertaking will be ordered to suspend business operations or have its business licence revoked.[204]

§3. Concentrations

91. The AML merger control rules and the relevant implementing regulations set out the jurisdictional, procedural, and substantive rules on notifiable transactions under the AML. This introduced a new merger control regime and replaced the merger control regime under the M&A Rules.[205] Whereas the M&A Rules applied only to foreign companies, the AML merger control regime applies equally to domestic Chinese companies and foreign companies. This section reviews the basic AML merger control rules, and the relevant implementing regulations are discussed in later chapters.

92. The AML provides that, as a basic principle, 'undertakings may implement concentrations in accordance with the law through fair competition and voluntary combination to expand business scope and enhance market competitiveness'.[206] The main provisions of the merger control regime are set out in Chapter IV of the AML.[207] A concentration of undertakings is defined as: (1) a merger of undertakings; (2) an acquisition of control of another undertaking through the purchase of shares or assets; or (3) an acquisition of control of another undertaking, or of the ability to exercise decisive influence on another undertaking, through contract or other means.[208]

93. The AML does not define the terms acquisition of control and decisive influence, nor does it specify any notification thresholds.[209] An earlier draft of the Notification Measures provided that the acquisition of control of other undertakings shall mean: (1) the acquisition of over 50% of the voting rights or assets of another undertaking; or (2) in the absence of the acquisition of over 50% of the voting rights or assets of another undertaking, if the acquirer obtains the ability to decide the appointment of one or more board members and key management members, budgets, operations and sales, pricing, substantial investment or other important management and operational strategies through the acquisition of shares and assets or through contracts or other means. However, the final version of the Notification Measures does not contain any such definition. Currently, the issue of whether a transaction leads to the acquisition of control or decisive influence by one undertaking over another undertaking, especially where there is a minority stake acquisition, needs to be determined on a case-by-case basis and thus may cause uncertainty.

94. Documents required for notification. Under the AML, the documents required to be lodged for the notification of a concentration include: (1) an application; (2) information on competition in the relevant market; (3) the agreement of the proposed

204. *Ibid.*, Art. 40.

205. *See* para. 20 above for the development of China's merger control regime and paras 41–46 above for the relevant AML implementing regulations in relation to merger control.

206. AML, Art. 5.

207. *Ibid.*, Arts 20–31.

208. *Ibid.*, Art. 20.

209. The Notification Thresholds Rules prescribe the relevant thresholds. *See* discussion at para. 460 below.

concentration; (4) the parties' audited financial reports for the preceding accounting year; and (5) other documents as requested by the MOFCOM.[210]

95. The preliminary review. Concentrations that meet the notification thresholds must be notified to the MOFCOM. The MOFCOM has a preliminary review period of thirty days following the receipt of the notification within which to decide whether or not a further review will be conducted. The preliminary review period of thirty days cannot be extended. A notifiable concentration cannot be implemented before the MOFCOM makes a decision on whether or not to conduct a further review. If the MOFCOM fails to reach a decision within the preliminary review period, the proposed concentration is deemed to be cleared.[211]

96. The further review. The further review period is ninety days, which can be extended by a further sixty days under specified circumstances upon the MOFCOM giving written notice to the undertakings involved. These circumstances include: (1) the undertakings concerned agree to extend the time limit; (2) the documents submitted by the undertakings concerned are inaccurate and need further verification; or (3) relevant circumstances have significantly changed following the receipt of the notification.[212] During the course of the further review, the MOFCOM shall prohibit the concentration if it concludes that the proposed concentration may eliminate or restrict competition, unless the parties can prove that: (1) the proposed concentration will improve the conditions of competition and the pro-competitive effect of the concentration will obviously outweigh its anticompetitive effect; or (2) the proposed concentration is in accordance with public interest.[213] The MOFCOM may conditionally clear a concentration.[214]

97. The review decision. The MOFCOM is required to publish its prohibition decisions and conditional clearance decisions in a timely manner.[215] The AML does not require that the MOFCOM publish its unconditional clearance decisions. Unconditional clearance decisions were unavailable to the public until November 2012, when the MOFCOM announced that it will publish information of unconditional clearance decisions it has made since 1 August 2008, in accordance with the Regulations on the Disclosure of Government Information.[216] Since then, the MOFCOM has published lists of unconditional clearance decisions on a quarterly basis, providing case name, parties to the concentrations as well as the date of completion of review.[217]

98. Remedies for non-compliance. Remedies for non-compliance with the AML merger control rules include orders to cease the implementation of the concentration, dispose of shares or assets, divest a business within a given time period, or take other

210. AML, Art. 23. *See* paras 455–456 below for further requirements on notifiable materials under the Notification Measures.
211. AML, Art. 25.
212. AML, Art. 26.
213. *Ibid.*, Art. 28.
214. *Ibid.*, Art. 29.
215. AML, Art. 30.
216. *See* announcement of the MOFCOM (in Chinese) at http://fldj.mofcom.gov.cn/aarticle/xxfb/201211/20121108436852.html%20(CN)%20 , 15 Nov. 2012.
217. MOFCOM's unconditional merger clearance decisions (in Chinese) are available at http://fldj.mofcom.gov.cn/article/zcfb/.

necessary measures to restore the market to its state prior to the concentration. A fine up to CNY 500,000 may also be imposed.[218]

§4. Other Prohibitions

99. Administrative monopoly. Monopoly conduct, a concept covering restrictive agreements, abuse of dominance and anticompetitive concentrations, is the principal subject matter of the AML. However, the AML also prohibits the abuse of administrative powers to eliminate or restrict competition, commonly referred to as administrative monopoly. Administrative agencies and organisations empowered by laws or regulations with responsibilities for public affairs administration (collectively, 'public authorities') are prohibited from abusing their administrative powers to participate in designated transactions, hinder the free movement of goods among regions, restrict non-local undertakings' bidding activities in the local market, restrict non-local undertakings' investment and establishment of subsidiaries in the local market, force undertakings to engage in monopoly conduct or promulgate anticompetitive rules.[219]

100. Although the AML generally prohibits administrative monopoly, the AMEAs have not secured substantial jurisdiction over administrative monopoly. Under the AML, where a public authority engages in administrative monopoly conduct, its superior agency shall order the public authority to make a correction, and the persons directly in charge and others directly responsible shall be subject to disciplinary sanctions in accordance with the law. The AMEAs may only make proposals on the handling of administrative monopoly to the relevant superior agency.[220]

101. It is noted that the enforcement mechanism vis-à-vis administrative monopoly is weak and cannot provide sufficient deterrent effect. Furthermore, the standard tools of competition law in general are less relevant to the treatment of anticompetitive actions of the government and the political challenges of dealing with them are more difficult to surmount. Meta laws in the form of constitutional and treaty provisions are a key instrument in preventing anticompetitive actions of government in the US, Europe, and Australia. In contrast, China does not have such meta laws or constitutional provisions and, at this early stage of the AML, there does not seem to be a systematic approach, well-grounded with high-level political support. Thus there is a gap in China's legal arrangements to deal with administrative monopoly.[221] However, there were several cases related to administrative monopoly in recent years. In particular, with the promulgation of *Opinion on Establishing Fair Competition Review System in Marketplace (*'Opinion*')* in June 2016, the NDRC has strengthened its supervision on administrative monopoly. In the ensuing six months, the NDRC initiated investigations on more than twenty cases. By the end of 2016, the administrative monopoly cases that NDRC published include: (1) Shenzhen Education Bureau unlawfully pre-fixed

218. AML, Art. 48.
219. AML, Arts 32–37.
220. AML, Art. 51.
221. Allan Fels, *Administrative Monopoly – A Comparison of China, Australia, the USA and the EU* (Chinese version), in *Issues Surrounding the Enforcement of the Anti-Monopoly Law*, 308–321 (Xiaoye Wang ed., Beijing: Social Sciences Academic Press, 2010).

the lowest price in the tender process for students' uniforms, and imposed discriminatory conditions/requirements for bidders' eligibility and evaluation criteria, which was in violation of the AML. (2) Shanghai Transportation Committee, in administering the cruise ship industry, led the business operators to form price alliance and forced the operators to join public platform and set a unified ticket price. Although it restored order to the industry, it completely eliminated price competition in the market at issue in violation of the AML. (3) Beijing Municipal Committee of Housing and Urban-Rural Development, in implementing the minimum price for quality control for ready-mixed concrete, organised the business operators to reach a price monopoly agreement in violation of the AML. (4) Certain government-designated power supply companies in twelve provinces/municipalities including, *inter alia*, Chongqing, Jilin, and Hebei, were mandated to be the only contractor available for building electricity supply and transmission equipment in newly built residential areas and entitled to charge a unified price, which allegedly amounted to administrative monopoly that eliminated competition. After relevant competition regulators' investigation and intervention from higher-level supervisory authorities, such activities at issue were suspended and rectified. [222]

102. Abuse of intellectual property rights. The AML stipulates that it does not apply to the conduct of undertakings in exercising their intellectual property rights in accordance with applicable laws and regulations; however, the conduct of undertakings to eliminate or restrict competition by abusing their intellectual property rights shall be governed by the AML.[223] The AML does not stipulate or clarify the types of behaviour that would be construed as an abuse of intellectual property rights, or the legal liabilities flowing from an abuse of intellectual property rights. This vagueness has caused concerns among commentators and businesses.[224] The SAIC has promulgated the *IPR Regulation* on 7 April 2015.[225] However, because this regulation does not regulate price-related activities (i.e., issues relating to licence fees for intellectual property rights), it has limited application. It is important to appreciate that legislation other than the AML, such as the Contract Law and the Patent Law, may be relevant in this context. *See* the discussion on technology licensing at paragraphs 299–314 below.

222. *See* news report by The Paper, Departments from 15 Provinces Penalized by NDRC, Decision of Administrative Penalty, http://www.thepaper.cn/newsDetail_forward_1589750, 29 Dec. 2016.
223. AML, Art. 55.
224. H. Stephen Harris, Jr. & Rodney J. Ganske, *The Monopolization and IP Abuse Provisions of China's Anti-Monopoly Law: Concerns and a Proposal*, 75 Antitrust Law Journal 218–221 (2008).
225. Provisions on the Prohibition of the Abuse of Intellectual Property Rights to Exclude or Restrict Competition were promulgated by the SAIC on 7 Apr. 2015, official Chinese text available at http://www.saic.gov.cn/fldyfbzdjz/zcfg/xzgz/201507/t20150724_233535.html.

§5. Tests of Illegality

I. Per Se Prohibitions and Naked Restraints

103. Regarding the prohibition of monopoly agreements, the AML does not draw a distinction between hardcore restraints and less problematic practices or per se prohibitions and those subject to a rule of reason test. However, hardcore cartels, such as price-fixing, output restriction, market sharing, and bid rigging, seriously impede competition and the undertakings involved may not be able to prove that such conduct provides consumers with benefits as required by the AML exemption rule. As demonstrated by the recent enforcement activities of the NDRC and the SAIC, hardcore cartels may be treated as per se illegal under the AML.

II. Balancing Tests

104. Exemptions of monopoly agreements. Under the AML, the prohibition of monopoly agreements, which includes horizontal and vertical agreements, shall not apply if the undertakings involved can prove that the agreement is for the purpose of: (1) improving technology or researching and developing new products; (2) upgrading product quality, reducing cost, enhancing efficiency, unifying specifications and standards of products or implementing a division of labour based on specialisation; (3) improving operational efficiency and enhancing the competitiveness of small and medium-sized undertakings; (4) realising social public interest such as energy conservation, environmental protection, and disaster relief; (5) moderating serious sales decreases or production surpluses during a period of economic depression; (6) safeguarding the legitimate interest of foreign trade and economic cooperation; or (7) other circumstances as stipulated by law or by the State Council.[226] The last is a sweeping clause that enables the AMEAs to exempt restrictive agreements that are not specified in the AML. The AML further stipulates that, except for those agreements aimed at safeguarding the legitimate interest of foreign trade and economic cooperation or falling within those other circumstances as stipulated by law or the State Council, the undertakings in question must also prove that the agreement will not substantially eliminate competition in the relevant market and that consumers will be able to share the benefits derived from such agreement.[227] As indicated by the statutory text, the AML exemption scheme implies a balancing test for monopoly agreements by looking at multilayer and non-exhaustive standards that mix considerations of efficiencies, trade and industrial policy, and social public interest.

105. Exemptions of monopoly agreements are not available under the AUCL, the Price Law or the Bidding Law.

106. Justifications for otherwise abusive behaviour. Under the AML, certain types of conduct may constitute abusive behaviour by dominant undertakings and are prohibited if such behaviour cannot be justified. These include below-cost sales, refusal

226. AML, Art. 15(1)–(7).

227. *Ibid.*, Art. 15, para. 2.

to deal, exclusive dealing, tying and imposing other unreasonable terms, discriminatory treatment, and other abusive behaviour as determined by the AMEAs.[228] Under the AML, justifications can be proffered as a potential defence against an allegation of abuse of dominance.

107. The AUCL and the Price Law both list a number of circumstances where selling below the cost is permitted, including the sale of fresh, live, or seasonal products, disposal of products near expiry or sale of goods at lower prices for paying off debt, changing productions lines or closing of business.[229] Justifications for other types of prohibited abusive behaviour are not available under the AUCL and the Price Law.

III. Merger Tests

108. Under the AML, a concentration may be challenged if it has or is likely to have the effect of eliminating or restricting competition, unless the parties can prove that the positive effects of the concentration on competition significantly outweigh its negative effects or that the concentration is in public interest.[230]

109. The MOFCOM shall take the following factors into consideration when conducting a substantive assessment of a concentration: (1) the market share of the participating undertakings in the relevant market and their ability to control the market; (2) the concentration level in the relevant market; (3) the effect of the proposed concentration on market entry and technology development; (4) the effect of the proposed concentration on consumers and other relevant undertakings; (5) the effect of the proposed concentration on the development of the national economy; and (6) other factors affecting the market competition that are considered relevant by the MOFCOM.[231] The MOFCOM may approve a concentration unconditionally or with restrictive conditions to reduce the anticompetitive effects arising from the proposed concentration.[232]

110. The AML does not provide sufficiently clear rules on substantive tests for merger control. Thus the Merger Assessment Measures should be referred. The Merger Assessment Measures are formulated pursuant to the AML and stipulate that the MOFCOM should, where relevant to the circumstances of the case, comprehensively assess the competitive effects of a merger pursuant to the factors listed in Article 27 of the AML. When assessing a merger, the MOFCOM will first consider whether the merger will cause or strengthen a single undertaking's ability to eliminate or restrict competition (unilateral effects). If the relevant market is controlled by a few undertakings, the MOFCOM will consider whether the merger will cause or strengthen the undertakings' collective ability to eliminate or restrict competition (coordinated effects). The incentive and the likelihood of unilateral and coordinated effects will be considered. For vertical and conglomerate mergers, the MOFCOM will assess the adverse effect of the merger

228. AML, Art. 17(2)–(7).
229. AUCL, Art. 11; Price Law, Art. 14(2).
230. AML, Art. 28.
231. AML, Art. 27.
232. *Ibid.*, Art. 29.

on the upstream, downstream, and neighbouring markets (foreclosure effects and portfolio effects).[233]

111. The Merger Assessment Measures state that the market share of the merging parties is an important indicator of market power and the level of concentration in the market (measured by the Herfindahl-Hirschman Index and concentration ratios) will be a significant consideration in the MOFCOM's merger review. The Merger Assessment Measures also provide a list of other factors relevant to the assessment of market power. These include the competitive situation of the market, whether the merging parties are close competitors, whether other undertakings in the market have surplus capacity, countervailing buyer power, any financial and technological advantages of the merging parties and countervailing buyer power as a form of competitive pressure on the merging entity. The Merger Assessment Measures further consider the effect of a merger on market entry, technological progress, consumer welfare, upstream and downstream market participants, the national economy, and public interest. The efficiency defence (such as economies of scale and scope and cost reduction) and the failing firm defence are also recognised.[234]

233. Merger Assessment Measures, Arts 1, 3–4.
234. Merger Assessment Measures, Arts 5–12.

Chapter 4. Overview of Main Notions

§1. UNDERTAKING

112. Under the AML, the term of undertaking is defined as 'a natural person, a legal person or any other organisation that engages in the manufacture of or trading in goods or the provision of services'.[235]

113. A textual reading of this definition means that public authorities are not undertakings for the purpose of the AML, although the AML prohibits administrative monopoly, that is public authorities abusing their administrative powers to eliminate or restrict competition. This may illustrate the difficult relationship between the administrative monopoly prohibition and the remedy rules under the AML. The AML provides that an undertaking shall bear civil liabilities to those injured by the undertaking's monopoly conduct. However, the AML does not provide that injured parties are entitled to damages from public authorities engaging in administrative monopoly.[236] Therefore, the design of both public and private enforcement mechanisms under the AML vis-à-vis administrative monopoly is weak.

114. Undertakings belonging to the same group and having the status of parents and subsidiaries may have distinct legal personalities. To date, the AML implementing regulations and the AMEAs decisional practice have yet to specify whether different undertakings form part of the same group are considered as one undertaking under the AML rules on restrictive agreements. However, such undertakings are treated, for the purpose of the AML merger control regime, as one and the same undertaking and are exempted from the notification obligation. The AML stipulates that a notifiable concentration should not be implemented without a prior notification and a clearance. An exception from prior notification is provided where: (1) an undertaking concerned already holds more than half of the voting rights or assets of all other undertakings involved in the concentration; or (2) an undertaking not involved in the concentration holds more than half of the voting rights or assets of all other undertakings involved in the concentration.[237]

115. The AUCL provides a definition for the term of undertaking that is similar to that under the AML. The AUCL defines an undertaking to be 'a legal person or any other economic organisation or an individual engaged in business of goods or profit-making services'.[238] Although the AUCL refers to profit-making services, it is noteworthy

235. AML, Art. 12, para. 1.
236. AML, Arts 50–51.
237. AML, Art. 23.
238. AUCL, Art. 2, para. 3.

that, in the past, the SAIC has held that non-profit hospitals and schools are undertakings for the purposes of the AUCL.[239]

116. Trade Associations. The AML specifically prohibits trade associations from organising undertakings to reach monopoly agreements and stipulates that trade associations should guide undertakings towards lawful competition.[240] To date, the AML implementing regulations and the AMEAs decisional practice have not specified how associations of professionals (lawyers, accountants, etc.) will be treated under the AML.

§2. Relevant Market

117. The concept of the relevant market was introduced by the *Interim Provisions on the Prohibition of Monopolistic Pricing Behaviour 2003* (hereinafter 'Interim Provisions on Price Monopoly') but was not defined.[241] The AML defines the concept of relevant market as 'the scope of product or territory within which undertakings compete against each other for specific products or services during a certain period of time'.[242] In order to provide further guidance on the definition of the relevant market and enhance the transparency of enforcement, the AMC issued the Market Definition Guidelines in May 2009. The Market Definition Guidelines adopt similar approaches to market definition as those used in the EU and the United States and are in line with the prevailing international practice. Key aspects of the Market Definition Guidelines include an explanation of the relevance of market definition in competition analysis, a list of factors relevant to the definition of product and geographic markets, and an explanation of the basic analytic framework, including the use of the hypothetical monopolist test for arriving at a view of the market.

118. The role of the market definition.[243] The Market Definition Guidelines provide that defining the relevant market is a starting point for analysing competitive behaviour and is an important step in AML enforcement. The Market Definition Guidelines recognise that all competitive activities occur within specific market boundaries and that the market definition exercise is for the purpose of identifying the scope of the market in which undertakings compete against each other. Market definition has a significant impact on important issues such as identifying competitors and potential competitors, assessing the market share of the undertakings and market concentration levels, as well as determining the market positions of the undertakings.

239. SAIC Reply on Whether Public Schools Shall Be Governed by the Anti-Unfair Competition Law, Gong Shang Gong Zi (2006) No. 90; SAIC Reply on Whether Non-profit Medical Institutions Shall be Governed by the Anti-Unfair Competition Law, Gong Shang Gong Zi (2001) No. 248.

240. AML, Arts 11 & 16.

241. *See* the Interim Provisions on Price Monopoly, Art. 3. The Interim Provisions on Price Monopoly were promulgated by the NDRC on 18 Jun. 2003, effective on 1 Nov. 2003 and repealed on 1 Feb. 2011 when the Measures on the Prohibition of Price Monopoly entered into force, official Chinese text available at http://fldj. mofcom. gov. cn/accessory/200812/1228439272213. pdf, English translation available by subscription at www.lawinfochina.com.

242. AML, Art. 12, para. 2.

243. Market Definition Guidelines, Art. 2.

119. The relevant product and geographic market. According to the Market Definition Guidelines, the relevant product market and the relevant geographic market should be defined for the purpose of AML enforcement.[244] A 'relevant product market' refers to a market that comprises a group or type of products considered to be close substitutes for each other on the demand side due to factors such as product characteristics, intended use, and price. As such products demonstrate a strong competitive relationship with each other, they may be deemed as the product scope within which the undertakings compete against each other.[245] A 'relevant geographic market' refers to the geographic scope within which the demand side obtains relatively close substitutes. Because such geographic regions demonstrate a strong competitive relationship, they may be deemed as the geographic scope within which undertakings compete against each other.[246]

120. The Market Definition Guidelines also emphasise that the temporal aspect of the relevant market should be considered if the products are clearly characterised by features such as the production cycle, expiration period, seasonality, prevalence and fashion, and the protection period of intellectual property rights.[247] In addition, the Market Definition Guidelines provide that the definition of the relevant technology market may be necessary and factors such as intellectual property rights and innovation will be considered in cases involving technology transfer and licensing agreements.[248]

121. Fundamental basis for defining the relevant market: analysis of substitutability. The Market Definition Guidelines provide that the size of the relevant market is largely dependent on the extent of substitutability between products or geographic regions. In market competition, the existence of products considered to be close substitutes or the geographic regions where such products can be offered are the immediate and effective competitive constraints on an undertaking's behaviour. Thus, defining the relevant market mainly involves demand-side substitution analysis. Supply side substitution may also be considered if the competitive constraints on an undertaking's behaviour arising from the supply side are similar to those competitive constraints on the demand side.[249]

122. Demand-side substitution refers to the determination of substitutability among different products based on factors such as demand-side requirements for functionality, quality recognition and price acceptance, and accessibility of products.[250] Supply side substitution refers to the assessment of the extent of substitutability among different products from the perspective of the supply side, by taking into account factors such as the investment required by other undertakings to convert production facilities, risk factors, and time required to enter the target market.[251]

123. Methodologies for defining the relevant market. The Market Definition Guidelines emphasise that there is more than one method to define the relevant market. In addition to a substitution analysis from the demand side and the supply side, the

244. Market Definition Guidelines, Art. 3, para. 1.
245. *Ibid.*, Art. 3, para. 2.
246. *Ibid.*, Art. 3, para. 3.
247. Market Definition Guidelines, Art. 3, para. 4.
248. *Ibid.*, Art. 3, para. 5.
249. Market Definition Guidelines, Art. 4.
250. Market Definition Guidelines, Art. 5.
251. *Ibid.*, Art. 6.

'hypothetical monopolist test' may apply where the market scope is unclear or difficult to define. The Market Definition Guidelines also encourage the use of economic analysis based on objective and accurate data and emphasise that whatever methods are used to define the relevant market, the basic attributes of the products, that is meeting consumers' needs, should always be the focus and serve as the basis to adjust any obvious deviations that arise during the definition of the relevant market.[252]

124. The Market Definition Guidelines list a series of illustrative factors to be considered when defining the relevant product market and the relevant geographic market, based on analysing demand-side substitution and supply side substitution. These factors include evidence of switching between products or services, product characteristics, intended use, price differences, sales channels, transport costs, regional trade barriers of the products as well as consumer preference and dependence on the products.[253]

125. The SSNIP test. The Market Definition Guidelines adopt the hypothetical monopolist test, that is the 'Small but Significant and Non-transitory Increase in Price' test (hereinafter 'SSNIP test'), to determine the relevant market. This reflects that the AMC has adopted a more economic approach to market definition. The Market Definition Guidelines provide detailed steps for applying the SSNIP test and recognise that practical problems may arise from using the SSNIP test, including the 'cellophane fallacy' and the often forgotten impact of differences between consumer groups and geographic regions.[254] For example, with respect to the cellophane fallacy, the Market Definition Guidelines state that, in principle, when applying the SSNIP test, the benchmark price should be the prevailing price in a market with sufficient competition. However, where the prevailing price obviously deviates from the competitive price, using the prevailing price may result in irrational market definition. Under such circumstances, the current prevailing price should be adjusted and a more competitive price should be used.[255]

126. The AUCL, the Price Law, the Bidding Law, and their relevant implementing regulations do not adopt the concept of relevant market.

§3. Market Power/Dominant Position

127. The AUCL, the Price Law, and the Contract Law adopted the concept of monopoly.[256] The Provisions on Public Utilities introduced the concept of advantageous

252. Market Definition Guidelines, Art. 7.
253. Market Definition Guidelines, Arts 8–9.
254. Market Definition Guidelines, Arts 10–11.
255. Market Definition Guidelines, Art. 11, para. 1. 'Cellophane fallacy' is named after the subject matter of the *Cellophane* case in the US. In this case the Supreme Court erroneously accepted Du Pont's argument that cellophane was not a separate market, but competed with other flexible packaging materials such as aluminium foil, polythene, and wax paper. The Supreme Court however failed to consider whether the cross-elasticity between cellophane and other packaging materials was only high because Du Pont was already exercising market power. *See United States v. EI du Point de Nemours & Co* 351 US 377 (1956).
256. AUCL, Art. 6; Price Law, Art. 14(2); Contract Law, Art. 329.

position in 1993 but did not define it.[257] The concept was later developed to dominant market position by the Interim Provisions on Price Monopoly in 2003, which provided that a market dominant position should be determined mainly on the basis of the market share of an undertaking in the relevant market, the degree of substitutability of the product in question, and the degree of difficulty for competitors attempting to enter the market.[258] However, a definition of market dominant position and further guidance regarding the level of market share, the degree of substitutability or entry barriers have not been provided in the Interim Provisions on Price Monopoly.

128. The concept of dominant market position was formally adopted by the AML in 2007. Under the AML, a dominant position refers to the market position possessed by one undertaking or several undertakings as a whole that enable the undertaking(s) to control prices, product quantities or other trading terms in the relevant market, or to restrict or affect entry into the relevant market.[259]

129. The SAIC provides guidance on what would be considered to be other trading conditions relevant to the assessment of a dominant position. Under the Measures on the Prohibition of Abuse of Dominance, other trading terms refer to factors other than prices and quantities of products that can impose material influence on market transactions, including product quality, payment terms, delivery methods, and after-sales services.[260] Furthermore, the Measures on the Prohibition of Abuse of Dominance provide that the ability to restrict or affect entry of the relevant market refers to the ability to exclude the entry of other undertakings into the relevant market, delay the entry of other undertakings into the relevant market within a reasonable time, or result in a situation where, although other undertakings can enter into the relevant market, the increased entry cost makes it difficult for such undertakings to compete effectively in the market.[261]

130. Indicators of dominance. The AML provides a non-exhaustive list of illustrative factors to help determine whether a dominant market position exists. These factors include: (1) the market share of the undertakings in question and the competitive conditions in the relevant market; (2) the ability of the undertakings in question to control the sales market or the raw materials-purchasing market; (3) the financial and technical conditions of the undertakings in question; (4) the extent of dependence of other undertakings on the undertaking in question; and (5) how difficult it is for other undertakings to enter the relevant market. The AML also provides a sweeping clause that recognises other factors relating to the dominant market position of the undertakings in question.[262] Although this list is non-exhaustive, it should be noted that a time element is missing because these factors indicating dominance should be considered over a sufficient period of time in order to evaluate their competitive effect and to avoid unjustified regulatory interference into the marketplace.

131. The presumption of a dominant position. Under the AML, the presumption of a dominant position arises if: (1) the market share of one undertaking accounts for

257. Provisions on Public Utilities, Art. 3.
258. Interim Provisions on Price Monopoly, Arts 2 & 3.
259. AML, Art. 17, para. 2.
260. Measures on the Prohibition of Abuse of Dominance, Art. 3, para. 2.
261. *Ibid.*, Art. 3, para. 3.
262. AML, Art. 18.

one-half of the relevant market; (2) the combined market share of two undertakings as a whole accounts for two-thirds of the relevant market; or (3) the combined market share of three undertakings as a whole accounts for three-quarters of the relevant market.[263] This presumption of dominance can be rebutted by an undertaking that is presumed to hold a dominant market position if the undertaking can provide evidence to prove that it does not hold a dominant market position.[264] Moreover, no undertaking with a market share of less than 10% shall be considered to hold a dominant position.[265] The Measures on the Prohibition of Abuse of Dominance provide that, if an undertaking that is presumed to hold a dominant market position can prove that it does not have the ability to either control prices, product quantities or other trading terms in the relevant market or restrict or affect entry of the relevant market, the undertaking will not be found to hold such a dominant position.[266]

132. Although the AML makes it clear that the presumption of dominance is rebuttable if the undertaking can provide evidence to prove that it does not hold a dominant market position, it is unclear whether a finding of lack of dominance will be precluded by the presumption where an undertaking accounts for less than 50% of the market. In practice, some of the M&A transactions with less than 50% market share involved have drawn attention from anti-monopoly authorities. For example, in June 2014, MOFCOM prohibited the Maersk Line, Mediterranean Shipping Company SA, and CMA CGM's proposed cooperative joint venture. The primary reason for the injunction was that such alliance would take up nearly 46.7% market share in Euro-Asia route sector of the shipping market.[267] In addition, the notion of 'joint dominant market position' has caused criticism. For example, it is noted that the concept of a joint dominant market position is contrary to the prevailing norms, and the concept of collective dominance in the EU and German competition laws require additional evidence of coordinated conduct to be identified.[268]

§4. Agreements and Concerted Practices

133. The AML prohibits monopoly agreements, which are defined as 'agreements, decisions or other concerted practices that eliminate or restrict competition'.[269] However, the AML does not define the concepts of agreement and concerted practice. To give further guidance, the Measures on the Prohibition of Monopoly Agreements provide that agreements can be in written or oral format, and concerted practices refer to the

263. AML, Art. 19, para. 1.
264. *Ibid.*, Art. 19, para. 2.
265. *Ibid.*, Art. 19, para. 3.
266. Measures on the Prohibition of Abuse of Dominance, Art. 12.
267. Ministry of Commerce, Anti-Monopoly Review on Maersk Line, Mediterranean Shipping Company, CMA CGM, http://fldj.mofcom.gov.cn/article/ztxx/201406/20140600628586.shtml, 17 Jun. 2014.
268. H. Stephen Harris, Jr. & Rodney J. Ganske, *The Monopolization and IP Abuse Provisions of China's Anti-Monopoly Law: Concerns and a Proposal*, 75 Antitrust L. J. 221–224 (2008).
269. AML, Art. 13.

situation that, in the absence of expressly concluded written or oral agreements or decisions, coordinated actions virtually exist among undertakings.[270]

134. The Measures on the Prohibition of Monopoly Agreements further provide a series of factors to be considered when determining whether a concerted practice exists, including whether: (1) the action of the undertakings demonstrates uniformity; (2) there are communications of intent or exchanges of information among the undertakings; and (3) the undertakings can offer reasonable explanations for the concerted practices. Furthermore, the structure of the relevant market, competitive conditions, market change, and sector conditions should also be considered.[271] The Measures on the Prohibition of Price Monopoly provide similar provisions on agreements and concerted practices.[272]

§5. Restriction of Competition

135. The AML does not define the concept of restriction of competition or restraint. However, guidance can be found in the concept of monopoly agreement, which is defined as an agreement, decision or concerted practice that eliminates or restricts competition.[273] In addition, the AML does not distinguish monopoly agreements by object or by effect, but provides an illustrative list of the prohibited horizontal and vertical agreements that eliminate or restrict competition.[274] Until early 2013, the track record of NDRC's and the SAIC's AML enforcement activities vis-à-vis restrictive agreements has primarily targeted naked cartels. Based on the NDRC's and the SAIC's decisional practice against hardcore cartels and vertical restraints, it seems that the AMEAs tend to take formalistic approaches when determining whether or not an agreement eliminates or restricts competition and, thus, is prohibited under the AML.

136. As discussed at paragraph 75 above, *de minimis* rules have not been established under the AML or other competition-related laws and regulations. It is unclear whether the AML prohibition would be applicable to agreements that have an insignificant effect on competition, for example, because of the weak position of the parties involved. Of note is that the AML does exempt agreements that aim to improve operational efficiency and enhance competitiveness of small and medium-sized enterprises on the conditions that such agreements do not substantially restrict competition in the relevant market and will enable the consumers to share the benefits derived from the agreements.[275]

270. Measures on the Prohibition of Monopoly Agreements, Art. 2, para. 4.
271. Measures on the Prohibition of Monopoly Agreements, Art. 3.
272. Measures on the Prohibition of Price Monopoly, Arts 5–6.
273. AML, Art. 13.
274. *Ibid.*, Arts 13–14.
275. AML, Art. 15(3).

§6. Monopolisation and Abuse of Dominance

137. The AML does not provide a legal definition of abuse of dominance, but provides a non-exhaustive list of prohibited abusive behaviour, plus a catch-all provision.[276] There can be no abuse without a dominant position having been established pursuant to the AML. The AML prohibits undertakings with market dominant positions from abusing their positions in the following ways: (1) selling products at unfairly high prices or buying products at unfairly low prices; (2) selling products at prices below cost without justification; (3) refusing to enter into transactions with other parties without justification; (4) requiring that other parties enter into transactions exclusively with them or with undertakings designated by them without justification; (5) tying products without justification or imposing any other unreasonable terms in the course of the transaction; (6) applying dissimilar prices or other transaction terms to equivalent trading parties that are in the same position without justification; and (7) engaging in other conduct amounting to abuse of dominant market position as determined by the AMEAs.[277] The wording of the AML regarding abuse of dominance seems to suggest a formalistic approach. Therefore, close attention must be given to the practice of the AMEAs and the courts to ascertain how abuse of dominance will be defined and assessed under the AML. The AML seems to adopt an objective concept of abuse because a strict textual reading of the AML indicates that the subjective intent of the wrongdoer plays no role in the finding of abusive behaviour.

138. The Measures on the Prohibition of Abuse of Dominance detail the AML prohibition on non-price-related abusive behaviour including refusal to deal, exclusive dealing, tying or imposing other unreasonable transaction terms and discriminatory treatment:[278]

(1) *Refusal to deal.* A dominant undertaking is prohibited from, without justification, curtailing the volume of existing transactions with a counterparty, delaying or suspending existing transactions with a counterparty, refusing to enter into new transactions with a counterparty, making it difficult for a party to continue transactions by setting restrictive conditions, or refusing to grant access to essential facilities to a party.[279]
(2) *Exclusive dealing.* A dominant undertaking is prohibited from, without justification, requiring that a party enter into transactions only with itself or any undertaking designated by it or not enter into transactions with the dominant undertaking's competitors.[280]
(3) *Tying or imposing other unreasonable transaction terms.* A dominant undertaking is prohibited from, without justification, tying sales or imposing other unreasonable transaction terms. These include: (a) compulsory bundling or grouping of different products which is contrary to common business practices, consumption habits or product functionality; (b) imposing unreasonable restrictions on contract duration,

276. AML, Art. 17.
277. *Ibid.*, Art. 17.
278. Measures on the Prohibition of Abuse of Dominance, Arts 4–7.
279. Measures on the Prohibition of Abuse of Dominance, Art. 4.
280. Measures on the Prohibition of Abuse of Dominance, Art. 5.

payment terms, transport and delivery terms, and service terms; (c) imposing unreasonable restrictions on the sales region, target customers, and after-sales services; and (d) imposing transaction terms irrelevant to the subject matter of the transaction.[281]

(4) *Discriminatory treatment.* A dominant undertaking is prohibited from, without justification, discriminating between parties who are in comparable positions with respect to transaction terms such as transaction quantity, product variety, product quality, quantity discounts or other preferential conditions, payment and delivery terms, and after-sales services.[282]

139. The Measures on the Prohibition of Price Monopoly prohibit price-related abusive behaviour including unfair pricing, below-cost sales, refusal to deal through unfair pricing, exclusive dealing through price discount, imposing an unreasonable fee other than transaction price, and price discrimination.[283]

140. Justification. The AML does not specify what circumstances may be considered as acceptable justification for engaging in abuse of dominance conduct. However, guidance for justification of specific types of abuse can be found in the Measures on the Prohibition of Abuse of Dominance and the Measures on the Prohibition of Price Monopoly.[284]

§7. Concentrations

141. The concept of concentration and its definition are outlined in paragraphs 91–93 above.

§8. Joint Ventures

142. Transactions that constitute concentrations of undertakings are potentially subject to the merger notification requirement under the AML. An early draft of the Notification Measures provided that a lasting and an independently operated enterprise jointly established by two or more undertakings constituted a concentration of undertakings within the meaning of the AML.[285] However, this provision was deleted when the MOFCOM issued the final Notification Measures. This has led to uncertainty with respect to the notifiability of joint ventures. However, the MOFCOM's recent practices have suggested that the creation of joint ventures would be subject to AML merger control review and thus be notifiable to the MOFCOM where there is an acquisition of control and the notification thresholds are met.

281. Measures on the Prohibition of Abuse of Dominance, Art. 6.
282. Measures on the Prohibition of Abuse of Dominance, Art. 7.
283. Measures on the Prohibition of Price Monopoly, Arts 11–16.
284. *See* Measures on the Prohibition of Abuse of Dominance, Art. 8 and Measures on the Prohibition of Price Monopoly, Arts 12–14.
285. MOFCOM Draft Interim Measures on the Notification of Concentrations of Undertakings (March 2009 version) (copy on file with the authors), Art. 3, para. 2.

143. The concept of a full-function joint venture does not exist in Chinese law. The AML and other competition-related provisions do not distinguish between full-function and non-full-function joint ventures. It should be noted that the relevant agreements and conduct relating to a joint venture might also be construed as being monopoly agreements and, thus, fall within the jurisdiction of the SAIC or the NDRC. Nevertheless, how jurisdiction over joint venture agreements will be allocated among the MOFCOM, the SAIC, and the NDRC remains to be seen.

Chapter 5. Consequences of Violations and Enforcement

§1. Administrative Enforcement

I. The Antitrust Authorities

A. Formation, Composition

144. Pursuant to the AML, the AMC was established in 2008 as a consultative and a coordinating organ and the MOFCOM, the SAIC, and the NDRC, all of which are AMEAs, were designated with powers to enforce the AML.[286]

145. The AMC. The AMC is a consultative and a coordinating organisation and its authorities and responsibilities include: (1) formulating competition policy; (2) organising the investigation and assessment of the overall competition conditions and generating evaluation reports; (3) formulating and publishing anti-monopoly guidelines; (4) coordinating the enforcement work by the AMEAs; and, (5) other responsibilities as stipulated by the State Council.[287]

146. The day-to-day work of the AMC has been assigned to the MOFCOM. Until March 2013, the AMC had been chaired by China's former Vice Premier Wang Qishan, and the successor is Vice Premier Wang Yang. It has four vice chairmen (the heads of the MOFCOM, the NDRC, the SAIC, and a deputy secretary general of the State Council) and consists of fourteen commissioners (the incumbent deputy heads of fourteen ministries and institutions under the State Council). These ministries and institutions include: (1) the NDRC; (2) the SAIC; (3) the MOFCOM; (4) the SASAC; (5) the MIIT; (6) the Ministry of Transport; (7) the Ministry of Finance; (8) the Ministry of Supervision; (9) the State Intellectual Property Office (SIPO); (10) the CBRC; (11) the CSRC; (12) the CIRC; (13) the State Electricity Regulatory Commission (SERC); and (14) the Legislative Affairs Office of the State Council.[288] The First Session of the twelfth NPC in March 2013 approved the Plan of Reform and Transformation of Functions of the Institutions under the State Council.[289] New heads of the relevant ministries and commissions were announced following the annual session of the NPC.

---

286. AML, Arts 9–10; *See* the *Reform Plan of the Institutions under the State Council*, approved at the First Session of the 11th NPC in March 2008 and the *Circular Concerning Organizational Structure of the State Council* (Guo Fa [2008] No. 11).

287. AML, Art. 9.

288. *See* the *Circular of the General Office of the State Council on the Main Responsibilities and Commissioner Appointment of the Anti-Monopoly Commission* (Guo Ban Fa [2008] No. 104).

289. *See* the *Plan of Reform and Transformation of Functions of the Institutions under the State Council*, issued by the State Council on 10 Mar. 2013, official Chinese text available at http://www.gov.cn/2013lh/content_2354443.htm, English translation available by subscription at www.lawinfochina.com.

147. The NDRC. The NDRC is one of China's three AMEAs and is responsible for price-related infringements of the AML in the areas of restrictive agreements, abuse of dominance, and administrative monopoly. The responsible unit within the NDRC is the Price Supervision and Anti-Monopoly Bureau, which also has other regulatory roles pursuant to the Price Law. There are ten divisions under the Price Supervision and Anti-Monopoly Bureau, including: (1) the Comprehensive Division; (2) the Legislative Affairs Division; (3) the Supervision and Guidance Division; (4) the Price Investigation Division; (5) the Fee Investigation Division; (6) the Market Price Supervision Division I; (7) the Market Price Supervision Division II; (8) the Anti-Price Monopoly Investigation Division I; (9) the Anti-Price Monopoly Investigation Division II; and (10) the Competition Policy and International Cooperation Division. The Anti-Price Monopoly Investigation Division I, the Anti-Price Monopoly Investigation Division II, and the Competition Policy and International Cooperation Division are the working units responsible for the NDRC's role in AML enforcement and international cooperation.[290] In practice, the two Market Price Supervision Divisions also handle some of the AML investigations.

148. The SAIC. The SAIC is one of China's three AMEAs and is responsible for non-price-related infringements of the AML in the areas of restrictive agreements, abuse of dominance, and administrative monopoly. The responsible unit within the SAIC is the Anti-Monopoly and Anti-Unfair Competition Enforcement Bureau (hereinafter 'Competition Enforcement Bureau'). The Competition Enforcement Bureau has eight divisions, including: (1) the Comprehensive Division; (2) the Anti-Monopoly Enforcement Division I; (3) the Anti-Monopoly Enforcement Division II; (4) the Anti-Monopoly Legislative Affairs Division; (5) the Anti-Unfair Competition Division; (6) the Case Supervision and Coordination Division; (7) Direct Sale Regulation Division; and (8) Anti Pyramid Selling Division. The Anti-Monopoly Enforcement Division and the Anti-Monopoly Legislative Affairs Division are the working units responsible for the SAIC's role in AML enforcement.[291]

149. The MOFCOM. The MOFCOM is one of China's three AMEAs and is solely responsible for enforcing the merger control regime under the AML and coordinating the work of the AMC.[292] The responsible unit within the MOFCOM is the Anti-Monopoly Bureau, which has seven divisions, including: (1) the General Office; (2) the Competition Policy Division; (3) Merger Review Division (I); (4) Merger Review Division (II); (5)Merger Review Division (III); (6) the Supervision and Enforcement Division; and (7) the AMC Coordination Division.[293]

290. *See* Main Functions of the NDRC Price Supervision and Anti-Monopoly Bureau (in Chinese) at http://jjs.ndrc.gov.cn/jgsz/default.html.

291. *See* Composition of the SAIC Competition Enforcement Bureau (in Chinese) at www.saic.gov.cn/fldyfbzdjz/jgsz/.

292. The MOFCOM and the SAIC were jointly responsible for merger review pursuant to the M&A Rules. The SAIC ceased to be responsible for merger review after the AML took effect in 2008 and the subsequent amendment of the M&A Rules in 2009.

293. *See* Composition of the MOFCOM Anti-Monopoly Bureau (in Chinese) at http://fldj.mofcom.gov.cn/article/gywm/200811/20081105868495.shtml.

150. The AMEAs' local bureaus. The AML provides that, based on the needs of the enforcement work, the AMEAs may authorise their corresponding organs at the provincial level to be in charge of the AML enforcement work.[294]

151. The Procedural Measures on Monopoly Agreements and Abuse of Dominance Cases further provide that the SAIC may authorise its local bureaus at the provincial level to investigate and handle monopoly conduct occurring or mainly occurring within their corresponding administrative regions. Such authorisation should be decided on a case-by-case basis and the authorised local bureaus should not further delegate the cases to lower-level bureaus.[295]

152. The Procedural Measures on Price Monopoly Cases also provide that the NDRC may authorise its local price bureaus at the provincial level to investigate and handle price monopoly cases occurring within their corresponding administrative regions. The NDRC may designate relevant price bureaus at the provincial level to investigate and handle cross-region price monopoly cases, but the NDRC shall organise the investigation of major price monopoly cases directly.[296] Local price bureaus at the provincial level are allowed to delegate the investigation of price monopoly cases to the price bureaus at the next level down. The delegated price bureaus shall conduct the investigation on behalf of the delegating price bureaus and shall not entrust others to conduct the investigation.[297]

B. Investigating Powers

153. See discussion at paragraphs 385–390 below.

C. Adjudicating Powers (Ascertaining and Sanctioning)

154. The principal feature of the administrative enforcement of the AML is the combination of investigative, adjudicative, and prosecutorial functions. Apart from wide and substantial investigative powers, the AML grants the AMEAs the power to accept commitments, reopen proceedings, find infringements, adopt decisions, and impose fines and other penalties.[298] Other relevant laws and regulations, such as the AUCL and the Price Law, do not contain detailed provisions on the adjudicative powers of the enforcement agencies.

155. Commitments. Under the AML, where undertakings under investigation are committed to implementing specific measures within prescribed timeframes to eliminate the consequences of alleged monopoly conduct, the AMEAs may decide to suspend the investigation without making a finding as to whether there has been an infringement of the AML.[299]

156. The AMEAs shall monitor the undertakings' performance of such commitments and may terminate the investigation upon fulfilment of the commitments

294. AML, Art. 10, para. 2.
295. Procedural Measures on Monopoly Agreements and Abuse of Dominance Cases, Art. 3.
296. Procedural Measures on Price Monopoly Cases, Art. 3.
297. *Ibid.*, Art. 4.
298. AML, Arts 44–49.
299. AML, Art. 45, para. 1.

by the undertakings.[300] The investigation will be resumed if: (1) the undertakings fail to perform the commitments; (2) there has been a material change to the facts upon which the decision to suspend the investigation was made; or (3) the decision to suspend the investigation was made based on incomplete or false information provided by the undertakings.[301]

157. The AML and the relevant the relevant implementing regulations do not exclude the applicability of the said commitment rules to hardcore restrictions and are silent on whether the AMEAs can modify the commitment proposed by the undertakings. There have been precedents where the AMEAs accepted commitments made by the undertakings under investigation. For instance, in September 2016, SAIC published an investigation termination notice related to alleged anticompetitive activities of Hai'an Power Supply Company, which is a subsidiary of Jiangsu Power Company. The termination notice states that 'authorized by SAIC, Jiangsu AIC conducted an investigation on Hai'an Power Supply Company on 19 August 2013 for its alleged abuse of dominant market power to apply discriminatory treatment. On 5 September 2014, Jiangsu AIC issued a suspension decision for investigation of the case. On 19 August 2016, Jiangsu AIC decided to terminate the investigation pursuant to Anti-Monopoly Law and Provisions of the State Administration for Industry and Commerce on the Procedures of Handling Monopoly Agreement and Abuse of Market Dominance Cases, because the company had fulfilled its commitment to rectify its anti-competitive activities without triggering any legal ground for restoring the investigation.'[302] Besides, anti-monopoly enforcement officers from NDRC once indicated that they have evaluated whether China Telecom and China Unicom had fully fulfilled their commitments to rectification and whether such rectification had remedied the consequences or the impact of the alleged anticompetitive activities, and made its decision in accordance with the results of their evaluation. [303]

158. Leniency. The AML establishes a leniency mechanism to detect and combat cartels. No leniency provisions are available under the AUCL, the Price Law, or the Bidding Law. Under the AML, where an undertaking involved in a monopoly agreement, on its own initiative, reports important evidence relating to the making of the monopoly agreement to an AMEA, that undertaking may be given a reduced punishment or be exempted from punishment at the authorities' discretion.[304]

159. To increase the effectiveness of the leniency mechanism and to provide legal certainty to whistle-blowers regarding the conditions that a cartel member has to meet in order to receive immunity from the penalties, the relevant AML implementing regulations provide further guidance on leniency. For example, under the Measures on the Prohibition of Monopoly Agreements, important evidence means evidence that enables the SAIC and its local bureaus to initiate investigations or that plays a key role in the determination of monopoly agreements, for example, information that

300. AML, Art. 45, para. 2.
301. *Ibid.*, Art. 45, para. 3.
302. *See* http://www.saic.gov.cn/zwgk/gggs/jzzf/201609/t20160929_171498.html.
303. *See* Chinanews.com, NRDC: Decision on Anti-Monopoly Case of China Telecom and China Unicom http://news.xinhuanet. com/english2010/database/2010-01/21/c_13145387.htm, 9 Feb. 2014.
304. AML, Art. 46, para. 2.

relates to the parties to the agreements, the product scope involved, the way the agreements are reached, the content of the agreements, and the implementation of the agreements.

160. Under the Measures on the Prohibition of Monopoly Agreements, in granting leniency, the SAIC shall take into account the sequence of the undertakings' voluntary reports, the importance of the evidence provided, the circumstances surrounding the making and the implementation of monopoly agreements as well as the cooperation that the undertakings provided during the investigations.[305] An undertaking shall be exempted from penalties if it is the first to voluntarily report relevant information and material evidence regarding a monopoly agreement and offers comprehensive and voluntary cooperation during the investigation. For other undertakings that voluntarily report relevant information and material evidence regarding a monopoly agreement, the AMEA may impose reduced penalties by taking those circumstances into consideration.[306]

161. However, inconsistencies on the granting of leniency exist between the AML implementing regulations promulgated by the SAIC and the NDRC respectively. Under the NDRC's Procedural Measures on Price Monopoly Cases, the first undertaking which reports the circumstances of a price monopoly agreement and provides material evidence may be exempted from punishment; the second undertaking which reports the circumstances of a price monopoly agreement and provides material evidence may receive a penalty reduced by no less than 50%; and any other undertaking which reports the circumstances of a price monopoly agreement and provides material evidence may receive a penalty mitigated by no more than 50%.[307] In contrast, the SAIC's Measures on the Prohibition of Monopoly Agreements are silent on the percentage by which penalties are reduced for undertakings which report the circumstances of a non-price-related monopoly agreement and provide material evidence. A discretionary marker system, as what is adopted in the EU, is yet to be established under the AML.[308]

162. Furthermore, the SAIC's Procedural Measures on Monopoly Agreements and Abuse of Dominance Cases make it clear that the leniency provisions shall not apply to the ringleaders of cartels.[309] An early draft of the NDRC's Procedural Measures on Price Monopoly Cases contained a similar provision; however this was removed from the final version.[310] These inconsistencies and the resulting uncertainties may discourage whistle-blowers to come forward and thus compromise the effectiveness of the leniency regime under the AML. In addition, the AML and the relevant AML implementing regulations do not clarify whether an undertaking that seeks leniency

305. Measures on the Prohibition of Monopoly Agreements, Art. 11, para. 2.

306. *Ibid.*, Art. 12.

307. Procedural Measures on Price Monopoly Cases, Art. 14, para. 2.

308. The discretionary marker system adopted by the European Commission means, where justified, a leniency applicant can be accepted on the basis of limited information and the applicant is granted time on a case-by-case basis to gather information and evidence required for immunity. *See* Commission Notice on Immunity from Fines and Reduction of Fines in Cartel Cases [2006], OJ C 298/17, II. Immunity from Fines (14)–(15).

309. Procedural Measures on Monopoly Agreements and Abuse of Dominance Cases, Art. 20, para. 2.

310. Draft Procedural Measures on Price Monopoly Cases (June 2009 version) (copy on file with the authors), Art. 22.

would be given immunity from civil claims. There is currently no protection on the documentations filed by leniency applicants against requests of third parties aimed at collection evidence for follow-on actions. Further implementing regulations are, therefore, required to enable the AML leniency regime to become functional. Because of the insufficient transparency of the AMEAs' enforcement activities, it is unclear whether any on-site inspections carried out to date were based on leniency applications. In February 2016, NDRC, on behalf of the AMC, released a *Draft Guidelines for the application of Leniency Rules in Horizontal Monopoly Agreement.* [311]The exact time when it will take effect is still unknown.

163. Limitation period for the delivery of decisions. The AML and its implementing regulations to date do not provide any limitation period for the NDRC and the SAIC to deliver decisions regarding monopoly agreements and abuse of dominance cases. The MOFCOM is under a strict time limit to deliver merger review decisions.[312] In practice, NDRC rendered its final decision on the Qualcomm case in February 2015, which lasted for one year and three months in total since NDRC opened the investigation in November 2013. [313]SAIC rendered its decision on the Tetra Pak case in November 2016, which lasted for four years and ten months in total since SAIC opened the investigation in January 2012.[314]

164. Publication of decisions. Under the AML, the AMEAs may publish the decisions regarding monopoly agreements and abuse of dominance, which means that the publication of decisions is at the discretion of the NDRC and the SAIC.[315] The MOFCOM is required to publish its merger review decisions that prohibit or conditionally approve the proposed concentrations, but it is not required to publish unconditional merger clearance decisions.[316]

D. Other Institutional Tasks (Consultancy to Parliament/Government)

165. The AML does not explicitly provide that the AMEAs shall provide consultation to the NPC, the local people's congresses or the government. It is important to appreciate that the AML prohibits administrative organs from promulgating rules that eliminate or restrict competition.[317] The AMEAs may play a competition advocacy role and raise concerns if the rule-setting interferes with competition more than is necessary. In addition, as noted in paragraphs 99–101 above, the AML prohibits administrative monopoly but provides that the prohibition be handled and sanctioned by the superior authority of the public authority that engages in anticompetitive behaviour. The AML also provides that the AMEAs may make suggestions as to how to handle the administrative monopoly case in accordance with the law to the relevant

311. *See* http://jjs.ndrc.gov.cn/fjgld/201602/t20160203_774287.html for the Chinese text.
312. AML, Arts 25–26; also *see* a discussion at paras 475–477 below.
313. NDRC, Decision of Administrative Penalty No.1(2015), available at http://jjs.ndrc.gov.cn/fjgld/201503/t20150302_666170.html, 9 Feb. 2015.
314. *See* SAIC Competition Enforcement Decision No. 10 2016, available at http://www.saic.gov.cn/zwgk/gggs/jzzf/cfjd/201611/P020161116513025279743.pdf.
315. AML, Art. 44.
316. *Ibid.*, Art. 30.
317. AML, Art. 37.

superior authority.[318] The reported cases of the AMEAs' advocacy role are limited. However, as indicated by the Guangdong AIC's investigation into a municipal government's administrative monopoly conduct, consultancy to the legislature and the government has become part of the AMEAs' competition advocacy activities.

166. Local AIC bureau in Guangdong province investigated and handled administrative monopoly conduct in relation to GPS services.[319] In January 2011, three companies complained to the Guangdong AIC, a local bureau of the SAIC, alleging that a municipal government of Guangdong Province had abused its administrative power to eliminate or restrict competition in the market for global positioning system (GPS) services for motor vehicles. The three companies also applied to the Guangdong Province Legislative Affairs Office for administrative review of the municipal government's conduct in March 2011.

167. This was the first reported administrative monopoly case handled by an AIC authority pursuant to the AML. The Guangdong AIC found that the municipal government had abused its administrative power to eliminate or restrict competition and infringed the AML. The Guangdong AIC found that the municipal government, through the issue of minutes of meetings and work plan regarding the compulsory use of GPS monitors, had designated a particular GPS service provider as the municipality's GPS tracking and monitoring platform. All other GPS service suppliers were required to upload their monitoring data onto the platform and the designated GPS service provider was allowed to collect service charges of no more than CNY 30 per vehicle per month from other GPS service suppliers. The municipal government had also requested that the traffic administration department not allow those vehicles that failed to upload monitoring data to the designated platform to pass the annual vehicle examination. The Guangdong AIC found that the municipal government's conduct had exceeded its legitimate authorities, intervened in the normal operation of the business, and severely restricted competition in the GPS service market.

168. Guided by the SAIC and acting pursuant to the *Measures on the Prohibition of Abuse of Administrative Power to Eliminate or Restrict Competition* (an AML implementing regulation issued by the SAIC), the Guangdong AIC proposed that the Guangdong Provincial Government rectify the municipal government's conduct in accordance with the law. In June 2011, the Guangdong Provincial Government issued an administrative review decision holding that the municipal government's conduct had violated Articles 8 and 32 of the AML, as well as Article 13 of the *Law on Motor Way Safety*, and thus should be revoked. Since the AML became effective in 2008, NDRC and SAIC have published several cases on administrative monopoly, including cases concerning toll for highway, bid and tender for medical product, and cartels formed by local governments, etc. Those cases normally have significant impact on the society.

318. *Ibid.*, Art. 51.

319. China Industry & Commerce News, *Meeting Minutes Designated Business Operators; Administration for Industry and Commerce Bureaus Exercised the Consultation Right the First Time* (in Chinese), http://www.cicn.com.cn/content/2011-07/27/content_102134.htm, 27 Jul. 2011.

II. Government Direct Enforcement Activities

169. The enforcement of the AML and competition provisions of the AUCL and the Price Law is entrusted to the AMEAs, which can directly impose penalties on monopoly conduct without the involvement of other agencies or the courts. The AML and other competition-related laws and regulations do not entrust the direct enforcement powers to the State Council.

170. In June 2016, State Council released Opinion on Establishing Fair and Equitable Competition Review System in Marketplace ('Competition Review Opinion'). As the Competition Review Opinion mentions, fair competition is one of the fundamental principles of market economy, and the important foundation for an effective market mechanism. However, due to the existence of local protectionism, regional block, trade barrier, monopolistic enterprises, illegal government subsidies or preferential policies, and other means that are detrimental to market players' interests and in contravention of the principles of a unified national market and fair competition, China needs to put in place a mechanism in the market for the purpose of fair competition review, in order to ensure the government refrains from taking any anticompetitive executive actions or issuing measures and policies with effects of eliminating or restricting competition, and gradually abolish any regulations and approaches that get in the way of a unified national market and fair competition. The Competition Review Opinion states that the targets of fair competition review are regulations, regulatory documents, and other policies which may impact market players' economic activities, which include the administrative laws and regulations and policies from the State Council and other local rules. The criteria for review contain (1) market entrance and exit; (2) free-trading of products; (3) impact on the cost of production and operation; and (4) impact on production and operation activities. It further pointed out that based on the principle of 'who makes the rule shall clean up the rule', self-review by governments who promulgate the regulations and policies should be crucial during the fair competition review process. It means that any administrative regulations without fair competition review shall not be released. According to the Opinion, starting from July 2016, State Council, Provincial Government and their departments ('Reviewing Authorities') shall conduct fair competition review amidst their policy-making and legislation. Starting from 2017, the provincial government shall, based on how fair competition review fares, take away important experience/lessons therefrom, and guide the municipal and county governments through in their conducting of fair competition review. What's more, according to Competition Review Opinion, NDRC, State Counsel's Legislative Affairs Office, MOFCOM, SAIC, and other relative departments shall promptly study and devise the detailed implementation rules in terms of particularly the content, scope and method of the fair competition review, and guide the Reviewing Authorities to conduct fair competition review and revoke non-compliant policies to secure the orderly implementation of fair competition review. Needless to say, the AMEAs shall play a key role in carrying out fair competition review.[320]

320. Sina, Opinion on Establishing Fair and Equitable Reviewing System in Marketplace, http://finance.sina.com.cn/roll/2016-08-26/doc-ifxvixsh6709984.shtml, 26 Aug. 2016.

III. Other Administrative Agencies Applying Antitrust Rules

171. Although competition-related provisions of other laws and regulations, such as those under the AUCL and the Price Law, coexist with the AML, these provisions are primarily enforced by the SAIC, the NDRC, and each agency's local bureaus at the provincial level.

172. However, as discussed in paragraphs 47–49 and 58–63 above, sector-specific laws and regulations sometimes include competition-related provisions, a fact that may result in concurrent jurisdiction between the AMEAs and the sector regulators.

IV. Administrative Fines

173. Under the AML, the AMEAs may impose fines between 1%–10% of an undertaking's annual turnover in the preceding year for an infringement of the prohibitions on monopoly agreement or abuse of dominance.[321] To date, it is unclear which portion of an undertaking's turnover (i.e., worldwide, China-wide, or market-specific) will be subject to the fines. In cases where the monopoly agreement has not been implemented, a fine of up to CNY 500,000 may be imposed. Furthermore, a fine of up to CNY 500,000 may be imposed for industry associations that organise undertakings to reach monopoly agreements.[322] *See* paragraph 160 above for the AMEAs' powers to impose fines where leniency is granted, and paragraph 224 below where there is an obstruction of investigation by the undertaking concerned.

174. Pursuant to the AML, the implementation of an anticompetitive concentration in violation of the AML merger control rules is liable to a fine up to CNY 500,000.[323]

175. When deciding the amount of fines, the AMEAs are required to take into account the nature, extent, and duration of the illegal conduct.[324] To date, no further guidance on the calculation of fines has been provided. The AMC's proposed legislation Guideline on Determining Illegal Income and the Amount of Fine is still in the process of seeking public comments.[325]Although the AML enforcement history is relatively short and limited, information on how the fines were actually calculated and imposed can be obtained from the published decisions. For example, in the decision made by SAIC on Tetra Pak's abuse of dominant market position, it expressly imposed a fine on Tetra Pak of an amount of 7% of its turnover derived from sales of relevant products in Mainland China in 2011. [326] In the decision made by NDRC on Qualcomm's abuse of dominant market position in February 2015, it expressly imposed a fine of 8% of its turnover made in China in 2013.[327]

321. AML, Arts 46 & 47.
322. *Ibid.*, Art. 46, paras 2–3.
323. AML, Art. 48.
324. AML, Art. 49.
325. *See* http://jjs.ndrc.gov.cn/fjgld/201606/t20160617_807541.html for the Chinese text.
326. *See* SAIC Competition Enforcement Decision No. 10 2016, available at http://www.saic.gov.cn/zwgk/gggs/jzzf/cfjd/201611/P020161116513025279743.pdf.
327. *See* NDRC Decision of Administrative Penalty N o.1 (2015), available at http://jjs.ndrc.gov.cn/fjgld/201503/t20150302_666170.html.

176. See paragraphs 82, 87, and 90 above for the AMEAs' powers to impose fines under the AUCL, the Price Law, and the Bidding Law.

V. Administrative Injunctions and Other Restrictive Orders

177. Penalties for monopoly agreements and abuse of dominance: cease-and-desist orders and confiscation. Apart from imposing fines, if the NDRC or the SAIC finds that a monopoly agreement or an abuse of dominant market position violates the AML, it may order that the undertaking ceases its violations and confiscates the illegal gains.[328] In 2013, in the case related to six LCD major panel makers including Samsung, LG (both are South Korea enterprises), and Chimei and AU Optronics (both are Taiwanese enterprises), NDRC imposed aggregate penalties of RMB 353 million on those enterprisers (of which RMB 171.74 million were refunded to Mainland TV producers, RMB 36.75 million were confiscated as illegal income, and RMB 144,045 million were levied as a fine).[329] In the ensuing anti-monopoly decisions, it has been rare for anti-monopoly enforcement agencies to impose an administrative fine and confiscate illegal income at the same time. It is because, on the one hand, calculation of the amount of illegal income is difficult. On the other hand, pursuant to Article 50 of the AML, the business operators that carry out monopolistic conducts and have caused damages to others shall bear the civil liability under the applicable law. It means that because of the collusion of the LDC panel makers, the TV consumers have to pay the extra price. Under this circumstance, the consumers have the right to sue the LDC panel makers for damages based on NDRC's sanction decision. In the event that NDRC, as the enforcement authority, confiscates illegal income received by the LDC panel makers, the consumers' claims for compensation is unlikely to be sustained. Thus, theoretically, there are issues with Articles 46 and 47 of the AML that stipulates AMEAs have the power to confiscate illegal income.

178. In cases where industry associations organise undertakings to reach monopoly agreements and the circumstances are serious, the industry associations concerned may be deregistered by the competent registration authorities.[330]

179. Penalties for implementing anticompetitive concentrations: cease-and-desist orders and other remedies. For implementing anticompetitive concentrations in violation of the AML merger control rules, apart from imposing fines, the MOFCOM may order that the undertaking in question cease the implementation of the concentration, dispose of the shares or assets, transfer the business within a given time limit or to take other necessary measures to restore the market to its state prior to the concentration.[331]

180. Penalties for administrative monopoly: correction orders and disciplinary sanctions. Under the AML, the superior authority of the public authority engaging in administrative monopoly shall order the latter to rectify its conduct. The persons directly in charge and others who are directly responsible for the administrative

328. AML, Art. 46, para. 1 & Art. 47.
329. ChinaDaily, The Overview of Anti-Monopoly of LCD Panel Maker, http://www.chinadaily.com.cn/hqgj/jryw/2013-01-04/content_7925341.html, 04 Jan. 2013.
330. AML, Art. 46, para. 3.
331. AML, Art. 48.

monopoly are subject to disciplinary sanctions. The AMEAs may make proposals to the relevant superior authority on the handling of the case.[332] There are already precedents in this respect. Take a case involving a telecommunication regulator as an example. In 2014, Yunnan DRC noticed that Yunnan Telecommunication Bureau abused its administrative authority by guiding business operators into reaching a price monopoly agreement to eliminate and restrict market competition, which is in violation of the AML. Under NDRC's guidance, Yunnan DRC made investigation and requested Yunnan Telecommunication Bureau to rectify. After the investigation, it is revealed that during the period from August to October in 2009, Yunnan Telecommunication Bureau took the lead to organise several negotiations among China Mobile, China Telecom, China Unicom, and China Tietong and reached an agreement named *Agreement on Regulating Various Gift/Complimentary Activities Conducted by Yunan Basic Telecommunication Operators* at the end of 2009. The agreement required the four operators to unify the scope, amount, and frequency of their complimentary activities, and prescribed that a fine would be imposed upon the companies that do not comply with the agreement. Yunnan Telecommunication Bureau's aforementioned actions have violated Article 36 of the AML, which prescribes that 'no administrative organs or organizations empowered by law or administrative regulation to administer public affairs may abuse its administrative power to compel business operators to engage in monopolistic activities that are prohibited by this Law'. The Yunnan DRC had ordered the Yunnan Telecommunication Bureau to rectify and stop the actions. In the meantime, NDRC communicated further with the Ministry of Industry and Information Technology. The latter promised that it would guide Telecommunication Bureaus in all of the provinces, autonomous regions, and municipalities across China to study the AML in order to boost their administration capability, and correct similar illegal actions. Besides, Yunnan DRC imposed a fine on three operators that were parties to the colluded agreement at an amount of 2% of their last year's turnover from the relevant products and RMB 200,000 for TieTong, which was a party to the colluded agreement but did not perform it. The total amount of the fines levied in this case is RMB 13.18 million.[333]

VI. Interim Measures

181. The AML and its implementing regulations to date do not expressly provide the AMEAs with powers to take interim measures in relation to a possible infringement of the AML that may result in irreparable damage. There are no reported cases to date that establish that the AMEAs have such powers.

182. It should be noted that, pursuant to the AUCL, the enforcement agencies have the power to impose interim measures by ordering that the undertakings under investigation provide information on the source and quantity of products, suspend sales, and wait for the investigation. The undertakings under investigation cannot

332. AML, Art. 51.

333. *See* press release at http://jjs.ndrc.gov.cn/gzdt/201506/t20150602_694801.html

remove, conceal or destroy the property in question.[334] In addition, under the Price Law, enforcement agencies may order the undertakings under investigation to suspend sales and may register and preserve evidence if it might be destroyed or difficult to obtain later on.[335] However, to date there are no reported cases where interim measures have been imposed pursuant to the AUCL and the Price Law.

§2. Civil Enforcement

183. Prior to the enactment of the AML, enterprises in China were actively seeking a legal basis in the existing framework, for example, by relying on the AUCL and the Contract Law, to challenge their competitors' alleged monopoly conduct. High-profile cases included *Sichuan Dexian v. Shanghai Sony Guangdian Electonics* (hereinafter '*Dexian v. Song*'), on leveraging and bundling of consumables in an aftermarket, and *Dongjin v. Intel*, on bundling and intellectual property rights disputes.[336] At the same time, Chinese judges tried cases involving monopoly disputes based on broad principles in existing statutes.[337] In *Dexian v. Sony*, the court held that the plaintiff failed to proffer convincing evidence that Sony applied digital recognition code on Sony digital cameras and camcorders as well as the bundled batteries and, by doing so, abused its intellectual property rights so as to restrict competition from non-Sony batteries. In *Dongjin v. Intel*, the parties reached a settlement and the plaintiff withdrew the compliant.[338]

184. Under the AML and other competition-related laws, undertakings shall be responsible for civil liabilities if they infringe the relevant provisions and their conduct causes damages to others.[339] This means that civil enforcement of the AML and other competition-related laws is allowed and private parties can bring actions in the courts to challenge the alleged conduct and to claim damages. However, the AML and other competition-related laws themselves do not prescribe, for example, any procedures for seeking damages, evidentiary rules or guidelines for determining compensation. Instead, civil liabilities and litigation procedures are generally governed by the *General Principles of Civil Law 1986* (hereinafter 'Civil Law Principles') and the *Civil Procedure*

334. AUCL, Art. 17(3); also *see* para. 441 below.
335. Price Law, Art. 34 (3) & (4); also *see* para. 442 below.
336. Zhihong Hou, *Sichuan Dexian Sued Sony in Shanghai for Monopolizing Behaviour* (in Chinese), China Securities Daily (30 Jun. 2006); People's Daily Online, *Review: Causes and Consequences of Dongjin's Counterclaim against Intel* (in Chinese), http://it. people. com. cn/ GB/8219/68399/68409/4621379. html, 24 Jul. 2006.
337. Kong Xiangjun & He Zhonglin, *Establishing China's Anti-Monopoly Civil Litigation Regime* (in Chinese), in *Report on Competition Law and Policy of China 2010*, 24–25 (China Society for World Trade Organization Studies ed., Beijing: Law Press 2010).
338. *See Ibid.*, at 24–25 and 28–29.
339. AML, Art. 50; AUCL, Art. 20; Price Law, Art. 41; Bidding Law, Art. 53.

Law 1991 (amended 2007 and 2012) (hereinafter 'Civil Procedure Law').[340] Therefore, the Civil Law Principles and the Civil Procedure Law also govern private competition litigation. On 8 May 2012, the Supreme People's Court published the *Provisions on Several Issues Concerning the Application of Law in the Trail of Civil Dispute Cases Arising from Monopoly Conduct*.[341]The AML Judicial Interpretations state that they are promulgated in accordance with the AML, the Civil Law Principles, the Tortuous Liability Law, the Contract Law, the Civil Procedure Law, and other relevant laws.[342]

185. Pursuant to the AML, individuals and entities are entitled to bring private actions in respect of monopoly conduct, including restrictive agreements, abuse of dominance, and anticompetitive mergers, and to claim damages.[343] The scope for private actions under the AML is wide and recent court practice has indicated that stand-alone litigation is allowed.

186. It has been reported that, from 1 August 2008 when the AML came into effect to the end of 2015, the courts in China have accepted 430 private actions brought under the AML, of which 366 have been concluded. One of the notable features of anti-monopoly civil litigation is that it has been increasing consecutively every year. Especially in 2015, there were 156 case heard by the court and 116 were judged.[344] All of them were stand-alone claims. Among them, most of the cases involved alleged abuses of dominant market positions and a typical case is Qihoo *v.* Tencent for which the SPC made a final judgment in 2014. There were also cases involving vertical monopoly agreement and a typical case is Beijing Raibow *v.* Johnson & Johnson ruled by Shanghai Supreme People's Court in 2013. [345] Half the cases involved new technologies; and around one-third of the cases were settled or withdrawn.[346] In cases where judgments were rendered, the claims were all dismissed either because the plaintiffs failed to prove the relevant markets, the defendants' dominant position, or

340. The Civil Law Principles were promulgated by the NPC on 12 Apr. 1986, effective on 1 Jan 1987 and amended in 2009, English translation available at www.npc.gov.cn/englishnpc/Law/2007-12/12/content_1383941.htm The Civil Procedure Law was promulgated by the NPC on 9 Apr. 1991, effective on the same day and amended in 2007 and 2012, English translation available at www.npc.gov.cn/englishnpc/Law/2007-12/12/content_1383880.htm and www.npc.gov.cn/englishnpc/Law/2009-02/20/content_1471601.htm.

341. Official Chinese text of the Supreme People's Court Provisions on Several Issues Concerning the Application of Law in the Trail of Civil Dispute Cases Arising from Monopoly Conduct (hereinafter 'AML Judicial Interpretations') is available at http://www.court.gov.cn/xwzx/xwfbh/twzb/201205/t20120508_176702.htm.

342. *See* AML Judicial Interpretations, Preamble.

343. AML, Art. 50.

344. Supreme People's Court, *Press Interview regarding the Provisions on Issues Concerning the Application of Law in the Trail of Monopoly Civil Dispute Cases (draft for comments)*' (in Chinese), www.court.gov.cn/xwzx/yw/201104/t20110426_19885.htm, 26 Apr. 2011, and *see* http://blog.sina.com.cn/s/blog_5a81db850102w7kw.html.

345. *See* http://blog.sina.com.cn/s/blog_54dbb6fa0101lln5.html.

346. Kong Xiangjun & He Zhonglin, *Establishing China's Anti-Monopoly Civil Litigation Regime* (in Chinese), in *Report on Competition Law and Policy of China 2010*, 30–35 (China Society for World Trade Organization Studies ed., Beijing: Law Press 2010).

that the defendants abused dominant positions, or dismissed on limitation grounds.[347] However, there have recently been some cases where the plaintiff won in the end, including Beijing Rainbow *v.* Johnson & Johnson adjudicated and decided by Shanghai Supreme People's Court in 2003 and Huawei *v.* IDC adjudicated and decided by Guangdong Supreme People's Court in 2013. [348] These cases demonstrated that Chinese companies have started to use the AML as a weapon to fight against foreign competitors who have secured a dominant market position. On the contrary, these Chinese companies have shown improved capabilities of manoeuvring through anti-monopoly litigations.

187. Sursen v. Shanda.[349] The first judgment rendered in a private enforcement action brought under the AML was in relation to a case brought by Beijing Sursen Electronic Technology Co., Ltd (hereinafter 'Sursen') against Shanda Interactive Entertainment Ltd. (hereinafter 'Shanda') and Shanghai Xuanting Entertainment Co. Ltd (hereinafter 'Xuanting'). Both Sursen and Shanda and Xuanting own websites hosting digital books. An author commissioned by Shanda and Xuanting had written one of the most popular online novel series in China in 2008, called 'Star Change'. Xuanting owned the copyright to Star Change. Sursen then commissioned two authors to write a series of online novels entitled 'Star Change Sequel', which was also very popular. The content of Star Change Sequel was very similar to that of the Star Change. Shanda and Xuanting accused the authors of Star Change Sequel and Sursen of violating Xuanting's copyright. The authors of Star Change Sequel apologised to Shanda and Xuanting and promised to stop writing 'Star Change Sequel'. Sursen then brought an action under the AML and accused Shanda and Xuanting of abusing their dominant position in the market for online literature by restricting the ability of the authors of Star Change Sequel to enter into a business relationship with Shanda and Xuanting's competitors. Sursen also claimed CNY 16,820 for damages and legal fees. Shanda and Xuanting denied that they held a dominant position in the market for online literature and argued that the two authors stopped writing voluntarily since they realised that they had violated the Xuanting's copyright in the original novel. On 23 October 2009, the Shanghai No. 1 Intermediate People's Court delivered its judgment and rejected Sursen's claims, holding that Beijing Sursen had failed to provide sufficient evidence to prove that Shanda and Xuanting held a dominant position in the market for online literature. The AML Judicial Interpretations confirm that a case shall be accepted and heard when the plaintiff directly brings a civil action or brings a civil action after a decision made by the AMEA on the monopoly conduct becomes effective, provided that other acceptance criteria specified by law are satisfied.[350]

347. Legal Daily, *Only Ten Monopoly Cases Were Accepted by the Courts During the Past Two Years* (in Chinese), http://epaper. legaldaily. com. cn/fzrb/PDF/20100830/05. pdf, 30 Aug. 2010.

348. No.306 Adjudication of Guangdong Provincial Higher People's Court (2013) and No.306 Adjudication of Guangdong Provincial Higher People's Court (2013)

349. Ao Yingjie, *Judgment of the First Internet Monopoly Case Delivered Today* (in Chinese), www.chinacourt.org/html/article/200910/23/378581.shtml, 23 Oct. 2009.

350. AML Judicial Interpretations, Art. 2

188. Renren v. Baidu.[351] In *Renren v. Baidu*, the court for the first time conducted substantive analyses on the market definition, the presumption of dominance, and the evidentiary standards required for a finding of an abuse of dominance. Tangshan Renren Information Service Ltd. (hereinafter 'Renren') operates a medical information website while Baidu, Inc. (hereinafter 'Baidu') is a leading search engine provider in China, which offers natural as well as paid search rankings. Renren accused that Baidu had abused its dominant position in the search engine market by blocking Renren's website from natural search ranking after Renren reduced payment for listing in Baidu's paid search results. Renren claimed damages of CNY 1.106 million and sought an order for Baidu to cease its conduct. Baidu denied that it held a dominant position in China's search engine market but admitted that it had blocked Renren's website and argued that the blocking measures were taken indiscriminately pursuant to Baidu's policy of banning websites with junk links. The Beijing No. 1 Intermediate People's Court dismissed Renren's claim in December 2009, holding that: (1) Renren had failed to provide sufficient evidence to establish that Baidu held a position of dominance; and (2) Baidu's measures against Renren were justified and there was no relationship between Baidu's technical blocking measures and Renren's reduction of payment for rankings.

189. Zhou Ze v. China Mobile.[352] Zhou Ze, a customer of China Mobile, accused that China Mobile had abused its dominant position by imposing discriminatory tariffs to existing and new customers of mobile phones. Zhou alleged that China Mobile held a 70% market share in the market for mobile telecommunications. China Mobile argued that China's telecommunications market is competitive and denied that it held a dominant position in the market. The case was settled in October 2009 and China Mobile gave Zhou Ze a prize of CNY 1,000 for his help in improving China Mobile's services.

190. Li Fangping v. China Netcom.[353] In *Li Fangping v. China Netcom*, the plaintiff, a non-permanent resident in Beijing, accused China Unicom for abuse of dominance through discriminatory treatment between customers who have permanent resident status in Beijing and those who do not. The plaintiff alleged that when applying for installation of landline phones with China Netcom, post-pay contracts were only available for permanent Beijing residents, or non-permanent residents with guarantee. The court found that there was a relatively high degree of substitutability between landline and mobile telephony services and between cable and wireless Internet services. The court also found that China Netcom's terms and conditions for post-pay landline

351. Wang Wenbo, *The Baidu Case is Heard Today* (in Chinese), http://bj1zy.chinacourt.org/public/detail. php?id=612, 22 Apr. 2009; Yang Qinghui, *Judgment of the First Monopoly Case in Beijing Delivered* (in Chinese), http://bj1zy.chinacourt.org/public/detail. php?id=675, 23 Dec. 2009.

352. China Daily, *China Mobile 'Monopoly Case' Settled; Plaintiff Awarded a 'Prize" of 1,000 Yuan* (in Chinese), www.chinadaily.com.cn/zgzx/2009-10/28/content_8860663.htm, 28 Oct. 2009.

353. Shi Yan, *China Netcom Discrimination Case Referred to the Beijing No. 2 Intermediate People's Court* (in Chinese), www.chinacourt.org/html/article/200810/29/327718.shtml, 29 Oct. 2008; Huang Chenfeng, *China Netcom Discrimination Case Thrown Out* (in Chinese), http://tech.sina.com.cn/t/2009-12-25/16543712368.shtml, 25 Dec. 2009.

telephony were justified for control of credit risks. The claim was later rejected by the court because of insufficient evidence of dominance presented.

191. Rainbow v. J&J.[354] On 1 August 2013, the Shanghai Higher People's Court overturned the decision of the first instance court and ordered that Johnson & Johnson Medical (China) Ltd. and its Shanghai branch (hereinafter 'J&J') pay CNY 530,000 to its former distributor, Rainbow Medical Equipment & Supply Co. (hereinafter 'Rainbow'), for violating the AML. The case originated from a distribution agreement under which J&J set price floors that Rainbow could charge for surgical sutures. In July 2008, after finding that Rainbow had quoted suturing products in a bid below the price floor, J&J deducted Rainbow's deposit, terminated its distribution rights in several allocated hospitals, and, since August 2008, stopped the delivery of suturing products. Rainbow then filed a lawsuit in the Shanghai No. 1 Intermediate People's Court under Article 14(2) of the AML, seeking CNY 14 million in damages. However, the first instance court rejected Rainbow's claims, relying on a three-pronged test: (1) whether J&J engaged in the alleged monopoly conduct; (2) whether losses were suffered by Rainbow; and (3) whether there was a causal link between Rainbow's losses and J&J monopoly conduct. The first instance court held that Rainbow had failed to provide the requisite evidence on the market share of the disputed products, the competition conditions in the relevant market and the necessary causal link between the alleged RPM and the losses.

192. In contrast to the first instance court, the appellate court set down four criteria that must be satisfied for a defendant to bear civil liabilities arising out of RPM conduct: (1) whether there is sufficient competition in the relevant market; (2) whether the defendant possesses a strong market position; (3) the motivation of the defendant to engage in the RPM conduct; and (4) the impact of RPM on competition. After taking all the four factors into consideration, the court concluded that J&J has a strong market position in the surgical sutures market in China, in which there is insufficient competition, and that the RPM conduct eliminated intra-brand competition and restricted inter-brand competition. It found that J&J had breached Article 14(2) of the AML and ordered it to pay damages equal to Rainbow's loss of profits in 2008, which was calculated with reference to the retail prices and profit margins of other surgical sutures makers.

193. Huawei v. IDC. [355]This case was the first anti-monopoly case related to Standard Essential Patents ('SEPs') and adjudicated by People's Court with a final judgment rendered. Huawei, the plaintiff in this case, is a wireless communication equipment provider while IDC, the defendant in this case, has a lot of essential patent rights in wireless communication area that are compatible with 2G, 3G, and 4G

354. Press release on the *Rainbow v. J&J* Judgment of the Shanghai Higher People's Court (in Chinese) is available at http://www.hshfy.sh.cn/shfy/gweb/xxnr.jsp?pa=aaWQ9Mjc5NjgwJnhoPTEPdcssz; Official text of the *Rainbow v. J&J* Judgment (in Chinese) is available at http://www.hshfy.sh.cn:8081/flws/text.jsp?pa=ad3N4aD01JnRhaD2jqDIwMTKjqbumuN/D8cj9KNaqKdbV19a12jYzusUmd3o9z.

355. Shenzhen Intermediate People's Court, *Huawei v. InterDigital*, 4 Feb. 2013, [2011] Shen Zhong Fa Zhi Min Chu Zi No. 857; and No. 858; and Guangdong High People's Court, *Huawei v. InterDigital*, 16 Oct. 2013, [2013] Yue Gao Fa Min San Zhong Zi No. 305 and Guangdong High People's Court, *Huawei v. InterDigital*, 21 Oct. 2013, [2013] Yue Gao Fa Min San Zhong Zi No. 306.

standards. The parties have had multiple commercial negotiations regarding the licensing of these SEPs since November 2008 but failed for IDC's much higher licence fee charged to Huawei compared to that to Apple and Samsung. In July 2011, IDC sued Huawei in a United States federal court for injunction on Huawei's alleged infringement. On 6 December 2011, Huawei brought two lawsuits to the Intermediate People's Court of Shenzhen City, Guangdong Province. In one of these two lawsuits, Huawei requested court to stop IDC's abuse of dominant market position and claim for compensation. In the other lawsuit, Huawei requested the court to determine the licence fee IDC should charge Huawei on a fair and equitable basis. In February 2013, the Intermediate People's Court of Shenzhen City, Guangdong Province handed out the first verdict, and in October 2013, Guangdong Supreme People's Court gave the final judgment. There are several anti-monopoly issues in relation to SEPs considered in this case. The first issue concerns whether IDC has the dominant market position in terms of the SEPs. The second issue relates to how to determine the amount of the FRAND licence fee IDC should charge Huawei. The third issue concerns whether IDC has the right to request the court to issue an injunction against Huawei or bring a cause of action under patent infringement against Huawei. The court hearing the case took the view that as IDC holds the essential patents for WCDMA, CDMA2000, TD-SCDMA standards in global 3G communication business, and given such essential patents are unique and irreplaceable for these industrial standards, IDC has achieved market dominance position to the extent of the market where the SEPs at issue are concerned. In determining the FRAND licence fee of IDC's SEPs, the Court believes the fee level itself may be examined, or a comparison with fee rates charged to other licences for the same patents. If there is a large gap in the fees charged to one licensee and another in a similar position, then this constitutes evidence proving the existence of abuse of dominant market position by the licensor. Based on the then available evidence (particularly a comparison with the fees charged to Apple), the court rules that the fee rate IDC charges Huawei should not exceed 0.019%. On the issue of IDC's injunction claim in the United States federal court, the Court holds that considering Huawei had been acting in good faith during its negotiation with IDC, IDC's injunction claim basically serves to force Huawei to accept its unreasonable licence fees and aims to stop Huawei from exporting its products to the US market. This is not only a violation of its FRAND duty as the holder of essential patents for 3G standard but also of the AML. Taking into account the fact that both parties involved in this case are global leaders in the field of wireless communication, this judgment was highly publicised in China and abroad, and became a precedent in studying the SEPs and the AML.

194. Qihoo 360 v. Tencent.[356] The plaintiff, Qihoo 360, is a provider of free antivirus software with around 300 million users and has a reputation as the protector of Internet safety. The defendant, Tencent, is a provider of free instant messaging software and related service in the Internet sector with around 800 million users. On 11 November 2011, the plaintiff filed an anti-monopoly civil suit to the Guangdong Supreme People's Court, arguing on 3 November 2010, Tencent announced it would refuse to provide software services to users with any Qihoo software, forcing many to pick from one or the other. As a result, a large number of QQ software users deleted Qihoo's software. In addition, Tencent bundled its QQ Software Manager product with

356. *See* news report, http://legal.people.com.cn/n/2014/1016/c42510-25847888.html.

its instant messaging software, and under the pretext of updating the QQ Software Manager forced its users to instal QQ Doctor. As a result, the plaintiff was suing Tencent for abusing its dominant market position in the relevant instant messaging and related service market, constituting 'restrictive trade' and 'tying and bundling' that are prohibited by the AML. The Guangdong Supreme People's Court dismissed all of the plaintiff's claims on 28 March 2013. The plaintiff later appealed to the SPC which ultimately upheld the lower court's decision. This is the first and to date only anti-monopoly case heard by the SPC and thus drew public interest domestically and abroad. In the 115-page long judgment, the SPC elaborates on a series of important anti-monopoly legal issues, including the definition of relevant market, the criteria for determining market dominance, the principles and methods used to analyse the abuse of market dominance, etc., in the Internet industry. On the issue of relevant market, the SPC in its judgment points out that Hypothetical Monopolist Test (HMT) has a general application as one way of analysis in determining the relevant market. In practice, how the HMT will be set up depends on the area of market competition and the specifics of relevant data attainable. If the product in the particular market has high homogeneity and pricing is an important element of competition, the Small but Significant and Non-transitory Increase in Price Test (SSNIP) is the better approach. However, if there is obvious product differentiation and quality, service, innovation, consumer experience, and other non-pricing factors form the major elements of competition, then SSNIP may not be the best. It was hard to apply the HMT based on price increase in this case, but a modified version such as test on decrease in quality may be adopted. The definition of relevant market will primarily be determined using consumer substitution analysis, supplemented by the provider's perspective. Both qualitative and quantitative analyses can provide a definition of relevant market in practice, and there is no need for quantitative analysis if qualitative analysis does the job. Considering the above, the SPC defines the relevant market as instant messaging services in Mainland China. On whether Tencent has achieved market dominance, the SPC believes despite Tencent holding a large market share, market share is only a rough indicator of market dominance. When market entry is easy, high market share correlates operating efficiency or products with better quality, or products that are not in the relevant market impose strong competitive constraints to the company, high market share does not automatically translate into market dominance. This is especially true given the highly dynamic nature of the Internet industry where boundaries in markets are much vaguer than in traditional businesses. As such, a high market share should not be overestimated as an indicator, and more concrete facts and evidence such as market entry, market behaviour of operator, and the impact on competition, etc., should be looked into. Given that the Mainland Chinese instant communication market has adequate competition, easy market entry, and a large number of successful new entrants, the SPC ruled that there is not enough evidence suggesting the defendant has market dominance. On whether Tencent has abused its market dominance, the SPC points out that in cases where the market boundaries are vague and it is unclear whether the defendant has even achieved market dominance, further analysis of the defendant's impact on competitors is needed before concluding its market dominance. A comprehensive assessment of the negative and positive impact on consumers and competition due to the defendant's behaviour might also be necessary. The AML is not concerned with any particular operator's benefits, but whether as a whole healthy competition has been adversely affected or destroyed. During the one day Tencent implemented its 'incompatibility policy', all its main competitors, including MSN, Fetion, and Alibaba, saw relatively large increases in users, except Qihoo. Its (Qihoo) antivirus software only saw a 3.3% drop in market share, from 74.6% to 71.3%. Accordingly, there is no evidence suggesting Tencent through its incompatibility and product bundling extended its dominant position in instant messaging to the antivirus sector. Despite causing inconvenience to users, Tencent did not achieve any meaningful market exclusion or restriction, hence not violating prohibition on the abuse of market dominance set out in the AML.

195. Legal basis for bringing civil claims. The principal legal basis for the civil enforcement of competition law in China is the AML, which entitles individuals and entities to bring private actions in respect of monopoly conduct and to claim damages.[357] Similar provisions also exist under the AUCL, the Price Law, and the Bidding Law.[358]

196. Standing and causes of actions. The Supreme People's Court has confirmed that, if a party who brings civil litigation based on the AML meets the standing criteria set out in Article 119 of the Civil Procedure Law, the people's courts should accept the case.[359] These criteria include: (1) the plaintiff must be a natural person, a legal person or any other organisation that has direct interest in the disputed matter; (2) the identity of the defendant is definite; (3) the claim, facts, and reasons are concrete; and (4) the claim is within the jurisdiction of the court.[360] The Supreme People's Court is considering how direct interest should be refined when determining who has standing to bring civil competition litigation.[361] The AML Judicial Interpretations entitle individuals, legal persons, and other organisations that suffer losses from monopoly conduct or have disputes arising from agreements or rules of trade associations in violation of the AML to bring civil actions before the court.[362]

197. Specified anti-monopoly causes of actions. The Supreme People's Court promulgated the *Amendments to the Provisions on Causes of Actions in Civil Cases* (hereinafter 'Amended Provisions on Causes of Actions') on 18 February 2011, which took effect on 1 April 2011. In particular, the Amended Provisions on Causes of Actions classify competition disputes as Class I causes of actions and specify the causes of actions based on monopoly disputes pursuant to the AML. Specified causes of actions under the AML include disputes relating to: (1) horizontal monopoly agreements; (2) vertical monopoly agreements; (3) monopoly pricing; (4) predatory pricing; (5) refusal

357. AML, Art. 50.

358. AUCL, Art. 20; Price Law, Art. 41; Bidding Law, Art. 53.

359. *See* the *Supreme People's Court Notice on the Study and Implementation of the Anti-Monopoly Law* issued on 28 Jul. 2008.

360. Civil Procedure Law, Art. 119.

361. He Zhonglin & Zhu Li, *Principal Questions of Civil Anti-Monopoly Litigation: Report of the Consultation Meeting of Civil Anti-Monopoly Litigation and Judicial Interpretation* (in Chinese), *People's Court Daily*, 6, available at http://rmfyb.chinacourt.org/public/detail. php?id=130778, 6 Aug. 2009.

362. AML Judicial Interpretations, Art. 1.

to deal; (6) designated transactions; (7) bundling transactions; (8) discriminatory treatment; and (9) concentrations of undertakings.[363]

198. Time limits for bringing civil claims. The AML and other competition-related laws do not provide a limitation period within which a claim must be brought for a breach of the relevant laws. Hence the limitation period under the Civil Law Principles applies, which is two years from when the claimant knew or should have known of the alleged infringement of his or her rights.[364] The two-year time limit is subject to a long-stop limitation period of twenty years from when the rights were infringed.[365] The AML Judicial Interpretations further stipulate that the limitation period stops from the day the plaintiff reports the alleged monopoly conduct to the AMEA. If the AMEA decides not to accept the case, withdraws the case or terminates the investigation, a new limitation period begins from the day the plaintiff knew or ought to have known of the AMEA's decision. If the AMEA finds that the reported conduct constitutes monopoly conduct, a new limitation period begins from the day the plaintiff knew or ought to have known of that decision. If, at the time the plaintiff brings the action, the alleged monopoly conduct has continued for more than two years and the defendant raises the limitation period as a defence, the calculation of damages shall cover the two-year period prior to the date when the plaintiff files the lawsuit.[366]

199. Burden of proof. As a general rule under the Civil Procedure Law, the burden of proof lies with the claimants.[367] Therefore, in civil competition litigation, the plaintiff and defendant each bears the burden to prove the claims and defences respectively. Of note is that the burden of proof may reverse in some circumstances as specified under the AML, including exemptions for monopoly agreements, the rebuttal of the presumption of dominance and justifications for the conduct of dominant undertakings.[368] The AML Judicial Interpretations confirm the shifted burden of proof. If the alleged monopoly conduct falls into the agreements prohibited under Articles 13(1)–(5) of the AML (i.e., horizontal price-fixing, output restriction, market allocation, restriction on technology developments, and joint boycott), the defendant bears the burden of proof that the alleged agreement does not have the effect of eliminating or restricting competition. If the alleged monopoly conduct falls into an abuse of dominance prohibited under Article 17 of the AML, the plaintiff bears the burden of proof on the dominant position of the defendant in the relevant market and its abuse of such dominant market position. The burden of proof then shifts to the defendant to prove that its conduct is justifiable.[369]

200. In addition, the AML Judicial Interpretations recognise the presumed dominant position and stipulate that if the defendant in an abuse of dominance case is a public utility enterprise or an enterprise with a statutory monopoly status, the court may, on the basis of market structure and competition conditions, find that the defendant

363. Official text of the Amended Provisions on Causes of Actions in Chinese is available at www.court.gov.cn/xwzx/fyxw/zgrmfyxw/201103/t20110320_18959.htm.
364. Civil Law Principles, Art. 135.
365. *Ibid.*, Art. 137.
366. AML Judicial Interpretations, Art. 16.
367. Civil Procedure Law, Art. 64.
368. AML, Arts 15, 17 & 19.
369. AML Judicial Interpretations, Arts 7–8.

holds a dominant position in the relevant market unless there is sufficient evidence to the contrary. The plaintiff may use information publicly disclosed by the defendant to prove the defendant's dominant position. If the publicly disclosed information is sufficient to prove the defendant's dominant position, the court may find that the defendant holds a dominant position in the relevant market unless there is sufficient evidence to the contrary.[370]

201. Evidentiary value of decisions rendered by the anti-monopoly enforcement agencies. Official documents prepared by China's government agencies in their official capacity should generally carry more weight than other types of documentary evidence when submitted to prove a fact.[371] Therefore, a decision rendered by an AMEA is expected to be prima facie evidence of infringement in the related follow-on civil litigation. The Draft AML Judicial Interpretations once confirmed this principle and stipulated that the plaintiff may use a decision made by the AMEAs against monopoly conduct in a follow-on private suit to prove the existence of the alleged monopoly conduct, unless the defendant can provide rebuttal evidence.[372] Nevertheless, evidentiary value of decisions made by the AMEAs is controversial. Concerns had been raised and it had been suggested that this evidence rule should not discourage undertakings from cooperating with the AMEAs.[373] The finalised AML Judicial Interpretations do not include the use of the decisions of the AMEAs as prima facie evidence to prove monopoly conduct.

202. Expert witnesses and expert reports. The parties may apply to the court to engage one or two experts to appear in court and explain specialised issues relevant to the case. In Qihoo 360 v Tencent, both parties hired respective counsels as well as expert witnesses, some of whom formerly served as anti-monopoly officials in foreign governments. The parties may apply to the court to engage professional institutes or experts to conduct market research or undertake economic reports on specialised issues relevant to the case. Upon approval of the court, the parties may negotiate the choice of professional institutes or experts and if the parties fail to reach a consensus, the court shall designate the professional institutes or experts.[374]

203. Joint actions and representative actions. Under the Civil Procedure Law, joint actions and representative actions are available for multiple claimants. A joint action refers to the situation where the subject matter of separate proceedings is the same or similar and, with the consent of all parties, the court decides to combine the proceedings into one proceeding.[375] The AML Judicial Interpretations stipulate that if two or more plaintiffs bring multiple actions to the same court with competent jurisdiction

370. AML Judicial Interpretations, Arts 9–10.

371. *See* Some Provisions of the Supreme People's Court on Evidence in Civil Procedures (hereinafter 'Evidence Rules of Civil Procedures'), Art. 77. The Evidence Rules of Civil Procedures were promulgated by the Supreme People's Court on 21 Dec. 2001, effective on 1 Apr. 2002 and amended in 2008, official Chinese text available at www1.china.com.cn/chinese/PI-c/92700.htm, English translation available by subscription at www.lawinfochina.com.

372. *See* Draft AML Judicial Interpretations, Art. 11, para. 2. The Draft AML Judicial Interpretations were published on 25 Apr. 2011, official Chinese text available at http://www.court.gov.cn/gzhd/zqyj/201104/t20110425_19850.htm

373. Yang Xun & Jessica Su, *Anti-Monopoly Suits Heat Up*, 23 China L. & Prac. 25 (2009).

374. AML Judicial Interpretations, Arts 12–13.

375. Civil Procedure Law, Art. 52.

against the same monopoly conduct, the court may consolidate the trials of such cases. If two or more plaintiffs bring multiple actions to different courts with competent jurisdiction against the same monopoly conduct, the court that accepted the case later shall refer the case to the court that accepted the case earlier. The court accepting the referral may consolidate the trials of such cases. The defendant is obliged to provide information of actions in other courts against the same monopoly conduct to the court during its defence.[376]

204. Under the Civil Procedure Law, a representative action refers to the situation where a joint action has a large number of plaintiffs or defendants and the multiple parties elect to be represented by representative plaintiffs or defendants to carry on with the proceeding on their behalf.[377] If the number of litigants is not determined at the time a representative action is filed, the court may issue a public notice and claimants can opt in by registering with the court.[378] However, it has been suggested that the application of representative actions in competition-related cases should be limited because of concerns over the courts' ability to handle complicated competition cases involving multiple claimants.[379] The AML Judicial Interpretations removed the provisions on representative actions that existed in the previous draft and it remains to be seen whether representative actions will be allowed in the future pursuant to the Civil Procedure Law.

I. Competent Civil Courts

205. Civil competition-related actions may be brought before the courts if the alleged violation is committed within China. Furthermore, the courts may assert jurisdiction over anticompetitive conduct occurring outside China which has the effect of eliminating or restricting competition in China's domestic market.[380] Both hierarchical jurisdiction and territorial jurisdiction need to be considered when determining which courts have jurisdiction over civil competition-related actions.

206. Hierarchical jurisdiction. Hierarchical jurisdiction, or jurisdiction by level of courts for the trial of civil cases in the first instance, mainly depends on the nature and the significance of the disputed matters. As a general rule, basic people's courts have jurisdiction in the trial of cases unless otherwise prescribed by the Civil Procedure Law.[381] Intermediate people's courts have jurisdiction in the trial of cases involving significant subject matters, including: (1) major cases involving foreign elements; (2) cases with a major impact on the judicial district of the intermediate people's courts; and (3) cases as determined by the Supreme People's Court to be within the jurisdiction

376. AML Judicial Interpretations, Art. 6.

377. Civil Procedure Law, Art. 53.

378. *Ibid.*, Art. 54.

379. He Zhonglin & Zhu Li, *Principal Questions of Civil Anti-Monopoly Litigation: Report of the Consultation Meeting of Civil Anti-Monopoly Litigation and Judicial Interpretation* (in Chinese), People's Court Daily, 6, available at http://rmfyb. chinacourt. org/public/detail. php?id=130778, 6 Aug. 2009.

380. AML, Art. 2.

381. Civil Procedure Law, Art. 17.

of the intermediate people's courts.[382] Higher people's courts have jurisdiction in the trial of cases that have a major impact on the judicial districts of the higher people's courts.[383] The Supreme People's Court has jurisdiction in the trial of cases with nationwide impact and cases that the Supreme People's Court considers that it should exercise jurisdiction.[384] In practice, proceedings of significance are usually brought to the intermediate people's courts at the first instance.

207. Before the AML Judicial Interpretations were promulgated, it was unclear which level of courts will be the competent courts for the trial of private competition actions. It was expected that the intermediate people's courts would have first-instance jurisdiction over civil competition litigation. First, the Supreme People's Court issued the *Provisions on Causes of Actions in Civil Cases* (hereinafter 'Provisions on Causes of Actions') in February 2008, which categorised monopoly disputes as a subset of intellectual property right disputes.[385] In July 2008, just before the effective date of the AML, the Supreme People's Court issued a notice regarding the implementation of the AML. To be consistent with the Provisions on Causes of Actions, the notice requires that the intellectual property tribunals of the people's courts trial claims brought under the AML, including disputes over the abuse of intellectual property rights and other types of competition disputes.[386] It should be noted that most intellectual property tribunals reside within the civil divisions of the people's courts above the basic level. Second, since the AML entered into force, the first wave of civil competition cases were brought to the intermediate people's court or were transferred from basic people's courts to their corresponding intermediate courts for first-instance trial.

208. The AML Judicial Interpretations specify that the first-instance trial of anti-monopoly civil disputes should be heard by the intermediate people's courts located in: (1) the capital cities of provinces and autonomous regions; (2) the municipalities specifically designated under the State plan (i.e., Dalian, Qingdao, Ningbo, Xiamen, and Shenzhen); or (3) the municipalities directly under the State Council (i.e., Beijing, Shanghai, Tianjin, and Chongqing), or should be heard by other intermediate people's courts designated by the Supreme People's Court. Upon approval by the Supreme People's Court, basic courts may have first-instance jurisdiction over civil anti-monopoly litigation.[387]

209. Territorial jurisdiction. As a general rule, civil proceedings in China should be brought to the courts in the judicial districts where the defendants are located.[388] If an action involves multiple defendants located in different judicial districts, any of the

382. *Ibid.*, Art. 18.
383. *Ibid.*, Art. 19.
384. *Ibid.*, Art. 20.
385. *See* Provisions on Causes of Actions. It was reported that the Causes of Actions Measures were under revision and 'monopoly disputes' may become an independent cause of action separating from 'intellectual property disputes', *see* Kong Xiangjun & He Zhonglin, *Establishing China's Anti-Monopoly Civil Litigation Regime* (in Chinese), in *Report on Competition Law and Policy of China 2010*, 36 (Beijing: Law Press 2010).
386. *See* the *Supreme People's Court Notice on the Study and Implementation of the Anti-Monopoly Law* (28 Jul. 2008).
387. AML Judicial Interpretations, Art. 3.
388. Civil Procedure Law, Art. 21, paras 1–2.

appropriate courts can hear the case.[389] Special territorial jurisdiction rules apply where the general territorial jurisdiction is difficult to determine or where it is more appropriate to apply other rules of jurisdiction.[390] For example, contract dispute claims can be brought to the courts in the place where the contracts are performed.[391] For tort claims, actions can be brought to the courts where the defendants are located or where the alleged conduct occurred or is occurring.[392] The AML Judicial Interpretations confirm that territorial jurisdiction over civil anti-monopoly litigation shall be determined according to the specific facts of the case and the relevant provisions of the Civil Procedure Law and Judicial Interpretations on jurisdiction over tortious and contractual disputes.[393]

210. Appeal. Dissatisfied parties can appeal to the court at the next higher level within fifteen days after the date on which a judgment is served or within ten days after an order is served.[394] The Civil Procedure Law does not limit the grounds of appeal; therefore, appeal is available on both on questions of fact and questions of law. The enforcement of the first-instance judgment is automatically stayed upon the filing of an appeal within the prescribed time limits. Judgments rendered by the appellate court are final and enforceable.[395]

211. Time limits for adjudication. A first-instance trial generally concludes within six months after the case is filed. Under special circumstances, a six-month extension may be allowed upon approval from the president of the court. Any further extensions, if needed, shall be approved by the court at a higher level.[396] For expedited summary procedures, adjudication shall be made within three months after the case is filed and no extension of time is available.[397] An appellate court shall complete the hearing within three months after the appeal application is accepted. Further extensions, if needed, shall be approved by the president of the appellate court.[398]

212. Trial supervision. Trial supervision procedure, also known as a retrial procedure, is available for dissatisfied parties to challenge a final and enforceable judgment by approaching the court at the next higher level within six months after the effective date of the judgment.[399] Parties may apply for a trial supervision procedure on grounds such as insufficiency of evidence, error of law or deficiency of procedure.[400] The president of the court that rendered the judgment or a people's court and a people's procuratorate at a higher level may also invoke a trial supervision procedure.[401] Unlike

389. *Ibid.*, Art. 21, para. 3.
390. *Ibid.*, Arts 23–32.
391. *Ibid.*, Art. 23.
392. *Ibid.*, Art. 28.
393. AML Judicial Interpretations, Art. 4.
394. Civil Procedure Law, Art. 164.
395. *Ibid.*, Art. 175.
396. Civil Procedure Law, Art. 149.
397. *Ibid.*, Art. 161.
398. *Ibid.*, Art. 176.
399. Civil Procedure Law, Arts 199 & 205.
400. *Ibid.*, Art. 200.
401. *Ibid.*, Arts 198 & 208.

an appeal, the initiation of a trial supervision procedure by dissatisfied parties does not operate as an automatic stay of judgment unless otherwise ordered by the court.[402]

II. Sanctions

213. Pursuant to the Civil Law Principles, the court may impose any one or a combination of the following civil liabilities on an unsuccessful defendant: (1) cease infringements; (2) remove obstacles; (3) eliminate dangers; (4) return property; (5) restore the original conditions; (6) repair, rework or replace; (7) compensate for losses; (8) damages for breach of contract; (9) eliminate the ill effects and rehabilitate reputation; and (10) issue an apology.[403] It was expected that orders to cease the infringement, compensate for losses, and eliminate ill effects and dangers would be proper remedies for monopoly disputes brought before the courts.[404] The AML Judicial Interpretations confirm that if the defendant's monopoly conduct caused losses to the plaintiff, the court may order the defendant to cease the infringing conduct, pay damages or bear other civil liabilities based on the plaintiff's claims and the proven facts.[405]

A. Nullity

214. The AML and the Price Law do not specifically provide that agreements or other acts will be invalidated as a result of an infringement of the relevant competition provision. The AUCL and the Bidding Law provide that collusive bids are invalid.[406]

215. It is important to appreciate, however, that pursuant to the Civil Law Principles, civil acts shall be null and void if the acts: (1) are performed through collusive conduct that is detrimental to the interests of the State, a collective or a third party; (2) violate laws or public interest; or (3) are performed under the guise of legitimate acts to conceal illegal purposes. Civil acts that are null and void shall have no effect *ab initio.*[407] Furthermore, under the Contract Law, contract provisions that are in breach of any mandatory provision of laws and regulations are null and void and shall have no effect *ab initio.*[408] The Contract Law also provides that if a part of a contract is null and void, the remainder of the contract shall be valid if the invalid part can be severed from the contract without affecting the validity or enforceability of the rest of the contract.[409] Based on these provisions, the courts may declare that a

402. *Ibid.*, Arts 199 & 206.
403. Civil Law Principles, Art. 134.
404. *See* He Zhonglin & Zhu Li, *Principal Questions of Civil Anti-Monopoly Litigation: Report of the Consultation Meeting of Civil Anti-Monopoly Litigation and Judicial Interpretation* (in Chinese), People's Court Daily, 6, available at <http://rmfyb.chinacourt. org/public/detail. php?id=130778, 6 Aug. 2009.
405. AML Judicial Interpretations, Art. 14.
406. AUCL, Art. 27 and Bidding Law, Art. 53.
407. Civil Law Principles, Art. 58, para. 1(4), (5), (7) & para. 2.
408. Contract Law, Arts 52 & 56.
409. *Ibid.*, Art. 56.

monopoly agreement, an agreement containing monopoly provisions or part of such an agreement is null and void.

216. The AML Judicial Interpretations stipulate that the court shall invalidate the contents of contracts or rules of trade associations if they violate mandatory provisions of the AML or other laws and regulations.[410]

B. *Damages*

217. As a general rule, pursuant to the Civil Law Principles, the calculation of damages for civil liabilities includes compensation for the actual losses that the claimant has suffered, however it is debatable whether anticipated loss is included in that calculation.[411] Except for certain product liabilities, exemplary or punitive damages are generally not available in China.[412]

218. The AML, the Price Law, and the Bidding Law are all silent on the calculation of damages. The AUCL provides that, if the amount of loss suffered by the injured party is difficult to quantify, the amount of damages will be determined with reference to the profits derived from the infringement. The infringing party will also be liable to compensate the injured party for the reasonable costs of investigating the activities.[413] It is reported that punitive damages were under consideration for hardcore cartels in contravention of the AML but are not included in the Draft AML Judicial Interpretations. In addition, mitigated damages had been proposed for leniency applicants in administrative proceedings who are subject to private actions. Statutory damages had been proposed given the difficulty of proving actual losses arising from monopoly conduct.[414] However, neither punitive damages and mitigated damages nor statutory damages are provided in the finalised AML Judicial Interpretations. The AML Judicial Interpretations do confirm that, when calculating damages, the court may, upon request of the plaintiff, include reasonable expenses and costs incurred during the investigation and prevention of the alleged monopoly conduct by the plaintiff.[415]

219. In *Huawei v IDC*, Shenzhen Municipal Intermediate People's Court rules that as none of the parties provided concrete evidence showing 'the defendant profited or the plaintiff suffered loss due to the defendant's infringement on plaintiff's rights', taken into consideration the costs incurred by the plaintiff for attorney fees in China and the US, notary fees, loss of competitive interests, the nature of the infringement, subjective faults, and the seriousness of the impact to the plaintiff, the defendant is

410. AML Judicial Interpretations, Art. 15.
411. Civil Law Principles, Art. 117; also *see* Wei Zhenying, *Civil Law*, 724 (Chinese version) (Beijing: Peking University Press, 2000).
412. Injured consumers are entitled for double and decuple damages pursuant to Art. 49 of the *Law on Protection of Consumer Rights 1993* and Art. 96 of the *Food Safety Law 2009*, respectively.
413. AUCL, Art. 20.
414. He Zhonglin & Zhu Li, *Principal Questions of Civil Anti-Monopoly Litigation: Report of the Seminar of Civil Anti-Monopoly Litigation and Judicial Interpretation* (in Chinese), *People's Court Daily*, 6, available at http://rmfyb.chinacourt. org/public/detail. php?id=130778, 6 Aug. 2009.
415. AML Judicial Interpretations, Art. 14.

liable to the plaintiff for RMB 20,000,000 under economic loss due to monopoly. This decision was upheld by Guangdong Supreme People's Court as the final judgment.[416]

C. Interim Measures

220. Interim measures, including evidence preservation, property preservation, preservative measures, and advance enforcement, are available under the Civil Procedure Law and may be relevant to private anti-monopoly litigation. To date, there are no reported competition cases in which interim measures have been applied. It thus remains to be seen the extent to which interim measures will be relied upon in the civil enforcement of competition law in China.

221. Evidence preservation. Under the Civil Procedure Law, where there is a risk that evidence may be destroyed, lost or difficult to obtain later on, the parties may apply to the court for evidence preservation. The court may also take initiative to preserve such evidence.[417]

222. Preservative measures. If it may be difficult to enforce a judgment or any other damage may be caused because of the conduct of a party or other reasons, a court may, upon application of the opposing party, issue a ruling on preservation of the party's property, order the party to perform certain conduct, or prohibit the party from certain conduct. A court may order the applicant to provide a guarantee for taking a preservative measure and, if the applicant fails to provide guarantee, shall issue a ruling to dismiss the application. When it is necessary, a court may on its own initiative issue a ruling to take a preservative measure.[418]

223. Advance enforcement. Advance enforcement is available for cases involving urgent circumstances.[419] The Supreme People's Court interprets that urgent circumstances include situations where it is necessary to either: (1) cease the infringement and remove the obstacles; or (2) immediately cease certain conduct.[420] The court may order advance enforcement if: (1) the rights and obligations of the parties in dispute are clear and the applicant's life or business operation would be seriously affected without the advance enforcement; and (2) the respondent is capable of fulfilling the obligations involved in the advance enforcement.[421] When ordering advance enforcement, the court may require that the applicant provide a guarantee to cover any losses incurred by the respondent as a result of the advance enforcement order if the applicant is unsuccessful in the lawsuit. The application will be rejected if the applicant fails to provide such guarantee.[422]

---

416. Shenzhen Intermediate People's Court, *Huawei v. InterDigital*, 4 Feb. 2013, [2011] Shen Zhong Fa Zhi Min Chu Zi No. 857; and No. 858;

417. Civil Procedure Law, Art. 81.

418. Civil Procedure Law, Art. 100.

419. Civil Procedure Law, Art. 106(3).

420. *See* the *Supreme People's Court Several Opinions on the Application of the Civil Procedure Law* (promulgated on 14 Jul. 1992 and amended in 2008), Art. 107(1)–(2), official Chinese text available at www.people.com.cn/zixun/flfgk/item/dwjjf/falv/9/9-1-1-08.html.

421. Civil Procedure Law, Art. 107, para. 1.

422. *Ibid.*, Art. 107, para. 2.

§3. Criminal Enforcement

I. Criminal Sanctions for Antitrust Violations

224. Undertakings infringing the substantive rules on monopoly agreements, abuse of dominance, and concentrations under the AML are liable to administrative and civil liabilities. The AML does not provide for any criminal or individual liabilities for infringements of its substantive rules. However, fines may be imposed on individuals or entities obstructing investigations and if the obstruction constitutes a criminal offence, those individuals or entities may be prosecuted pursuant to the Criminal Law.[423]

225. Similarly, except for obstructing investigations, no criminal liabilities have been provided for conduct infringing the AUCL, the Price Law or the Bidding Law. However, it should be noted that the bid rigging offence and the forced transaction offence were introduced by the Criminal Law in 1997.[424] Companies responsible for criminal acts are liable for criminal fines and the person in charge and other personnel who are directly responsible are also liable for criminal penalties.[425]

226. The bid rigging offence under the Criminal Law. According to the Criminal Law, where bidders collusively submit bids that harm the interests of the tenderee and other bidders and when the circumstances are serious or where bidders and tenderee harm the legitimate interests of the State, collectives, and the public by colluding in the bidding, such bidders and/or tenderee are subject to imprisonment for a fixed term of up to three years, criminal detention, and/or fines.[426] Serious circumstances are defined as any of the following situations: (1) harming the legitimate interest of any of the tenderee, other bidders, the State, the collectives, and the public and causing economic losses of more than CNY 500,000; (2) the amount of illegal gains exceeding CNY 100,000; (3) the project price in the winning bid exceeding CNY 2 million; (4) engaging in illegal conduct, such as threat, fraud or bribery; or (5) repeat offenders who have been subject to administrative penalties for bid rigging on at least two prior occasions in the past two years and commit bid rigging again, even though the above quantitative threshold is not met.[427]

227. Forced transaction offence under the Criminal Law. According to the Criminal Law, where entities or persons violently or coercively force others to purchase or sell commodities or provide or accept services, and where the circumstances are serious, such entities or persons are subject to imprisonment for a fixed term of up to three years, criminal detention and/or fines.[428]

423. AML, Art. 52. Also *see* discussion at para. 439 below.
424. Criminal Law, Arts 223 & 226.
425. *Ibid.*, Art. 31.
426. Criminal Law, Art. 223.
427. *See* the *Supreme People's Procuratorate and the Ministry of Public Security Measures on the Criteria of Prosecution of Crimes (II) 2010* (promulgated on 7 May 2010), s. II, Art. 76, official Chinese text available at www.mps.gov.cn/n16/n1282/n3493/n3778/n4303/2417768.html.
428. Criminal Law, Art. 226.

II. Other Application of Criminal Law to Relevant Conducts

228. Monopoly conduct could potentially be criminally sanctioned if it constitutes bid rigging or is violent or coercive, subject to the criteria noted in paragraphs 226 and 227 above. Other monopoly conduct is currently not subject to criminal liabilities in China.

III. Role of Prosecutors

229. Pursuant to the *Criminal Procedure Law 1979* (amended 1996 and 2012) (hereinafter 'Criminal Procedure Law'), the people's procuratorates are responsible for conducting procuratorial work (including investigation) and initiating public prosecution at the people's courts.[429] That means that if a competition enforcement agency finds an infringement of the relevant competition provisions that may constitute a criminal offence, it must refer the case to a competent public security organ or a people's procuratorate to initiate a criminal proceeding. It remains to be seen to what extent the public security organs and the people's procuratorates play a role in competition cases.

IV. Competent Criminal Courts

230. The basic people's courts have jurisdiction as courts of first instance over ordinary criminal cases unless otherwise prescribed by the Criminal Procedure Law.[430] As a general rule for territorial jurisdiction, criminal cases are under the jurisdiction of the people's courts in the place where the crimes are committed. If it is more appropriate for the case to be tried by the people's court in the place where the defendant resides, then that court may have jurisdiction over the case.[431]

429. *See* Criminal Procedure Law, Art. 3. The Criminal Procedure Law was promulgated by the NPC on 7 Jul. 1979, effective on 1 Jan. 1980 and amended on 1996 and 2012, English translation available at www.npc.gov.cn/englishnpc/Law/2007-12/13/content_1384067.htm.

430. Criminal Procedure Law, Art. 19.

431. *Ibid.*, Art. 24.

Part II. The Application of the Prohibitions

Chapter 1. Restrictive Agreements

231. *See* paragraphs 78–80 above for an overview of the AML provisions on restrictive agreements. The AML and the competition provisions in other laws and regulations do not provide for a notification system for monopoly agreements. It is possible that the NDRC or the SAIC may adopt block exemptions and consultation procedures with respect to horizontal or vertical agreements in the future. At present, self-assessment by the parties to a horizontal or a vertical agreement is necessary in order to ensure compliance.

232. However, in order to clarify the general conditions and procedures for exemptions on monopoly agreements, the AMC of the State Council is organising the drafting of *the Guidelines on General Terms and Procedures for Exemptions from Monopoly Agreements*[432] in order for businesses to better understand and use the anti-monopoly agreement exemption system, guide relevant authorities as well as increase enforceability and transparency. The Draft General Terms put forward various factors that need to be considered for exemptions on monopoly agreements, and stressed that the AMC may, as it sees appropriate, issue guidelines with regard to the exemption of certain specific types of monopoly agreements and monopoly agreement for certain specific sectors.

§1. Horizontal Agreements

I. Cartels

233. Price-fixing, market allocation and output limitation are deemed to be hardcore cartels in mature antitrust jurisdictions and it is unlikely that hardcore cartels will satisfy the criteria for exemption or be treated under the reasonableness test. However, it is still unclear whether hardcore cartels will be treated as per se illegal under the AML or subject to the AML exemption rules, depending on the circumstances.[433] Apart from the AML, other competition-related laws, including the AUCL, the Price Law, and the Bidding Law, contain provisions governing cartel arrangements.

432. *See* http://jjs.ndrc.gov.cn/fjgld/201605/t20160512_801559.html for the Chinese text.
433. AML, Art. 15.

A. Price-Fixing

234. The AML prohibits the collusive fixing or changing of prices among competing undertakings.[434] Under the Price Law, undertakings are prohibited from colluding with each other to manipulate the market price and to harm the lawful rights and interests of other undertakings or consumers.[435]

235. The Measures on the Prohibition of Price Monopoly detail the circumstances in which horizontal price-fixing agreements are prohibited under the AML. Competing undertakings are prohibited from: (1) fixing or changing prices; (2) fixing or changing the range of price changes; (3) fixing or changing commissions, discounts or other fees that affect prices; (4) using an agreed price as a benchmark for negotiating with third parties; (5) setting a standard formula for pricing; (6) agreeing that prices may not be changed without other undertakings' consent; (7) fixing or changing prices through other means; and (8) other price-fixing agreements as determined by the NDRC.[436]

236. Cartel activities, especially price-fixing, have been widely reported in China over the years and appear to be commonplace, even after the enactment of the AML. As the enforcement authority responsible for price-related infringements under the AML and for the Price Law, the NDRC and its local bureaus have taken actions tackling a number of price-fixing cartels since the AML entered into force in 2008.

237. The Rice Noodle Cartel. In March 2010, the NDRC's local price bureau in the Guangxi province punished a number of local rice noodle producers for colluding to increase and fix prices for rice noodles. The local bureau found that the cartel leaders held meetings to discuss pricing, coerced other producers to join the cartel, and eventually reached an agreement to collectively increase prices and to share the profits derived from the price cartel. The local bureau relied on the AML and the Price Law and fined three leading producers of rice noodles CNY 100,000 each, and other eighteen producers of rice noodles between CNY 30,000 and CNY 80,000 each. Twelve producers of rice noodles received leniency in return for cooperation with the investigation.[437]

238. The Green Bean and Garlic Cartel. In July 2010, the NDRC Price Supervision Department, together with the MOFCOM Department of Market Supervision and the SAIC Department of Market Regulation, announced that three decisions had been made by local price authorities in Inner Mongolia, Shandong, Henan, and Guangdong in relation to collusion and manipulation of prices of green beans and garlic. It was alleged that the Jilin Corn Centre Wholesale Company led and cooperated with other companies, through meetings and other means, to fabricate and disseminate information on price increases and to collude to increase the price of green beans. It received a fine of CNY 1 million, which has been the most serious penalty to date since the enactment of the AML. Several cooperating companies received fines of CNY 500,000, and warnings were issued to 109 agricultural trading companies alleged to have joined

434. AML, Art. 13(1).

435. Price Law, Art. 14(1).

436. Measures on the Prohibition of Price Monopoly, Art. 7.

437. NDRC, *Rice Noodle Producers in Nanning and Liuzhou Investigated and Penalized for Colluding in Price Increases* (in Chinese), http://jjs.ndrc.gov.cn/fjgld/t20100331_338262.htm, 31 Mar. 2010.

the cartel. The trade associations and trading companies in the Henan and the Shandong provinces who were alleged to have colluded to increase the price of garlic were fined between CNY 80,000 and CNY 100,000 each.[438]

239. LCD producers panelised for price cartel.[439] In January 2013, the NDRC announced that it had investigated and penalised six LCD panel manufacturers from Korea (Samsung and LG) and Taiwan (AU Optronics, Chunghwa, Linolux, and HannStar) for fixing the price of LCD panels in China. This was the first time that the NDRC imposed penalties on an international cartel.

240. The NDRC began its investigations in December 2006. It found that, from 2001 to 2006, the six LCD panel manufacturers had held fifty-three 'crystal conferences' in Korea and Taiwan. These meetings were held almost on a monthly basis and used to exchange information about the LCD panel market and negotiate the price of LCD panels. The LCD panels sold in Mainland China by the six manufacturers were priced according to the negotiated prices or the exchanged information. The NDRC estimated that, from 2001 to 2006, LCD panels accounted for 70%–80% of the manufacturing cost of televisions. It found that the six manufacturers had sold over 5 million LCD panels into Mainland China during this period and made illegal gains of CNY 208 million. It found that the manufacturers had manipulated market prices and harmed the legitimate interests of other business operators and consumers, breaching Article 14(1) of the Price Law.

241. Pursuant to Articles 40 and 41 of the Price Law, the NDRC imposed aggregate penalties of CNY 353 million. It ordered the repayment of CNY 172 million to Chinese television manufacturers (nine in total), confiscated CNY 36.75 million, and imposed fines of CNY 144 million. The highest individual penalties were imposed on Samsung (CNY 101 million), LG (CNY 118 million), and Linolux (CNY 94.41 million). The NDRC stated it had reduced the penalties as the LCD panel manufacturers had voluntarily provided relevant information.

242. The six manufacturers also committed to strictly abide by China's laws, consciously maintain market competition order, and protect the legitimate interests of other business operators and consumers; use their best efforts to fairly supply China's television manufacturers and provide all customers the same opportunities to purchase high-end and high-tech products; and extend the warranty period on LCD panels sold in China from eighteen months to thirty-six months. It is estimated that the extension of warranty will save Chinese television manufacturers CNY 395 million in repair and maintenance costs. As the price-fixing conduct occurred from 2001 to 2006, which was prior to the AML coming into effect in August 2008, the penalties were imposed pursuant to the Price Law. The NDRC noted that, had the conduct been punished pursuant to the AML, it would have resulted in higher penalties. Under the AML,

---

438. NDRC, *NDRC, MOFCOM and SAIC Announced the Investigation against and Penalties Imposed on Hoarding and Price Collusion of Agricultural Products* (in Chinese)http://jjs.ndrc.gov.cn/gzdt/t20100702_358457.htm, 2 Jul. 2010.

439. NDRC, *Six Foreign Enterprises Panelized for Monopolizing LCD Panel Prices* (in Chinese), http://jjs.ndrc.gov.cn/gzdt/t20130117_523203.htm, 17 Jan. 2013; NDRC, *Answers to the Press regarding the LCD Cartel Case* (in Chinese), http://jjs.ndrc.gov.cn/gzdt/t20130117_523205.htm, 17 Jan. 2013.

penalties are calculated based on turnover whereas under the Price Law, they are based on illegal gains.

243. Price cartels formed by twelve Japanese auto parts manufacturers. The largest anti-monopoly fine to date was handed by NDRC on August 2014 to Japanese cartels of twelve auto parts manufacturers including Hitachi, Mitsubishi Electric, Fujikoshi, etc., amounting to RMB 1,235 billion. This fine involves two price cartels. According to the investigation, between January 2000 and February 2010 the eight Japanese auto parts manufacturers of Hitachi, Denso, Aisan, Mitsubishi Electric, Mitsuba, Yazaki, Furukawa, and Sumitomo in attempting to reduce competition and secure contracts at the most favourable rate, held bilateral or multilateral talks in Japan on multiple occasions to negotiate prices and implement order pricing agreements. Products involved in the price collusion which entered the Chinese market and received orders included starters, alternators, throttle bodies, wiring harnesses, and thirteen others. The parts whose prices were prefixed were used by over twenty models from Honda, Toyota, Nissan, Suzuki, and Ford, etc. As of the end of 2013, parts from the price collusions were still being supplied to the Chinese market. From 2000 to June 2011, the four bearing manufacturers of Nachi, Seiko, Jetway Tektronix, and NTN organised study seminars in Japan and market conferences in Shanghai to discuss the policies, timing, and magnitude of the increase in bearing price in the Asian and Chinese markets, and actually raised price accordingly.

244. The NDRC points that such acts by the twelve Japanese auto parts suppliers have violated the AML, excluded or restrained market competition, unlawfully influenced the respective prices for Chinese car's parts, full vehicle, and bearings, and thus damaged the rights of downstream manufacturers and interests of Chinese consumers. Punishments for price collusions of vehicle parts were: (1) Exemption of punishment for Hitachi which was the first to disclose the cartel and provided vital evidence, (2) About 4% of the turnover from the previous year for Denso which was the second to disclose and provided vital evidence, (3) About 6% of the turnover from the previous year from Yazaki, Furukawa, and Sumitomo which only participated in the price-fixing of one product, (4) About 8% of the turnover from the previous years from Aisan, Mitsubishi Electric, and Mitsuba which participated in the price-fixing of two products or more. Punishments for price-fixing bearings have been: (1) Exemption for Nachi which was the first to disclose the cartel and provided vital evidence, (2) About 4% of the turnover of the previous year for Seiko which was the second to disclose and provided vital evidence, (3) About 6% of the turnover from the previous year for NTN which left the Asian seminars but continued to attend the Shanghai conferences, (4) About 8% of the turnover of the previous year for Jetway Tektronix which organised conferences aimed at the Chinese market.

245. All the manufacturers involved proposed to take corrective measures set out as the following: (1) immediately adjust marketing polices based on existing Chinese law, (2) train all personnel to ensure compliance with relevant anti-monopoly regulations, (3) take steps to atone for past actions as well as to preserve the market order under full competition, and protect consumer rights.[440]

440. People.com, The Most Biggest Penalty: 12 Japanese Car Enterprises Imposed Fine of 1,225 million, http://auto.people.com.cn/n/2014/0820/c1005-25502326.html, 20 Aug. 2014.

B. Market/Client Allocation

246. The AML prohibits the allocation of sales market or raw material procurement market among competing undertakings.[441] The Measures on the Prohibition of Monopoly Agreements further set forth the AML rule on market allocation and prohibits competing undertakings from allocating: (1) sales regions, targets, categories, and volumes; (2) procurement regions, categories, and volumes of raw materials, semi-finished goods, parts and components, and related equipment; and (3) suppliers of raw materials, semi-finished goods, parts and components, and related equipment.[442]

247. Concrete manufacturer association penalised for market allocation. It is reported that, in early 2011, the Jiangsu Province Administration for Industry and Commerce, a local arm of SAIC, has penalised the Concrete Manufacturer Association of Lianyungang City for market sharing and fixing market shares. Officials at the Jiangsu Province Administration for Industry and Commerce said that, in March 2009, the association organised for sixteen members to reach several 'self-disciplinary agreements' that were aimed at coordinating competition and monopolising the market. The association allocated sales markets and units according to its members' capacities and equipment. Until August 2010, the association organised several meetings to discuss the allocation of projects and deterrent mechanisms. The association also obstructed its members' ability to enter into sales agreements with customers, which directly caused the suspension of several local construction projects. The Jiangsu Province Administration for Industry and Commerce found that the association breached the AML and imposed fines of CNY 730,723.19 on and confiscated illegal gains of CNY 136,481.21 of the association and the relevant parties.[443]

248. Another classic case of market allocation cartel is Hubei SAIC's administrative decision against the Insurance Industry Association of Hubei Province ('HAH') in 2016. According to investigation, since May 2005 HAH has been organising insurance companies in Hubei province to sign the 'Agreement on Unified Management of New Car Insurance in Wuhan City Vehicle Market', and established the Wuhan New Car Insurance Service Center ('New Car Center'), and handling other major issues involved in insuring new cars. Its primary function was to consolidate all the services previously provided by each insurance company separately and have all participating companies provide insurance based on previously reached agreement on premium share. For example, the first coordination decision stated that China People's Insurance Company would occupy a market share of 71.5%, China Ping An Insurance 12.5%, China Pacific Insurance 12.5%, and Tian An Insurance 3.5%. The market share coordination would be adjusted and agreement renewed on an annual basis. However, as the insurance industry expanded and more companies set up branches in Wuhan Province, the number of insurance companies that have established outlets in the New Car Center shot up

441. AML, Art. 13(3).
442. Measures on the Prohibition of Monopoly Agreements, Art. 5.
443. Xinhua News Agency, *Trade Association Allocated Market Share; Jiangsu Completed the First Anti-Monopoly Investigation* (in Chinese), www.js.xinhua.org/xin_wen_zhong_xin/2011-01/21/content_21923072.htm, 21 Jan. 2011; Global Competition Review, *SAIC Takes First Enforcement Steps*, www.globalcompetitionreview.com/news/article/29809/saic-takes-first-enforcement-steps/, 2 Mar. 2011.

to twenty-eight (representing the total number of licensed insurance companies in Wuhan) and the service outlets of the New Car Center increased from three to fifteen. When the AML came into effect, the IIAH published the 'Supplementary Agreement on the New Car Insurance and Centralized Service Convention in Wuhan' that reaffirmed each insurance company's market share and outlined market shares for new entrants and small companies. It also declared the respective number of new cars insurance companies underwrite in the New Car Center would be proportional to their respective current actual market share, calculated as the current market share percentage timed by the total new cars underwritten in the service centre to determine the number of new cars each insurance company would insure.

249. After Hubei SAIC began its investigation, IIAH on 23 October 2013 organised the insurance companies to sign the 'New Car Insurance Service Agreements in Wuhan', aimed at ensuring consumers' free will in choosing the insurance company, insurance method and types of policies, in order to protect against disturbances of any kind to market order or restrictions of any kind to market competition. On November of the same year, IIAH issued the 'Notice on the Abolishment and Amendment of Certain Self-Discipline Documents', cleaned up certain agreements signed with participating companies and emphasised the importance of abiding by AML. The relevant enforcement agency believed despite the lack of evidence suggesting refusals by insurance companies to insure new cars and price-fixing activities, IIAH, as the organiser of the relevant anticompetitive activities, did not abolish documents and agreements contrary to the AML until November 2013. Based on the above, the agency issued the 'Notice of Administrative Punishment Hearing' to IIAH based on violations of the AML, and imposed a fine of RMB 500,000 for monopolising the insurance market by organising participating companies into reaching a monopoly agreement. IIAH later sought leniency in its 'Statement of Counter-arguments'. The agency updated its decision, and after taking into account the IIAH's abolition of illegal documents and treaties as well as cooperation, which fits with the circumstances where penalty reduction applies under the Administrative Penalty Law, reduced the fine to RMB 200,000 based on Article 46, Clause 3 of the AML and Article 27 of the Administrative Penalty Law.[444]

C. Production/Innovation Limitation

250. The AML prohibits the limitation of production, sales, and innovation among competing undertakings.[445] With respect to limitations on production and sales, the Measures on the Prohibition on Monopoly Agreements further provide that competing undertakings are prohibited from: (1) restricting production volumes of products by means such as limiting or fixing production volumes or ceasing production; and (2) restricting sales volumes of products through refusing supply or limiting volumes of products available to the market.[446]

444. *See* SAIC Competition Enforcement Decision No. 6 2016, available at http://www.saic.gov.cn/fldyfbzdjz/jzzfgg/201703/t20170309_232285.html

445. AML, Art. 13(2) & (4).

446. Measures on the Prohibition of Monopoly Agreements, Art. 4.

251. With respect to limiting innovation, the Measures on the Prohibition on Monopoly Agreements further provide that competing undertakings are prohibited from: (1) restricting the purchase or use of new technologies or processes; (2) restricting the purchase, lease or use of new equipment; (3) restricting investment or research and development in new technologies, processes or products; (4) refusing to use new technologies, processes or equipment; or (5) refusing to adopt new technical standards.[447]

252. It should also be noted that the Contract Law provides that a technology contract that illegally monopolises technology or impedes technology development shall be null and void.[448] To date, there have been no reported cases in China regarding monopoly agreements that limit production and innovation. It, therefore, remains to be seen how the limitation on production or innovation will be assessed or treated under the AML and the Contract Law.

D. *Group Boycott*

253. The AML prohibits group boycotts.[449] The Measures on the Prohibition of Monopoly Agreements further provide that competing undertakings are prohibited from: (1) jointly refusing to supply or sell products to a particular undertaking; (2) jointly refusing to procure from or sell products of a particular undertaking; or (3) jointly preventing a particular undertaking from conducting business with other competing undertakings.[450]

254. To date, there have been no reported anti-monopoly cases in China regarding group boycotts. It, therefore, remains to be seen how group boycotts will be assessed and treated under the AML.

E. *Collusion on Other Objects*

255. *Bid rigging.* Bid rigging is commonly considered to be a type of hardcore cartel. The AML does not expressly prohibit bid rigging; rather it prohibits certain types of horizontal and vertical anticompetitive agreements. However, early drafts of the Measure on the Prohibition of Monopoly Agreements and the Measures on the Prohibition of Price Monopoly expressly prohibited bid rigging.[451] Although the provisions on bid rigging were not ultimately adopted, bid rigging may be construed as a type of monopoly agreement and prohibited pursuant to the catch-all provision under the AML. Prior to the AML, bid rigging was prohibited under the Bidding Law, the AUCL, and the Criminal Law.[452] *See* paragraph 226 above for a discussion on the bid rigging offence under the Criminal Law.

447. Measures on the Prohibition of Monopoly Agreements, Art. 6.

448. Contract Law, Art. 329; *see* a discussion at para. 308 below.

449. AML, Art. 13(5).

450. Measures on the Prohibition of Monopoly Agreements, Art. 7.

451. Draft Measures on the Prohibition of Monopoly Agreements (April 2009 version), Art. 6(5); Draft Measures on the Prohibition of Price Monopoly (August 2009 version), Art. 8.

452. Bidding Law, Arts 32 & 53; AUCL, Arts 15 & 27; Criminal Law, Art. 223.

256. It should also be noted that the Bidding Law Implementing Regulations provide further details on the prohibition of bid rigging.[453] In particular, the following activities between rival bidders are prohibited: (1) collusion between bidders on setting bidding prices or any other substantive content of the bidding documents; (2) collusion between bidders to determine the bid winner; (3) bidders agree beforehand that some bidders abandon bidding or win the bid; (4) concerted practices between bidders following instructions from the same trade associations; and (5) other concerted practices between bidders in order to win the bid or exclude specific bidders.

257. The prohibition of collusion between bidders under the Bidding Law, the AUCL, and the Criminal Law is in line with the generally accepted approach to treat bid rigging as a type of hardcore cartel between competitors. However, it is noteworthy that the prohibition of bid rigging under the Chinese law also covers collusion between bidders and tenderee. For example, the AUCL provides that 'bidders shall not act in collusion for bidding in order to raise or reduce the bid price. Bidders shall not collude with tenderee in order to eliminate other competitors from fair competition'.[454] In other words, big rigging in China may have both horizontal and vertical characteristics.

258. Bid rigging cases penalised pursuant to the AUCL. In 2002, three individuals were convicted of participating in a bid rigging conspiracy with respect to a bid to operate an aquafarm in the Zhejiang Province. The three individuals met and determined the bid winner and the winning price, and to compensate the losing bidders, they agreed to operate the aquafarm together. The bid was invalidated and the respondents were fined CNY 200,000, CNY 100,000, and CNY 50,000 respectively.[455] In another case, twenty-three construction companies were prosecuted for bid rigging on a contract for the construction of a housing project. The companies agreed that one of the construction companies would get the contract in exchange for payments to the other companies, and assigned one of the companies to calculate the bidding prices of all the candidates. The bid was invalidated and the companies involved were fined.[456]

259. As discussed in paragraphs 47–49 above, the AML does not expressly repeal competition-related provisions in other laws and regulations. However, conflicting legal norms do exist. For example, different legal liabilities are stipulated for bid rigging pursuant to each of the Bidding Law, the AUCL, and the Criminal Law. No reported cases on bid rigging that have been punished pursuant to the AML. It remains to be seen how the applicable law will be chosen and how bid rigging will be treated in the future.

II. Information Exchange Practices

260. To date, there are no clear rules on information exchange practices among competing undertakings. It can be presumed that where the exchange of information

453. Bidding Law Implementing Regulations, Arts 39, 40, 41 & 67.

454. AUCL, Art. 15.

455. State Administration for Industry and Commerce and Chinese Academy of Social Sciences International Law Research Centre, *Selected Anti-Monopoly Cases and Analysis on China's Anti-Monopoly Enforcement*, 132–134 (Chinese version) (Beijing: Law Press, 2007).

456. *Ibid.*, 129–132.

is harmless or beneficial to competition, the practice will not infringe the AML. However, as demonstrated by the *Rice Noodle Cartel* case discussed in paragraph 237 above, exchanges of sensitive price information as a mechanism for implementing or monitoring a cartel arrangement will be condemned by the AML and other competition-related laws and regulations.

III. Cooperation Agreements

261. To date, the AML and competition provisions in other laws and regulations do not provide clear rules regarding joint ventures and other beneficial horizontal arrangements, such as research and development agreements and specialisation agreements. Therefore, it remains to be seen whether cooperation agreements will be addressed specifically in the future.[457]

262. As discussed in paragraph 264 below, the Contract Law provides that a technology contract that illegally monopolises technology or impedes technological development shall be null and void.[458] However, it should be noted that the AML provides a general exemption mechanism for monopoly agreements, which may apply to agreements between competitors on research and development, specialisation, standardisation, as well as joint production, purchasing, and selling, provided that the agreements aim at improving quality, reduce costs and enhancing efficiency, and do not substantially restrict competition in the relevant market and allow consumers to share the resultant benefits.[459]

A. Research and Development

263. The AML prohibits competing undertakings from reaching a monopoly agreement to restrict the purchase or the development of new technology.[460] To date, except for the AML general exemption mechanism for monopoly agreements aiming to improve technology or research and develop new products, there are no further rules addressing competition issues in research and development agreements.[461]

264. In should be noted that the Contract Law covers technology contracts, which are defined as 'contracts the parties concluded for establishing their rights and obligations in respect of the development or transfer of technology, or in respect of technical consulting or service'.[462] Therefore, a research and development agreement is a type of technology contract and should comply with the Contract Law, which prohibits technology contracts that illegally monopolise technology or impede technological progress.[463]

457. *See* a discussion on when a joint venture will be construed as a type of concentrations at paras 142–143 above.
458. Contract Law, Art. 329; also *see* discussion at para. 308 below.
459. AML, Art. 15.
460. AML, Art. 13(4).
461. *Ibid.*, Art. 15(1).
462. Contract Law, Art. 322.
463. *Ibid.*, Art. 329.

265. To date, there have been no reported cases concerning competition issues relating to research and development agreements. It, therefore, remains to be seen how the competition aspect of research and development agreements will be assessed and treated under the AML and the Contract Law.

B. Specialisation

266. The AML prohibits competing undertakings from reaching a monopoly agreement to restrict the purchase or the development of new technology.[464] To date, except for the AML general exemption mechanism for monopoly agreements aiming to improve product quality, reduce costs, and improve efficiencies by way of specialisation, further rules addressing competition issues of specialisation agreements are unavailable.[465]

C. Standardisation

267. The AML prohibits competing undertakings from reaching a monopoly agreement to restrict the purchase or the development of new technology.[466] To date, except for the AML general exemption mechanism for monopoly agreements aiming to improve product quality, reduce costs, and improve efficiencies by way of standardisation, further rules addressing competition issues of standardisation agreements are unavailable.[467]

D. Joint Production

268. To date, there are no rules in the AML, the AML implementing regulations or any other laws or regulations that specifically address joint production agreements.

E. Joint Purchasing

269. To date, there are no rules in the AML, the AML implementing regulations or any other laws or regulations that specifically address joint purchasing agreements.

F. Joint Selling

270. To date, there are no rules in the AML, the AML implementing regulations or any other laws or regulations that specifically address joint selling agreements.

271. Government-led joint selling scheme of the coal industry may infringe the AML.[468] In 2013, the Shanxi Province has adopted a series of measures related to the coal industry. The *Joint Sales Implementation Plan for Coal Chemical Enterprises in*

464. AML, Art. 13(4).
465. *Ibid.*, Art. 15(2).
466. AML, Art. 13(2).
467. *Ibid.*, Art. 15(1).
468. Gao Liping, *Shanxin Province Proposes New Policies to Fix the Prices of Anthracite; Experts Alleged that the Policies Amount to Price Monopoly* (in Chinese), *Yicai*, http://www.yicai.com/news/2013/08/2907690.html , 2 Aug. 2013.

South East Shanxi Province (Discussion Draft) (hereinafter 'Joint Selling Plan') implements the *Measures on the Further Improvement of the Development Mode of the Shanxi Coal Economy to Achieve Sustainable Growth*, a government document promulgated on 25 July 2013 to curb the continuous downward trend of coal prices. Local coal industry bureaus and four large State-owned coal enterprises participated in the drafting of the Joint Selling Plan. The Joint Selling Plan intends to establish a series of concerted schemes, including coordinated actions of coal enterprises located in the same area, united sales strategies for coal products of the same quality, and regulated reference prices of coal chemical products. Strict disciplinary measures were also put in place to make sure that cheating does not occur. The *Current Conditions of the Coal Chemical Industry of Shanxi Province and Suggestions on Joint Actions* were also adopted to fix the prices of anthracite. Antitrust experts have commented that, given that the coal market has already been deregulated, those government documents could amount to a price cartel and thus infringe the AML.

§2. Vertical Agreements

272. The AML is the main competition legislation applicable to vertical agreements. The AML does not define the concept of a vertical agreement but prohibits undertakings from reaching monopoly agreements with their counterparties to fix resale prices or restrict minimum resale prices. The AML further provides a sweeping clause that prohibits undertakings from engaging in other types of vertical practices as determined by the AMEAs.[469] Vertical agreements that meet certain criteria may be exempted.[470]

273. Disputes arising from vertical agreements have been reported widely in China. For example, in July 2002, Changhong, the biggest consumer electronics producer in China, announced that it was terminating its supply of television sets to the Beijing outlets of Gome, a major electronics retailer in China. The termination was triggered by Gome's pursuit of an aggressive pricing policy without Changhong's consent.[471] The issue of whether there was a minimum resale price maintenance agreement between Changhong and Gome was not addressed as there was no relevant legal prohibition against that practice in 2002. Since the AML entered into force, there have been large number of news reports about vertical restraints in China.

274. Until early 2013, vertical agreements have not appeared to be an enforcement priority of the AMEAs. At the time of writing, there do not appear to be any reported decisions or other enforcement activities by the NDRC or the SAIC addressing vertical restraints other than resale price maintenance (RPM).[472] It remains to be seen whether the future development of the AML will include rules on franchising, exclusive distribution, selective distribution, and other distribution arrangements.

---

469. AML, Art. 14.

470. AML, Art. 15; *see* a discussion at para. 104 above.

471. Tianfu Zaobao, *Changhong Stops to Supply Gome Surprising the Industry* (in Chinese), available at www.people.com.cn/GB/channel3/23/20000731/166264.html, 31 Jul. 2000.

472. *See* discussions at paras 277–286 below.

275. Other relevant laws and regulations on vertical agreements. In addition to the AML, other relevant laws and regulations governing vertical agreements primarily include: (1) the Contract Law; (2) the Retailers and Suppliers Measures; (3) the Price Law and the accompanying Provisions on Administrative Penalties for Price Violations; (4) the Judicial Interpretations on Technology Contracts; (5) the Technology Import and Export Regulations; and (6) the Provisions on Regional Blockades.

276. For example, the Retailers and Suppliers Measures prohibit retailers and suppliers from impeding market transaction order and fair competition as well as from damaging the legitimate interests of their trading partners.[473] Several provisions of the Retailers and Suppliers Measures regulate vertical agreements. Retailers are generally prohibited from: (1) restricting suppliers' pricing ability where suppliers directly supply consumers and other business operators; and (2) restricting suppliers' ability to supply other retailers.[474] Suppliers are prohibited from tying and restricting retailers' ability to sell commodities of other suppliers.[475] The Retailers and Suppliers Measures provide that, if other laws or regulations provide similar rules on the prohibited behaviour, such other laws or regulations shall prevail; otherwise, the Retailers and Suppliers Measures are applicable. The liabilities of infringement include orders to rectify the conduct and fines of up to CNY 30,000.[476]

I. Distribution

277. Resale price maintenance. Resale price maintenance, in particular the fixing of resale prices and restricting minimum resale prices, is expressly prohibited under the AML and the Measures on the Prohibition of Price Monopoly.[477] In addition, the Judicial Interpretations on Technology Contracts and the Technology Import and Export Regulations prohibit the inclusion of clauses restricting the price the technology recipient can charge to its customers in relation to products or services developed from the transferred technology.[478] The Retailers and Suppliers Measures prohibit retailers from restricting the price that suppliers can charge when selling directly to consumers or to other business operators.[479]

278. Whether resale price maintenance will be treated as a per se infringement or analysed under a rule of reason standard remains to be seen. Although the wording of the AML suggests that an agreement containing a resale price maintenance provision may be exempted if the prescribed conditions are met, implementing measures of Article 14 or Article 15 of the AML are required to provide further guidance and clarify the circumstances in which exemptions might be available.

473. Retailers and Suppliers Measures, Art. 4.
474. *Ibid.*, Art. 7.
475. *Ibid.*, Art. 18.
476. *Ibid.*, Art. 23.
477. AML, Art. 14; Measures on the Prohibition of Price Monopoly, Art. 8.
478. Judicial Interpretations on Technology Contracts, Art. 10(3); Technology Import and Export Regulations, Art. 29(6).
479. Retailers and Suppliers Measures, Art. 7(1).

279. A clear tendency in law enforcement practice is when the case involves resale price maintenance, the People's Court would adopt a rule of reason analysis and would take into account more factors than the administrative law enforcement agencies. In the case of *Beijing Rainbow v. Johnson & Johnson* discussed earlier, Shanghai Supreme People's Court considered the following factors: (1) lack of adequate competition in the relevant market, (2) Johnson & Johnson's dominant position in the relevant market, (3) the motive behind the fixed resale price is to eliminate the competition between distributors, (4) anticompetitive effects of the resale price restriction which apparently outweigh any pro-competitive effects. [480]

280. Guangzhou Intellectual Property Court ruled on August 2016 that the fixed resale price agreement in the Gree case is legal and justifiable. This judgment differed greatly from previous rulings of the anti-monopoly administrative enforcement agencies, and raised many questions throughout the academia and the industry. The plaintiff is a dealer of Gree air conditioners, and is suing Gree Electronics' general distributor and wholesaler in the city of Dongguan for implementing agreements to fix the resale price. He was punished by Gree for breaching such agreement as a Gree dealer and is seeking court judgment against Gree for breaking the AML. The Court points that based on the tripartite agreement signed between the plaintiff and two defendants, the defendants restricted the minimum prices the plaintiff can sell Gree products. The Court, however, doesn't believe this constitutes monopoly agreement and thus violates the AML, namely because (1) Gree's air conditioners do not have absolute advantage in the Dongguan market (i.e., without dominant market position), which has many viable alternatives (i.e., customers are free to choose from competing brands with minimum resale prices on Gree's air conditioners); (2) there is no evidence suggesting Gree's fixed resale prices will affect its competitive relationship with related industries; and (3) while the fixed resale prices will impact how the particular dealer competes with others selling the same brand, factors such as presale marketing, promotion, and after-sales services also play vital roles in the internal competition. As a result, the Court does not see the act of the defendants as constituting monopoly per the AML. [481]

281. Premium liquor producers fined CNY 449 million for RPM. On 22 February 2013, the Guizhou Price Bureau and the Sichuan Development and Reform Commission (DRC) each announced that it had taken enforcement action against State-owned premium liquor producers, Moutai and Wuliangye, respectively, for retail price maintenance. Moutai was fined CNY 247 million and Wuliangye was fined CNY 202 million. The announcements by the Guizhou Price Bureau and the Sichuan DRC come after Moutai and Wuliangye each issued a press release on 15 and 17 January 2013,

480. The Adjudication of *Beijing Ruibangyong v. Johnson & Johnson*, http://www.cpahkltd.com/cn/info.aspx?n=20130819085542040689

481. Wei Shilin, The First Adjudication on Vertical Monopoly of GREE, http://blog.sina.com.cn/s/blog_5a81db850102wj7l.html, 1 Nov. 2016. *See also*, No.33 Adjudication of IP Court in Guangzhou.

respectively, stating that it was being investigated by the NDRC and the provincial bureau. These penalties are the first under the AML for RPM.[482]

282. The Guizhou Price Bureau stated that Moutai had fixed the minimum resale price to independent distributors and penalised distributors selling the products at a price lower than the minimum price. The Guizhou Price Bureau found that this conduct constituted a vertical monopoly agreement in breach of Article 14 of the AML. It also noted that Moutai had cooperated with the investigation, returned the deposit guarantee to its distributors, and rectified its policies promptly.

283. The Sichuan DRC stated that, since 2009, Wuliangye had reached agreements with more than 3,200 independent distributors to fix the minimum resale price of its product. It penalised distributors who did not implement the minimum price through measures such as limiting their business, reducing supply, deducting deposit moneys, deducting marketing support fees, and imposing fines. The Sichuan DRC noted that Wuliangye had stopped supplying a major Sichuan supermarket chain in 2011 to force the supermarket to promise not to sell its product below the specified minimum price and in 2012, it had punished fourteen distributors across eleven provinces and municipalities for selling at below minimum price, across regions, and across channels by deducting liquidated damages and marketing support fees. The Sichuan DRC found that Wuliangye had used its position of market strength to restrict the minimum resale price through measures such as contractual agreements, price controls, region monitoring, evaluations, and endpoint controls. It found that the conduct constituted a vertical monopoly agreement in breach of Article 14 of the AML.

284. The Sichuan DRC stated that Wuliangye was a leading liquor company that enjoys high brand awareness and consumer loyalty, and that by engaging in the conduct it had adversely affected fair market competition, economic efficiency, and consumer interests. First, it eliminated intra-brand competition between its distributors. Second, it restricted inter-brand competition. Wuliangye's price monopoly conduct had set a bad example for other liquor producers and other producers had begun to engage in similar conduct, further restricting and harming competition. Third, it harmed consumer interests as it eliminated the opportunity for consumers to buy lower-priced products, especially as Wuliangye has a strong position in the market for aromatic liquor and its products have low substitutability. The Sichuan DRC noted that Wuliangye had cooperated with the NDRC and the Sichuan DRC and had promptly publicly announced that it would rectify its conduct, removed the penalties, and returned the deducted marketing supporting fees. The penalty of CNY 202 million was 1% of Wuliangye's sales of the previous year.

285. Infant formula producers fined CNY 669 million for RPM.[483] On 7 August 2013, the NDRC announced that it had imposed fines on various infant formula

482. Disclosure of Wuliangye regarding the Decision Rendered by Sichuan DRC (in Chinese) is available at http://disclosure.szse.cn/m/finalpage/2013-02-23/62145581.PDF, 23 Feb. 2013; Disclosure of Maotai regarding the Decision Rendered by Guizhou Price Bureau (in Chinese) is available at http://static.sse.com.cn/disclosure/listedinfo/announcement/c/2013-02-22/600519_20130223_1.pdf, 23 Feb. 2013.

483. NDRC, *Biostime and Several Other Milk Powder Producers Breached the AML and Were Fined CNY 669 Million in Total* (in Chinese), http://www.ndrc.gov.cn/xwfb/t20130807_552991.htm, 7 Aug. 2013.

producers for RPM in breach of Article 14 of the AML. The NDRC had found that the anticompetitive arrangements had varied from producer to producer and included entering into RPM arrangements, punishments for non-compliance, reducing rebates, restricting supply, and terminating supply. It imposed record aggregate fines of CNY 669 million, with Mead Johnson being fined CNY 203.76 million (4% of last year's sales revenue), Danone Dumex CNY 171.99 million (3% of last year's sales revenue), Biostime CNY 162.9 million (6% of last year's sales revenue), Abbott CNY 77.34 million (3% of last year's sales revenue), Friesland Campina CNY 48.27 million (3% of last year's sales revenue), and Fonterra CNY 4.47 million (3% of last year's sales revenue). The penalty levels varied according to the producer's degree of cooperation with the NDRC in the investigation and whether it had voluntarily or actively implemented corrective measures. Wyeth, Meiji, and Beingmate were exempt from administrative sanctions as they had actively cooperated with the investigation, provided important evidence, and voluntarily and actively implemented corrective measures.

286. In addition to fines, the infant formula producers also put forward the following corrective measures: (1) stop the illegal conduct; (2) revise their distribution agreements and sales and business policies to comply with Chinese laws; (3) reorganise distribution systems and provide anti-monopoly training to employees; and (4) take action to eliminate the consequences of prior illegal actions and to benefit consumers. The NDRC's application of the leniency policy to vertical agreement cases was viewed as a response to the scarce antitrust enforcement resources of the agency.

287. When tackling vertical price restrictions, the NDRC has taken high-profile antitrust law enforcement actions in the automotive industry. In August 2014, the Hubei Provincial Price Bureau imposed a fine of RMB 248 million on FAW-Volkswagen Automobile Co. Ltd. This decision announced the start of an antitrust law enforcement wave in the automotive industry. Similar penalties imposed on Mercedes-Benz, General Motors, Dongfeng Nissan, and other car manufacturers. The scope of law enforcement concerns price-fixing practices in vehicle sales as well as in sales of auto parts. In April 2014, the China Automotive Maintenance and Repair Trades Association disclosed the 'parts-to-whole price ratio' (i.e., the ratio between the sales prices of auto parts and whole vehicles) of eighteen common car models. Among these, the parts-to-whole price ratio of the Benz C-class W204 model stands on top of the list with a ratio of 1,273%. This means that the price-to-manufacture replacements of all parts of such a car in China is sufficient to buy twelve new cars of the same model. The public in China therefore strongly urged the antitrust authorities to conduct investigations in the automotive industry. Restrictions on competition in the automotive industry include horizontal restrictions, vertical restrictions, and abuse of market dominance. Many of the cases involved vertical price-fixing cases. This means that the setting of resale price or minimum resale price is prevalent in the sales of entire vehicles or auto parts by OEMs in the automobile industry in China. For instance, in the case involving Audi vehicles, according to NDRC's Anti-Monopoly Bureau, the Audi Sales Department of FAW-Volkswagen Sales Company Ltd. repeatedly assisted ten car dealers in Hubei Province to enter into and implement monopoly agreements regarding vehicle sales and service maintenance prices since 2012. It also arranged for the dealers to sign the 'Limited Price List of Audi Vehicles in Wuhan' and 'Letter of Business operator on Pricing Scheme in Central China Area', and circulated to them the 'Notice on Strictly

Implementation of Audi Standard Price System in Hubei Province in Central China Area' and 'Service Marketing Management Regulations' in Hubei Province. The Sales Department also set up a 'Competition Order Regulation Team' to urge dealers to implement the price management regulations stipulated by FAW-Volkswagen Sales Company Ltd. NDRC's Anti-Monopoly Bureau pointed out that the above practices violated Article 14 of the AML, constituting illegal practices of 'fixing the resale prices of products to third parties' and 'fixing the minimum resale price of products to third parties. The Hubei Province Price Bureau imposed a fine against FAW-Volkswagen Sales Company Ltd. equal to 6% of its sales revenues in the relevant market of the preceding year, i.e., RMB 248,580,000, pursuant to Article 46 of the AML. [484]

288. Territorial restrictions and customer restrictions. The AML does not expressly prohibit territorial restrictions and customer restrictions. Notably, the SAIC identified other types of prohibited vertical agreements in a draft of the Measures on the Prohibition of Monopoly Agreements published for comments in April 2009. These included, for example, agreements containing territorial restrictions and exclusivity clauses that prohibit an undertaking from, without justification, making agreements that demand that its counterparties operate only within the allocated territories or deal exclusively with it or other designated undertakings.[485] These prohibitions were deleted in the final Measures on the Prohibition of Monopoly Agreements following negative comments from interested parties. Commentators noted that the proposed prohibitions would broaden the AML prohibition on exclusivity and the imposition of other unreasonable transaction terms, which applies only to dominant undertakings. In addition, it was noted that the SAIC failed to recognise that vertical agreements might be pro-competitive in certain circumstances, particularly where there is sufficient inter-brand competition.[486]

289. The Provisions on Regional Blockades aim to curb the barriers entry into regional markets that are erected by local governments and public authorities. The Provisions on Regional Blockades prohibit any entity or individual from restricting the flow of products and services originating in other regions within China to the relevant local market.[487] However, it is difficult to assess the exact scope and the effectiveness of this prohibition because reported cases were seldom dealt with pursuant to the Provisions on Regional Blockades.

A. Exclusive Distributorship

290. The AML vertical agreement rules do not contain provisions on exclusive distributorships but provide a sweeping clause to prohibit other vertical monopoly

484. *See* Money 163.com report: FAW-Volkswagen was Fined RMB 248 million for Organising Audi Dealers to Conduct Monopoly, http://money.163.com/14/0911/14/A5SC08U700254TI5.html.

485. Draft Measures on the Prohibition of Monopoly Agreements (April 2009 version) (copy on file with the authors), Art. 6(2)–(3).

486. AML, Art. 17(4) & (5); *see* Global Competition Review, *China Issues Draft Dominance Guidelines*, www.globalcompetitionreview.com/news/article/28504/china-issues-draft-dominance-guidelines/, 27 May 2010.

487. *See* the Provisions on Regional Blockades.

agreements as determined by the AMEAs.[488] However, it should be noted that the AML prohibits dominant undertakings from refusing to deal and from imposing unreasonable transaction conditions on their counterparties without justification.[489] Such prohibitions may be interpreted to cover exclusive distributorship arrangements.

291. To date, there have been no reported cases concerning competition issues in exclusive distributorship arrangements and it remains to be seen how exclusive distributorships will be assessed and treated under the AML.

B. Exclusive Dealing

292. The AML vertical agreement rules do not contain provisions on exclusive dealing but provide a sweeping clause to prohibit other vertical monopoly agreements as determined by the AMEAs.[490] However, it should be noted that the AML prohibits dominant undertakings from requiring, without justification, that parties enter into exclusive dealing agreements with them or designated undertakings.[491]

293. Notably, the Judicial Interpretations on Technology Contracts and the Technology Import and Export Regulations prohibit technology contracts or technology import-export contracts from containing clauses that restrict either the ability of the technology recipient to obtain the supplier's products from alternative sources or the freedom of the technology recipient to purchase competing technology.[492]

294. Furthermore, the Retailers and Suppliers Measures prohibit suppliers from restricting retailers' freedom to purchase products, including the supplier's own products, from other sources and prohibit retailers from restricting its supplier from selling its products or services to other retailers.[493]

C. Selective Distribution

295. To date, there are no rules in the AML, the AML implementing regulations or other laws or regulations that specifically address selective distribution.

D. Franchising

296. In principle, the AML prohibits vertical agreements that fix resale prices or restrict minimum resale prices and other vertical agreements that are determined by the AMEAs as having the effect of eliminating or restricting competition. The AML also provides an exemption mechanism. To date, there have been no AML implementing regulations or enforcement actions concerning franchising-related competition issues.

297. However, reference should be made to the State Council *Regulations on the Administration of Commercial Franchising 2007* (hereinafter 'Franchising

488. AML, Art. 14.
489. *Ibid.*, Art. 17(5).
490. AML, Art. 14.
491. *Ibid.*, Art. 17(4).
492. Judicial Interpretations on Technology Contracts, Art. 10(5); Technology Import and Export Regulations; Art. 29(5).
493. Retailers and Suppliers Measures, Arts 18(2) & 7(2).

Regulations'),[494] which replaced the MOFCOM *Administrative Measures on Commercial Franchising 2004* (hereinafter 'Franchising Measures').[495] Under the Franchising Regulations, a commercial franchise refers to a business activity where the franchisor licenses to the franchisee the right to use the franchisor's operational resources such as registered trademarks, enterprise logos, patents, and know-how, and the franchisee conducts the business under the unified business format agreed to in the franchise agreement and pays the franchisor franchise fees in return.[496]

298. It is noteworthy that, under the Franchising Measures, franchisors were prohibited from creating a market monopoly or impeding fair competition through franchising.[497] Franchisors were further prohibited from requiring that its franchisees purchase products from the franchisors, except where it was necessary to guarantee the quality of the franchised product. However, franchisors were entitled to require that the purchased products comply with certain quality standards or to list a number of suppliers from which the franchisees could choose.[498] The Franchising Measures, in this regard, provided no effective sanctions and remedies. The Franchising Regulations do not provide similar competition-related provisions, perhaps for the purpose of avoiding duplication with the AML implementing regulations in the future. How the AML prohibition and exemption rules will be applied to franchising arrangements, such as provisions commonly found in franchising agreements such as price restrictions, territorial restrictions, and non-compete obligations, will need to be addressed by the AML implementing regulations and the AMEAs' enforcement practice in the future.

II. Technology Licensing

299. The AML does not govern the conduct of undertakings to exercise their intellectual property rights under laws and relevant administrative regulations on intellectual property rights; however, undertakings' conduct to eliminate or restrict market competition by abusing their intellectual property rights shall be governed by the AML.[499] In addition, the AML prohibits competing undertakings from reaching monopoly agreements that restrict the purchase of new technology or equipment, restrict the development of new technology or products or implement joint boycotts.[500] Further, the exercise of intellectual property rights could in some circumstances infringe the AML as the AML also prohibits undertakings from fixing resale prices, restricting minimum resale prices, and abusing its dominant market position.[501] For example, an

494. The Franchising Regulations were promulgated by the State Council on 31 Jan. 2007 and effective on 1 May 2007, official Chinese text available at www.gov.cn/zwgk/2007-02/14/content_527207.htm.
495. The Franchising Measures were promulgated by the MOFCOM on 31 Dec. 2004 and effective on 1 Feb. 2005, official Chinese text available at www.chinacourt.org/flwk/show1. php?file_id=98686.
496. The Franchising Regulations, Art. 3.
497. The Franchising Measures, Art. 5.
498. *Ibid.*, Art. 10(4).
499. AML, Art. 55.
500. *Ibid.*, Art. 13(4)–(5).
501. *Ibid.*, Arts 14 (1)–(2) & 17.

undertaking with a dominant market position may abuse its dominant position if it refuses to trade with a party without justification.[502] Therefore, a dominant firm's refusal to license intellectual property rights might be construed as a refusal to deal, potentially leading to compulsory licensing. It should be noted that the AML specifies a number of circumstances under which the prohibited monopoly agreements may be exempted.

300. The AML neither specifies how IPR inclusive technology licensing agreements should be addressed under the AML, nor do they set out block exemptions for technology licensing agreements. In the absence of clear guidance regarding the extent to which the exercise of intellectual property rights can be considered as anticompetitive, it would be difficult to assess the anticompetitive effects of a technology licensing agreement under the general AML framework for monopoly agreements and abuse of dominance.

301. In this case, on 7 April 2015, SAIC published *IPR Regulation,*[503]which takes effect as of 1 August 2015. It should be noted that, as SAIC's authority in antitrust law enforcement does not cover price-related anticompetitive practices, the *IPR Regulation* does not apply to price-related monopoly practices. However, as most of the antitrust cases involving intellectual property rights are related to licence fees for intellectual property rights, the application of the *IPR Regulation* is in practice is rather limited.

302. According to Article 3 of the SAIC *IPR Regulation*, the abuse of intellectual property rights to eliminate or restrict competition refers to a business operator's exercise of intellectual property rights in violation of the AML – that is, implementation of monopoly agreements, abuse of a dominant market position, and other anticompetitive practices (excluding price monopoly conduct). Article 4 of the *IPR Regulation* provides that business operators shall not, by way of exercising intellectual property rights, conclude monopoly agreements prohibited under Articles 13 and 14 of the AML, unless the business operators involved are able to prove that the concluded agreements fall under Article 15 of the AML. Article 6 of the *IPR Regulation* provides that a business operator with a dominant market position shall not abuse its position to eliminate or restrict competition in the course of exercising intellectual property rights. A dominant market position is to be determined and presumed in accordance with Articles 18 and 19 of the AML. Article 7 of the *IPR Regulation* provides that where its intellectual property rights constitute an essential facility for production and operational activities, a business operator with a dominant market position shall not, without any justification, refuse to license other business operators to use its intellectual property rights on reasonable terms in order to eliminate or restrict competition. All of the following factors shall be considered at the same time in determining an 'essential facility': (1) the intellectual property right is not reasonably substitutable in the relevant market, and is essential for other business operators to compete in the relevant market; (2) refusal to license such intellectual property right will have an adverse effect on competition or innovation in the relevant market, and be detrimental to consumer

502. Ibid., Art. 17(3).

503. Provisions on the Prohibition of the Abuse of Intellectual Property Rights to Exclude or Restrict Competition were promulgated by the SAIC on 7 Apr. 2015, official Chinese text available at http://www.saic.gov.cn/fldyfbzdjz/zcfg/xzgz/201507/t20150724_233535.html.

benefits or public interests; and (3) the licensing of the intellectual property right will not result in unreasonable harm to the business operator. Articles 8–11 set forth the various practices by which a business operator with a dominant market position may abuse its intellectual property rights, including exclusive dealing, tying, imposing unreasonable restrictive conditions, and discriminatory treatment. These provisions describe these practices involving the exercising of intellectual property rights.

303. Article 12 of the *IPR Regulation* regulated issues where patent pools may raise issues of eliminating or restricting competition. This includes two circumstances: first, patent pool members may, by means of the patent pool, exchange competitively sensitive information in relation to output and market allocation, so as to conclude monopoly agreements prohibited by Articles 13 and 14 of the AML. Second, a patent pool management organisation with a dominant market position may, without any justification, engage in any of the following conduct amounting to an abuse of a dominant market position through the patent pool to eliminate or restrict competition: (1) restricting patent pool members from licensing their patents outside the patent pool as independent licensors; (2) restricting patent pool members or licensees either independently or in collaboration with third parties, from researching or developing technologies competing with the patents in the patent pool; (3) forcing licensees to exclusively grant back the technologies improved or developed by them to the patent pool management organisation or patent pool members; (4) prohibiting licensees from challenging the validity of the patents in the patent pool; (5) differentiating trading terms applicable to patent pool members or licensees in the same relevant market under the same conditions; or (6) other abuses of a dominant market position determined by SAIC.

304. Article 13 of the *IPR Regulation* provides that in the course of exercising intellectual property rights, holders of standard essential patents ('SEP') shall not eliminate or restrict competition by setting or implementing standards (including mandatory requirements in national technical specifications). The implementation of the following types of conduct without any justification is covered in the provision: (1) in the course of participating in setting standards, intentionally refraining from disclosing information on the patent to the standards-setting organisation, or explicitly waiving its patent right but nonetheless asserting the patent right against companies implementing the standard after the patent has been incorporated into the standard; and (2) refusing to grant a licence, tying products or imposing other unreasonable conditions on transactions in violation of the fair, reasonable, and non-discriminatory ('FRAND') principle in order to eliminate or restrict competition, after the patent has become a standard essential patent. For the purpose of the *IPR Regulation*, an SEP refers to a patent that is essential to the implementation of a standard.

305. Article 14 of the *IPR Regulation* describes the procedures for the authorities to undertake investigations in accordance with the AML and the relevant procedural provisions. Article 15 provides for the steps that can be taken by the authorities in analysing and determining whether a business operator has abused intellectual property rights to eliminate or restrict competition. Article 16 sets forth the factors that should be taken into consideration by the authorities in determining the impact on competition of a business operator's abuse of intellectual property rights. Article 17 provides for the legal consequences that may arise as a result of the abuse of intellectual property rights to eliminate or restrict competition.

306. In addition, there have been some reported anti-monopoly cases in which penalties or remedies have been imposed for the exercise of intellectual property rights. The eye-catching cases include the *Huawei v. IDC* case decided by the Chinese courts in 2013 and the Qualcomm case announced by NDRC in 2015. In the latter case, a record administrative fine of RMB 6,066 billion was imposed.

307. It is important to appreciate that certain provisions of intellectual property laws and regulations may be relevant. China's major legislation governing intellectual property rights and technology licensing include: (1) the Patent Law; (2) the *Copyright Law 1990* (amended 2001 and 2010) (hereinafter 'Copyright Law');[504] (3) the *Trademark Law 1982* (amended 1993, 2001, and 2013) (hereinafter 'Trademark Law');[505] (4) the Contract Law; (5) the Judicial Interpretations on Technology Contracts; (6) the Foreign Trade Law; and (7) the Technology Import and Export Regulations.

308. Under the Contract Law, a technology contract that illegally monopolises technology or impedes technological development is null and void.[506] Parties to a technology transfer contract may agree to the scope for the exploitation of a patent or know-how, provided that no restriction is imposed on competition and development in technology.[507] The Judicial Interpretations on Technology Contracts set forth the circumstances where a technology contract would be deemed to be illegally monopolising technology or impeding technology development. These circumstances include the following practices: (1) restricting technological improvements made by one party to a technology contract or imposing non-reciprocal conditions of sharing such technological improvements; (2) restricting a technology recipient's purchase of technology from other sources; (3) unreasonably restricting the volume, variety, price, sales channels or export markets of the technology recipient's products and services; (4) requiring that the technology recipient accept unnecessary ancillary conditions, including purchasing unnecessary technology, raw materials, products, equipment, and services; (5) unreasonably restricting the technology recipient's sources of supplies of raw materials, parts or equipment; or (6) prohibiting or restricting the technology recipient's ability to challenge the intellectual property rights that are the subject of the technology contract.[508]

504. The Copyright Law was promulgated by the NPC on 12 Mar. 1984, effective on 1 Apr. 1985 and amended on 4 Sep. 1992, 25 Aug. 2000, and 27 Dec. 2008, English translation available at www.fdi.gov.cn/pub/FDI_EN/Laws/law_en_info.jsp?docid=125096.

505. The Trademark Law was promulgated by the Standing Committee of the NPC on 23 Aug. 1982, effective on 1 Mar. 1983 and amended on 22 Feb. 1993, 27 Oct. 2001, and 30 Aug. 2013, English translation available at www.npc.gov.cn/englishnpc/Law/2007-12/13/content_1384018.htm, English translation of the 2013 amendments available by subscription at www.lawinfochina.com.

506. Contract Law, Art. 329.

507. *Ibid.*, Art. 343.

508. The Judicial Interpretation on Technology Contracts, Art. 10.

A. Patent Licensing

309. Pursuant to the Patent Law, where a patent holder grants another party the right to exploit its patent, a licensing agreement should be reached between the licensor and the licensee, the licensee should pay a patent royalty, and the licensee has no right to grant sublicences to any other entity or an individual for the purposes of exploiting the patent.[509] The Patent Law does not provide general rules regarding the duration, exclusivity, grant-back, non-compete obligations or other restrictions of licensing agreements. However, according to the Technology Import and Export Regulations,[510] certain restrictions are prohibited in patent or trade secret licensing agreements regarding technology imports. These prohibited restrictions include: (1) requesting that the licensee accept conditions that are unnecessary for the licence, including buying unnecessary technology, raw materials, products, equipment or services; (2) requesting that the licensee pay an exploitation fee for the technology or undertake other relevant obligations when the patent right expires or is invalidated; (3) requiring that the licensee improve the licensed technology or use improved technology; (4) restricting the licensee's ability to obtain either technology similar to the licensed technology from other sources or competing technology; (5) imposing unreasonable restrictions on the licensee's ability to purchase raw materials, parts and components, products or equipment from other channels or sources; (6) unreasonably restricting the quantity, variety or sales price of the licensee's products; and (7) unreasonably restricting the export channels for products manufactured using the licensed technology.[511]

310. Compulsory licensing. In December 2010, the SIPO released its *General Introduction to the Third Revision of the Patent Law of the People's Republic of China and its Implementing Regulations* (hereinafter 'General Introduction'). The General Introduction explains the main revisions made during the third round of revisions to China's Patent Law and its implementing regulations that were completed in 2010. Some of the main revisions to the Patent Law and its implementing regulations include amending the compulsory licence system, enhancing the threshold of patentability, amending the confidentiality examination system for applications to foreign countries, introducing pre-litigation evidence preservation measures and allowing parallel imports. As at 1 June 2010, SIPO has granted no compulsory licences.[512]

311. The Patent Law provides detailed conditions under which a party who is capable of exploiting a patent may apply to the SIPO for the grant of a compulsory licence to exploit the patent. A compulsory licence may be granted under two circumstances: (1) if a patent holder fails, within three years from the date of a patent being granted and four years from the date of a patent being filed, to exploit or

509. Patent Law, Art. 12.

510. The Technology Import and Export Regulations were promulgated by the State Council on 10 Dec. 2001, effective on 1 Jan. 2002, and amended on 8 Jan. 2011; official text in Chinese is available at www.gov.cn/zwgk/2005-06/03/content_4102.htm, English translation available by subscription at www.lawinfochina.com.

511. Technology Import and Export Regulations, Art. 29.

512. SIPO, *General Introduction to the Third Revision of the Patent Law of the People's Republic of China and its Implementing Regulations*,, http://english.sipo.gov.cn/laws/lawsregulations/201012/t20101210_553631.html, 10 Dec. 2010.

sufficiently exploit the patent without any justification; or (2) if a patent holder's exploitation of the patent is determined to be anticompetitive in accordance with the law and the compulsory licence is intended to eliminate or mitigate such adverse effect on competition.[513] A compulsory licence is granted on a non-exclusive basis and the grantee has no right to grant sublicences.[514]

312. The Patent Law also specifies that, for the purpose of public health, compulsory licences may be granted to manufacture and export patented pharmaceuticals into certain countries in accordance with the relevant international treaties to which China is a member.[515] Compulsory licences may also be granted where required in the event of a national emergency or other extraordinary state of affairs, or in public interest.[516] In addition, where a patent involves an important technical advance of considerable economic significance in relation to an earlier patent and the exploitation of the later patent depends on the exploitation of the earlier patent, the SIPO may, upon request, grant the owner of the later patent a compulsory licence to exploit the earlier patent. Upon request, the SIPO may grant the earlier patent owner a compulsory licence to exploit the later patent.[517]

B. Trademark Licensing

313. The Trademark Law governs trademark assignment and licensing but provides no specific rules related to competition issues in trademark licensing agreements.[518]

C. Know-How and Trade Secret Licensing

314. There is no specific legislation that governs know-how in China but trade secrets are protected under the AUCL. The illegal possession, discourse or use of trade secrets is an infringement of the AUCL.[519] There are no specific provisions related to competition issues in know-how and trade secret licensing agreements. However, reference should be made to the relevant provisions under the Contract Law and the Judicial Interpretations on Technology Contracts.[520]

513. Patent Law, Art. 48.
514. *Ibid.*, Art. 56.
515. Patent Law, Art. 50.
516. *Ibid.*, Art. 49.
517. *Ibid.*, Art. 51.
518. Trademark Law, Arts 42 & 43.
519. AUCL, Art. 10.
520. *See* discussion at para. 308 above.

Chapter 2. Dominant Undertakings' Prohibited Practices

315. The AML prohibits six types of abusive behaviour by dominant undertakings, including: (1) unfairly high or low pricing; (2) below-cost sales; (3) refusal to deal; (4) exclusive dealing; (5) tying and imposing other unreasonable terms; and (6) discriminatory treatment. The prohibition covers both exploitative and exclusionary practices. The AML also provides a catch-all clause to prohibit other types of abusive behaviour as determined by the AMEAs.[521] Both the SAIC and the NDRC have reported that they have received a number of complaints of abusive behaviour by enterprises and have been investigating a number of cases.[522]

316. In addition to the AML, the AUCL covers exclusionary practices and the Price Law covers both exploitative and exclusionary practices. According to laws and regulations other than the AML, abusive behaviour may be prohibited even if the entity engaging in the conduct does not possess a dominant position. *See* discussion at paragraphs 87–90 above for a discussion of such laws and regulations.

317. The AUCL has been applied frequently to prevent utility companies and other statutory monopolists from requiring that its customers purchase products from designated business operators. According to official statistics, the SAIC and its local bureaus have investigated and handled 5,188 cases from January 1995 to June 2005, involving sectors such as water, electricity and gas supply, railways, post and telecommunications, tobacco, oil, and salt.[523] Examples of violations include power stations promoting the use of power meters by threatening to withhold electricity from end users and post offices forcing users to participate in postal savings schemes.[524]

§1. Exploitative Practices

I. Excessive/Unfair Pricing

318. The AML prohibits undertakings with dominant market positions from selling or buying products at unfairly high or low prices.[525] However, the AML does not specify how the fairness of a price will be determined. The Measures on the Prohibition of Price Monopoly provide a number of factors that should be taken into account when determining whether a price is unfairly high or unfairly low. These

521. AML, Art. 17.
522. *See* Global Competition Review, *SAIC Already Investigating Monopoly Cases*, www.globalcompetitionreview.com/news/article/18645/, 1 Sep. 2009; Legal Daily, 'NDRC: *Complaints against Microsoft Lodged: Investigation against the Banking Fees Initiated* (in Chinese), available at http://politics. people. com. cn/GB/1027/7716875. html, 24 Aug. 2008.
523. State Administration for Industry and Commerce and Chinese Academy of Social Sciences International Law Research Centre, *Selected Anti-Monopoly Cases and Analysis on China's Anti-Monopoly Enforcement, 208* (Chinese version) (Beijing: Law Press, 2007).
524. *Ibid.*, at 12–13 & 51–53.
525. AML, Art. 17(1).

include: (1) whether the price is obviously higher or lower than that of the same kind of product that is sold or bought by other undertakings; (2) in circumstances where the cost is stable, whether the increase of the selling price or the decrease of the purchase price exceeded the normal margin; (3) whether the rate of increase in the price of a product is obviously higher than the rate of increase in its cost, or whether the rate of decrease in the purchase price is obviously higher than the rate of the cost decrease of the counterparties; and (4) any other relevant factors that need to be taken into account.[526]

319. Pharmaceutical companies fined for monopolising the pricing of medical raw material.[527] In November 2011, the NDRC imposed fines of CNY 7 million, confiscated illegal gains, and imposed a cease-and-desist order on two pharmaceutical companies for monopoly pricing. The decision was the first time that the NDRC has imposed significant penalties for a breach of the AML since the law became effective on 1 August 2008. The NDRC's investigation confirmed that Weifang Shuntong Pharmaceuticals (Shuntong) and Weifang Huaxin Pharmaceuticals (Huaxin) had engaged in monopoly pricing for promethazine hydrochloride, a raw material used to produce Reserpine, a type of affordable blood pressure drug listed in China's essential medicines. The NDRC found that, in June 2011, Shuntong and Huaxin had signed an exclusive distribution agreement with the only two manufacturers of promethazine hydrochloride in China. The agreement prevented the manufacturers from selling the raw material to any third party without Shuntong and Huaxin's permission. As a result of the exclusive arrangement, Shuntong and Huaxin monopolised the supply of promethazine hydrochloride and the cost of promethazine hydrochloride increased from CNY 200 per kilogram to as much as CNY 1,350 per kilogram. A number of Reserpine producers ceased their productions in July 2011 because of the rising costs and severe shortages of the supply of Reserpine began to arise.

320. Case Qualcomm.[528] In this case, NDRC found that Qualcomm holds a dominant position in the wireless SEP licensing market and charged unfair royalty rates through the following ways: (1) *Charging royalties for expired wireless SEPs. The authority found that a part of Qualcomm's patents had expired, including a certain amount of material wireless SEPs. Qualcomm had argued that every year a few patents would expire, while a larger quantity of new patents would be added to the patent portfolio. Therefore, the concern that Qualcomm charges unfair royalties for expired patents would be unfounded. However, NDRC held that, irrespective of whether Qualcomm's patent portfolio offered licensing without changes and whether new patents are continuously added to the patent portfolio, it was unreasonable by nature that Qualcomm did not provide a patent list for long-term or even non-fixed term licenses. Even if, as alleged by Qualcomm, new patents were continuously being added to the patent portfolio and in general the amount of patents in the patent portfolio are increasing, the amount of patents in the patent portfolio does not necessarily reflect its value. Therefore, the authority held that, the licensees should have been given the*

526. Measures on the Prohibition of Price Monopoly, Art. 11, para. 2.
527. NDRC, *Two Pharmaceutical Companies Panelized for Monopolizing the Pricing of Compound Reserpine* (in Chinese), http://jjs.ndrc.gov.cn/gzdt/t20111115_444599.htm, 15 Nov. 2011.
528. NDRC, Decision of Administrative Penalty No.1(2015), available at http://jjs.ndrc.gov.cn/fjgld/201503/t20150302_666170.html, 9 Feb. 2015.

opportunities of fair negotiation and should not have been charged royalties for expired patents. (2) Requiring licensees to cross-license patents free of charge. NDRC found that, during the licensing of wireless SEPs, Qualcomm forced some licensees to license relevant non-wireless SEPs held by them to Qualcomm, forced some licensees to cross-license patents free of charge, required some licensees not to asserts rights or file lawsuits based on the relevant patents held by the licensees against Qualcomm and its clients, and even refused to pay reasonable consideration to the licensees for patent cross-licenses. During the investigation in this case, Qualcomm put forward the following reasons for obtaining patent cross-licenses from licensees free of charge in three aspects: first, Qualcomm obtained patent cross-licenses by licensees to protect its baseband chips business and its customers from patent infringements; second, Qualcomm's requirement on licensees to cross-license patents free of charge is part of an overall value exchange with licensees; third, many licensees in China do not own patent portfolios that have material value to be exchanged. For the above-mentioned reasons, NDRC rejected the reasons put forward by Qualcomm, and concluded that it is unfair for Qualcomm to require licensees to cross-license patents free of charge. This is especially the case as some Chinese licensees also hold valuable patent portfolios. Qualcomm should not completely deny the value of the patents held by the Chinese licensees, in order to protect its baseband chips business and its customers from patent infringements, and impede license from asserting rights or filing lawsuits to enforce patents held by them. Qualcomm's argument that free cross-licensing is part of an overall value exchange with licensees lacks support in terms of fact and evidence. As a result, Qualcomm was deemed unable to prove the fairness of the free cross-licensing requirement on licensees. (3) Apart from the wireless SEPs which have an intrinsic value, offering quite some non-wireless SEP which are not necessary for wireless communications devices manufacturers as part of the patent portfolio to be licenses. Qualcomm's wireless SEPs are mainly related to the wireless communications technology, rather than a wireless communications device's enclosure, screen, camera, microphone, loudspeaker, battery, memory and operating system, etc. In this case, when licensing the wireless SEPs and non-wireless-SEPs as a package, the fact that Qualcomm took the net wholesale price of the entire wireless communications device as the basis for calculating the patent royalties was held to be unreasonable. From the perspective of the licensees, this means Qualcomm charged relatively high royalties, and calculated the patent royalties using the wholesale price of the entire device covered by Qualcomm's out-of-scope wireless SEPs as the basis, which was clearly deemed to be unfair and lead to excessive patent royalties.

321. NDRC found that Qualcomm, through the above-mentioned conduct taken together, directly or indirectly charged unfairly high royalties. This resulted in a breach of the rules prohibiting business operators with a market dominant position from charging unfairly high sales prices under Article 17(1)(1) of the AML.

322. Other relevant laws and regulations on excessive/unfair pricing. The Price Law prohibits unfair pricing activities including the obtaining of excessive profits that are in violation of laws and regulations, regardless of the presence of dominance.[529] As discussed in paragraph 19 above, the Price Law was enacted in 1997 mainly as a piece of price control legislation aiming to stabilise the overall price level of the

529. Price Law, Art. 14(7).

market.[530] There are overlaps between the Price Law and the AML, such as the prohibition on price collusion, below-cost sales, price discrimination, and excessive pricing or seeking excessive profits. However, the AML has a different rational on the prohibition of abusive behaviour. The similar prohibition under the AML and the Price Law thus result in different thresholds and criteria on determining whether conduct can be construed as excessive pricing under the AML or seeking excessive profits under the Price Law. The sanctions on prohibited behaviour are also different under the AML and the Price Law.[531] A practical implication is that pricing behaviour of a dominant undertaking may at the same time violate both the AML and the Price Law. How the enforcement agencies will reconcile the overlaps and the divergences remain to be seen.

II. Discrimination

323. The AML prohibits undertakings with dominant market positions from charging discriminatory prices or imposing otherwise discriminatory transaction terms, without justification, to transaction counterparties in comparable situations.[532] The Measures on the Prohibition of Abuse of Dominance set forth the types of conduct that amount to non-price-related discrimination, including discriminatory treatment, without justification, to parties in comparable situations regarding transaction quantity, variety, quality grade, rebates and discounts, payment and delivery terms, and after-sales services.[533]

324. The Draft Measures on the Prohibition of Price Monopoly once provided clarification on the types of reasons that would be considered to be acceptable justification for discriminatory pricing. These justifications included: (1) the price difference will not have any actual impact on competition in the counterparties' market; (2) the counterparties are able to obtain the same kind of goods or substitutes at a reasonable price from other undertakings; and (3) other justifications as determined by the NDRC.[534] However, the finalised Measures on the Prohibition of Price Monopoly do not contain similar guidance; hence legal and practical uncertainties remain.

325. However, the Measures on the Prohibition of Abuse of Dominance, although they do not specify what may be accepted as justifications, list two factors that should be taken into account when assessing whether otherwise abusive behaviour could be accepted as justifiable. These factors include: (1) whether the conduct is based on the undertaking's normal operating activities or interest; and (2) the impact of the conduct on economic efficiency, social public interest, and economic development. These factors should be considered when assessing the justifiability of non-price-related conduct of dominant undertakings, including discriminatory treatment, refusal to deal, exclusive dealing, and tying or imposing other unreasonable transaction conditions.[535]

530. *Ibid.*, Art. 1.
531. *See* discussion at para. 90 above.
532. AML, Art. 17(6).
533. Measures on the Prohibition of Abuse of Dominance, Art. 7.
534. Draft Measures on the Prohibition of Price Monopoly (August 2009 version), Art. 15, para. 2.
535. Measures on the Prohibition of Abuse of Dominance, Art. 8.

326. Huawei v. IDC. [536] The *Huawei v. IDC* case decided by the Shenzhen Intermediate People's Court and the Guangdong High People's Court is a typical case of prohibiting a business operator with a dominant market position to exercise discriminatory conduct. In the judgments, the courts not only considered the fact that IDC made a FRAND commitment to the standard-setting organisation, but also considered the fact that IDC, as a company with a dominant market position, should not apply differential treatment in relation to trading terms such as pricing, to trading counterparties in equivalent conditions, without reasonable justifications.

327. The judgments rendered by the courts pointed out that the central idea of a FRAND royalty is that the patent holder adheres to the reasonable and non-discriminatory principles to collect royalties. The key to the adherence of the two principles lies in the reasonableness of the royalties, which is demonstrated by the individual reasonableness of the royalty as well as the reasonableness reflected by comparison between the royalties paid by different licensees. The court first considered the individual reasonableness of the royalty. For instance, it considered the following factors: the amount of the royalty should be linked with the profits earned by exercising such patent or similar patents, and the proportion of the profit in relation to the profit or revenue generated by the licensee in selling the related products. The SEP holder should only charge a royalty for its SEPs, the total amount of which should not exceed a certain percentage of the profit generated by the products and the various patent holders behind a technology should appropriately allocate the royalty between themselves. However, the courts also believed that it was an idealistic approach to determine the royalty based on the above factors, since a high-tech product may involve a number of technical standards and even one technical standard may involve thousands of essential patents. In addition, there is a lack of practical experience in evaluating the quality of these essential patents and the degree of their contribution to the end products. As a result, the courts may encounter great difficulties in assessing the reasonableness of SEP royalties.

328. In this case, the courts focused on the 'non-discriminatory' principle in the FRAND commitment – i.e., whether IDC, as the holder of essential patents, charged basically the same royalties or royalty rates vis-a-vis other counterparties in equivalent conditions. The judgments pointed out that 'if an SEP holder applies a lower royalty rate to one licensee and a higher royalty rate to another, by making a comparison between the royalties, the latter has the reason to believe that it is treated discriminatorily and the SEP holder therefore violated its commitment to license on a non-discriminatory basis'. In this case, the court compared the conditions between IDC and several other IT companies. It mainly compared the royalties IDC demanded from Apple and Samsung for granting the licence. On the one hand, Apple and Samsung, as wireless communications equipment manufacturers, needed IDC's SEPs like Huawei does. On the other hand, the sales of mobile phones of Apple and Samsung rank top globally, far above the ranking of Huawei. The courts found that the royalty rates demanded by

536. Shenzhen Intermediate People's Court, *Huawei v. InterDigital*, 4 Feb. 2013, [2011] Shen Zhong Fa Zhi Min Chu Zi No. 857; and No. 858; and Guangdong High People's Court, *Huawei v. InterDigital*, 16 Oct. 2013, [2013] Yue Gao Fa Min San Zhong Zi No. 305 and Guangdong High People's Court, *Huawei v. InterDigital*, 21 Oct. 2013, [2013] Yue Gao Fa Min San Zhong Zi No. 306.

IDC from Apple and Samsung could serve as a convincing basis for the royalties payable by Huawei. However, considering that the royalty rates charged by IDC for its licence to Samsung was agreed upon in the context of legal proceedings while the royalty rates demanded from Apple was reached through equal consultations between the two parties, the courts mainly made a comparison of the patent royalties between IDC and Apple. From 2007 to 2014, IDC reportedly charged USD 56 million only as royalty from Apple for its worldwide licence. As the sales revenue Apple achieved during these seven years was estimated to be at least USD 300 billion, the courts assumed that the royalty rate paid by Apple to IDC was approximately 0.0187%. However, taking IDC's fourth licence offer to Huawei in 2012 as an example, for all tech products involving 2G, 3G, and 4G from 2009 to 2016, IDC in practice offered a royalty rate equal to 2% of Huawei sales revenues for the products during these seven years. In light of the above, the courts decided that the royalty rate demanded by IDC from Huawei was not fair. Referring to the rate charged by IDC from Apple, the courts held that the royalty rate IDC is entitled to demand from Huawei should not be higher than 0.019%.

329. IDC argued that it was wrong for the courts to convert the lump sum royalties charged by IDC from Apple to a royalty rate based on sales revenue of the products in order to determine the royalties chargeable from Huawei. However, the courts noted that, although a lump sum royalty is different from a royalty rate based on sales revenue of the products, the comparison was justified in this case, as IDC refused to disclose any information relating to its royalties during the court proceedings. Hence, the courts had no other means but making an estimation of the royalties according to IDC's annual report, the sales revenues of other licensees and other information, in order to determine the amount of royalties that IDC should charge from Huawei on FRAND terms. The courts decided that IDC engaged in discriminatory treatment and charged excessive patent royalties, violating its FRAND commitment made to the standard-setting organisation.

330. Other relevant laws and regulations on discrimination. The Price Law prohibits price discrimination against business operators with equal trading conditions for the same goods or services, regardless of the presence of dominance.[537]

§2. Exclusionary Practices

I. Predation

331. The AML prohibits undertakings with a dominant market position from selling products at prices below cost without justification.[538] The text of the AML does not require that a likelihood of recoupment is necessary for a finding of predatory pricing. An early draft of the Measures on the Prohibition of Price Monopoly once interpreted that selling goods at a price that is below-cost meant that an undertaking

537. Price Law, Art. 14(5). Also *see* discussion on the overlap and divergence between the AML and the Price Law in para. 322 above.
538. AML, Art. 17(2).

was continuously selling goods at a loss for the purpose of eliminating actual or potential competitors. However, the final Measures on the Prohibition of Price Monopoly do not adopt this interpretation.

332. The Measures on the Prohibition of Price Monopoly provide that below-cost sales are justifiable in the following circumstances: (1) selling fresh perishable goods, seasonal goods, goods nearing expiry or overstocked goods at reduced prices; (2) selling goods at reduced price due to debt repayment, switch in production or close of business; (3) promotions for the launch of new products; and (4) any other reasons that can prove the below-cost sales are justified.[539]

333. Other relevant laws and regulations on predation. The AUCL prohibits the sale of goods at a price that is below-cost for the purpose of excluding its competitors except for sales of fresh, seasonal or overstocked products, or sales for debt repayment, switch in production, or close of business. The Price Law prohibits the selling of goods at below-cost prices in order to squeeze out competitors or monopolise the market, except in the case of fresh products, seasonal products, and overstocked goods, where the prices are legally reduced.

II. Tying

334. The AML prohibits undertakings with dominant market positions from implementing tying arrangements or imposing other unreasonable transaction terms without justification.[540] The Measures on the Prohibition of Abuse of Dominance interprets that a prohibited tying arrangement pursuant to the AML means the bundling or grouping of different products and selling this bundle or group of products contrary to market practice, consumption habits or product functionality.[541]

335. Tying conduct of Wuchang Salt. The local price bureau of the NDRC in Hubei (hereinafter 'Hubei Price Bureau') has completed an investigation of a tying case. On 12 August 2010, the Hubei Price Bureau launched an investigation into the conduct of the Wuchang branch (hereinafter 'Wuchang Salt') of the Hubei Salt Industry Group (hereinafter 'Hubei Salt') in response to local media reports that Wuchang Salt had tied the sale of salt to the sale of a type of local brand washing powder. The Hubei Price Bureau found that Wuchang Salt's tying conduct was pursuant to a policy of 'developing businesses other than salt' that was adopted by Hubei Salt. Wuchang Salt had previously tied the sale of nutritious salt with ordinary salt. Wholesalers then either supplied the salt and the tied products to retailers separately or as a bundle. Most retailers, when selling to end users, did not tie the sale of salt to the sale of washing powder. During the investigation, Wuchang Salt bought back the unsold washing powder from the wholesalers and submitted a commitment to rectify its conduct and cease the tying. The Hubei Price Bureau held that the conduct of Wuchang Salt had infringed the AML. First, Wuchang Salt holds a dominant position in the local wholesale market for salt. Second, the conduct of Wuchang Salt constitutes a tying prohibited by Article 17(5) of the AML. Third, Wuchang Salt, as an undertaking having a status

539. Measures on the Prohibition of Price Monopoly, Art. 12.

540. AML, Art. 17(5).

541. Measures on the Prohibition of Abuse of Dominance, Art. 6(1).

as a statutory monopoly, infringed Article 7 of the AML, which requires that statutory monopolists should 'conduct business in accordance with laws in an honest and trustworthy manner, impose strict self-discipline, and accept supervision from the public...[and] should not harm consumer interest by taking advantages of their position'. In light of Wuchang Salt's cooperation with the investigation and actions to mitigate the consequence of its tying conduct, and the fact that the sales value and the social impact of the tying were limited, the Hubei Price Bureau decided to suspend its investigation and to issue a warning to Hubei Salt and Wuchang Salt pursuant to Article 45 of the AML. Wuchang Salt was required to correct its actions within one month and was subject to follow-up supervision restrictions for two months. Hubei Salt was required to supervise Wuchang Salt's performance of its commitment, to reinforce its management of the salt market, and to avoid similar abusive behaviour in the future.[542]

336. Case Tetra Pak. [543]In November 2016, SAIC issued an administrative penalty decision against Tetra Pak. This is a typical case involving unreasonable tying for a company with market dominance. According to the decision, the background was that the production of packaging materials has been standardised and customers have plenty of options in the market. With its dominant position in the relevant equipment market or in the technical services market, Tetra Pak used various methods to restrict and induce customers to use Tetra Pak's packaging materials. This practice essentially amounted to tying, by which Tetra Pak was deemed to be unreasonable and to have resulted in serious anticompetitive effects. In essence, through its tying practice, Tetra Pak was found to have unfairly leveraged its competitive advantage from the two former markets into the market of packaging materials. By doing so, Tetra Pak unreasonably strengthened its dominant position in the market of packaging materials by putting other manufacturers for packaging materials into an unfavourable competitive situation, and therefore unfairly restricted competition in that market.

337. After concluding that Tetra Pak had a dominant market position, the antitrust authority confirmed the following main issues:

(1) Tetra Pak committed tying of packaging materials while providing paper-based aseptic packaging equipment or technical services. The penalty decision stated that, from 2009 and 2013, Tetra Pak always entered into standard form contracts with its customers while selling or leasing paper-based aseptic packaging equipment. These contracts contained specific periods for performance validation and the warranty. The performance validation period was eight to twelve weeks after the customers commenced business production (i.e., eight to twelve weeks before the warranty period), aiming to make sure that the equipment actually reached the goals set up in the contract. The warranty period was twelve months after the production launch following equipment adjustment or eighteen months after shipment of the equipment. Tetra Pak requested from its customers that they use Tetra Pak packaging materials or packaging materials approved by Tetra Pak.

542. NDRC, *Tying Conduct of the Hubei Salt Industry Group, Wuchang Branch Was Investigated by the Hubei Price Bureau* (in Chinese), http://jjs.ndrc.gov.cn/gzdt/t20101115_380421.htm, 15 Nov. 2010.

543. *See* SAIC Competition Enforcement Decision No. 10 2016, available at http://www.saic.gov.cn/zwgk/gggs/jzzf/cfjd/201611/P020161116513025279743.pdf.

Although Tetra Pak made some amendments to the standard format contract after 2012, stating 'the buyer undertakes that the packaging materials to be used together with the equipment shall fulfill the minimum requirements of packaging materials as stipulated in the contract', 'the minimum requirements of packaging materials' only list the QSV code which is the code for Tetra Pak packaging materials. In addition, Tetra Pak was also found to engage in tying while providing technical services. For instance, the standard service agreement before 2011 required customers to use TP packaging materials mandatorily.

(2) There are no reasonable justifications for the tying of packaging materials. The authority recognised that, from the perspective of the functionality of products, in particular the demand and trading habits etc., the paper-based aseptic packaging equipment, technical services, and packaging materials are separate, independent products. As stipulated in the national standard Acceptance Specification of Packaging Equipment for Liquid Foods (GB/T19063–2009), '[p]roviders of equipment shall…discuss and agree with the customers to use packaging materials or containers for acceptance that are not lower than national or industry standard'. Currently, the common standard for paper-based aseptic packaging materials is Paper-Based Composite Aseptic Packaging Materials for Liquid Foods (GB/T 18192–2008). This shows that paper-based aseptic packaging materials are standardised products in China, which means that using Tetra Pak's packaging materials is neither a necessary condition for ensuring the Tetra Pak equipment operates in accordance with the predetermined level, nor a precondition for Tetra Pak to provide technical services. Moreover, the investigation showed that Tetra Pak's equipment was able to achieve the same mechanical efficiency even using other packaging materials. This means that the use of Tetra Pak packaging materials is not necessarily linked to the achievement of the predetermined performance goal of Tetra Pak equipment. In defence, Tetra Pak argued that 'if there are problems during the performance validation period due to the use of third-party packaging materials, we are unable to confirm timely whether it is because of the equipment or the packaging materials'. Nonetheless, the investigation showed that in practice it was easy to distinguish who should be responsible for any quality-related accident during the production process – i.e., whether it is the manufacturer of the packaging materials, or the manufacturer of the equipment or the manufacturer of liquid food products. Therefore, there was no need to restrict the use of packaging materials to those provided by the equipment manufacturer on the basis to keep responsibilities separate.

(3) Tying of packaging materials would harm competition in the market of packaging materials. SAIC concluded that the tying conduct of Tetra Pak would seriously affect customers' choice of packaging materials and harm competition in the packaging materials market. Taking the tying of packaging materials during the performance validation period as an example, if a customer switches to other packaging materials after this period, it would be necessary to readjust the equipment in order to ensure compatibility with the new packaging materials. This would become an additional cost for customers and therefore an obstacle for switching to other packaging materials. Although the performance validation period does not seem long, the tying practice during this period would have the

contestable demand' can only be met by the dominant business operator. In contrast, the 'contestable demand' can be met by business operators with or without a dominant position. The anticompetitive mechanism of loyalty rebates mainly lies in the fact that the dominant business operator can restrict and influence the contestable demand by taking advantage of its importance for the non-contestable demand. In that way, a dominant company can extend its market power from the non-contestable to the contestable demand part of the market. In this case, Tetra Pak was found to have implemented its royalty rebates under specific market conditions: (1) some customers rely on the product varieties and the volume offered by Tetra Pak; (2) the influence of Tetra Pak's tying the sale of packaging materials during its supply of equipment and technical services; (3) the influence of Tetra Pak's practice to simultaneously apply different rebates. The royalty rebates applied by Tetra Pak were found to have had a significant anticompetitive effect under the above-mentioned market conditions.

(3) SAIC decided that the loyalty rebates implemented by Tetra Pak impaired competition in the packaging materials market. The decision pointed out that Tetra Pak's loyalty rebates would force its competitors to offer higher discount rates in order to be able to compete, which may benefit customers in the short term. However, in order to secure a certain part of the purchase volume, the competitors not only need to offer a discount that is not lower than that offered by Tetra Pak in terms of non-contestable demand, but also need to make up for the discount in terms of the non-contestable demand if customers were to decrease their purchase volume from Tetra Pak. This requires that the price offered by Tetra Pak's competitors in terms of the contestable demand must be lower than the net price after the discount offered by Tetra Pak. Under the specific market conditions in this case, the contestable demand was limited and the price which competitors needed to match is low. Hence, competitors found it difficult to compete in the marketplace, and some competitors may even be forced to exit the market. Therefore, the ultimate consequence of the conduct is to eliminate and restrict market competition. In the long run, the loyalty rebates offered by Tetra Pak would result in restrictions to the sales volume and profits of competing packaging materials manufacturers. The insufficient use of their capacity would seriously impact their existence and development and, in consequence, harm competition in the packaging materials market and the interest of consumers.

342. Therefore, the royalty rebates of Tetra Pak were found to constitute '[an] other abuse of a dominant market position' prohibited in Article 17(1)(7) of the AML.

343. The Measures on the Prohibition of Abuse of Dominance prohibit non-price-related discrimination, including discriminatory treatment without justification to parties in comparable situations through granting quantity discounts.[546] It remains to be seen how rebates will be assessed and treated under the AML.

546. Measures on the Prohibition of Abuse of Dominance, Art. 7(2).

IV. Refusal to Deal

344. The AML prohibits dominant undertakings from refusing to trade with transaction counterparties without justification.[547] The Measures on the Prohibition of Abuse of Dominance provide further guidance on what would be considered as a refusal to deal under the AML. The prohibited practices include curtailing or suspending current transactions with counterparties or refusing to enter into new transactions with counterparties without justification. However, what may constitute a valid justification has not been specified.[548]

345. Article 7 of the *IPR Regulation* provides that where its intellectual property rights constitute an essential facility for production and operational activities, a business operator with a dominant market position shall not, without any justification, refuse to license other business operators to use its intellectual property rights on reasonable terms in order to eliminate or restrict competition. All of the following factors shall be considered at the same time in determining an 'essential facility': (1) the intellectual property right is not reasonably substitutable in the relevant market, and is essential for other business operators to compete in the relevant market; (2) refusal to license such intellectual property right will have an adverse effect on competition or innovation in the relevant market, and be detrimental to consumer benefits or public interests; and (3) the licensing of the intellectual property right will not result in unreasonable harm to the business operator.[549]

346. Essential facilities. The AML does not expressly address the issue of essential facilities. However, it should be noted that the Measures on the Prohibition of Abuse of Dominance prohibit dominant undertakings, without justification, from refusing to provide parties with access to essential facilities on reasonable terms. Factors that should be taken into account when determining whether an essential facility exists include the feasibility of separately investing, constructing or developing such a facility, the extent of the counterparty's reliance on such a facility for it to operate effectively, the possibility for the dominant undertaking to provide such a facility and the impact on the dominant undertaking's production and operations of providing such access.[550]

V. Price Squeeze

347. The AML does not expressly cover price squeezes, although it is possible that this concept may be developed under the catch-all clause that prohibits any other abusive behaviour as determined by the AMEAs.[551]

547. AML, Art. 17(3).
548. Measures on the Prohibition of Abuse of Dominance, Art. 4(1)–(4).
549. Provisions on the Prohibition of the Abuse of Intellectual Property Rights to Exclude or Restrict Competition were promulgated by the SAIC on 7 Apr. 2015, official Chinese text available at http://www.saic.gov.cn/fldyfbzdjz/zcfg/xzgz/201507/t20150724_233535.html.
550. Measures on the Prohibition of Abuse of Dominance, Art. 4(5).
551. AML, Art. 17(7).

348. In this case, even if China Telecom and China Unicom did not engage in discriminatory pricing for broadband wholesale access, this might still violate the AML, to the extent that their conduct constitutes an illegal margin squeeze. China Telecom and China Unicom provide both broadband wholesale and retail services – that is, they can provide Internet services directly to their own users). If their wholesale price is significantly higher than the retail price, then the ISPs providing Internet services on the basis of the broadband wholesale access provided by China Telecom or China Unicom will have no room to make profits and will be forced to exit the market.

349. In this case, China Telecom and China Unicom generally charged ICP website users an access price of RMB 100,000/G per month, sometimes even as low as RMB 30,000–50,000/G per month. In contrast, ISPs in competition with the two companies were generally asked to pay an access price of RMB 200,000–300,000/G per month, though for some ISPs the price could be as high as RMB 1.5 million/G per month. The result of this strategy was that a majority of ISPs were driven from the market, and brought about a situation where China Telecom and China Unicom had a monopoly over the ISP end users in Southern and Northern China, respectively, depriving consumers from the right to select Internet services of their choice.

350. Professor Kan Kaili from the Beijing University of Posts and Telecommunications had explained to the media that the problem stemmed from the fact that China Telecom and China Unicom are backbone network operators and – at the same time – provide broadband Internet service to end users. He said that the 'retail price' for broadband width offered by China Telecom and China Unicom to their major clients such as banks is just a fraction of the 'wholesale price' offered to some small and medium-sized ISPs. Accordingly, the wholesale price is higher than the retail price. Due to cost pressures, some tier 2 service providers were unable to compete with China Telecom and China Unicom through lower prices. Hence, this strategy allowed the two backbone network operators to achieve their goal of monopolising the market.[552]

552. Zhong Jingjing, The National Development and Reform Commission denies that the broadband monopoly case has been settled, and states that it has already obtained key evidence, BJNews, 22 Nov. 2011.

Chapter 3. Concentrations

351. Since the AML entered into force, the MOFCOM has been the most active of the AMEAs, enforcing the AML merger control regime diligently. To date, the MOFCOM has published twenty conditional clearance decisions and one prohibition decision.[553]

352. Substantive appraisal of concentrations. Under the AML, a concentration may be challenged by the MOFCOM if it has or is likely to have the effect of eliminating or restricting competition, unless the parties can prove that the positive effects of the concentration on competition significantly outweigh its negative effects, or that the concentration is in public interest.[554] The MOFCOM will take the following factors into consideration when conducting a substantive assessment of a concentration: (1) the market shares of the participating undertakings in the relevant market and their ability to control the market; (2) the level of concentration in the relevant market; (3) the effect of the proposed concentration on market entry and technology development; (4) the effect of the proposed concentration on consumers and other relevant undertakings; (5) the effect of the proposed concentration on the development of the national economy; and (6) other factors affecting the market that are considered relevant by the MOFCOM.[555] The AML does not provide separate rules on horizontal mergers, vertical mergers, market/product extension mergers, pure conglomerate mergers or joint ventures. However, guidance on and insights into the substantive aspects of merger analysis may be drawn from the published merger decisions to date.

353. MOFCOM's approach to market share and concentration levels. Pursuant to the AML, the MOFCOM shall take into account the market share of the merging parties in the relevant market and their ability to control the market, as well as the degree of concentration in the relevant markets.[556] Neither the AML nor the AML implementing regulations to date have provided any specific criteria for market share or concentration levels. It should be noted that the Merger Assessment Measures generally state that market concentration level is one of the important factors that should be considered when assessing the impact of a proposed transaction on competition. Under normal circumstances, the higher the concentration level of the relevant market is and the higher the increment of the concentration level post the transaction is, the more possibility of eliminative or restrictive effect on competition the proposed transaction will have.[557] In addition, the MOFCOM's decisions to date have indicated that the MOFCOM has paid close attention to market share and concentration levels of the merging entities.

553. Official Chinese text of the MOFCOM's announcements of these decisions is available at http://fldj.mofcom.gov.cn/article/ztxx/.

554. AML, Art. 28.

555. *Ibid.*, Art. 27.

556. AML, Art. 27(1).

557. Merger Assessment Measures, Art. 6.

354. In *Coca-Cola/Huiyuan*, the MOFCOM found that Coca-Cola had a 60.60% market share in the carbonated drinks market in China.[558] In *Mitsubishi Rayon/Lucite*, the MOFCOM found that Mitsubishi would obtain a post-transaction market share of 64% in the Chinese methyl methacrylate (MMA) market.[559] In *Panasonic/Sanyo*, the MOFCOM found that Panasonic would hold a post-transaction market share of 61.60% in the Chinese button-battery market.[560] In *Novartis/Alcon*, the MOFCOM found that the parties would have a combined global market share of over 60% for ophthalmological anti-infection products, although Novartis accounted for less than 1% of that market share. In addition, with respect to the market for contact lens care products in China, the MOFCOM found that the parties' combined market share would reach 20% and the merged entity would become the number two player in the market.[561] In *Pfizer/Wyeth*, in addition to market share, the MOFCOM considered the impact of the transaction on the Herfindhal-Hirschman Index (HHI), which is a measure of economic concentration in the market. The MOFCOM found that the merged entity would acquire a market share of 49.4% and a post-merger HHI of 2,182, resulting in an HHI increase of 336, and decided that the transaction would have the effect of eliminating or restricting competition.[562] However, the MOFCOM decisions to date have been brief and have failed to describe how the MOFCOM assessed the market share and concentration levels, and commentators have asserted that this lack of transparency creates legal uncertainty.[563]

355. In June 2014, MOFCOM prohibited the establishment of the joint venture by three European shipping companies – i.e., *Moller - Maersk A/S of Denmark, MSC Mediterranean Shipping Company S.A., and CMA CGM S.A.* [564]This decision is its second prohibition decision since the AML came into force. In this case, MOFCOM first defined the relevant market as the international container liner shipping services market and the relevant geographical market as the Europe-Asia route, the Trans-Pacific route and the Transatlantic route. MOFCOM then made an analysis on the transaction parties and the network centre they proposed to set up, including the parties' market

558. *See* MOFCOM Announcement [2009] No. 22 Regarding the Decision of Prohibition of Coca-Cola's Acquisition of Huiyuan, official Chinese text available at http://fldj.mofcom.gov.cn/aarticle/ztxx/200903/20090306108494.html.

559. *See* MOFCOM Announcement [2009] No. 28 Regarding Conditional Clearance of Mitsubishi Rayon's Acquisition of Lucite, official Chinese text available at http://fldj.mofcom.gov.cn/aarticle/ztxx/200904/20090406198805.html.

560. *See* MOFCOM Announcement [2009] No. 82 Regarding Conditional Clearance of Panasonic's Acquisition of Sanyo, official Chinese text available at http://fldj.mofcom.gov.cn/aarticle/ztxx/200910/20091006593175.html.

561. *See* MOFCOM Announcement [2010] No. 53 Regarding Conditional Clearance of Novartis' Acquisition of Alcon, official Chinese text available at http://fldj.mofcom.gov.cn/aarticle/ztxx/201008/20100807080639.html.

562. *See* MOFCOM Announcement [2009] No. 77 Regarding Conditional Clearance of Pfizer's Acquisition of Wyeth, official Chinese text available at http://fldj.mofcom.gov.cn/aarticle/ztxx/200909/20090906541443.html.

563. Mark Furse, *Merger Control in China: The First Year of Enforcement*, 31 Eur. Competition L. Rev. 98 et seq (2010).

564. MOFCOM Announcement No. 46 of 2014, http://fldj.mofcom.gov.cn/article/ztxx/201406/20140600628586.shtml

share, market control power, market concentration levels, difficulties of market access, the impact on consumers and related business operators, and other factors. Finally, the authority concluded that the transaction at hand may have the effect of eliminating or restricting competition in the container liner transport service market on the Europe-Asia route.

356. MOFCOM decided that this transaction had anticompetitive effects on the following basis: (1) the transaction was found to constitute a concentration between business operators, falling under MOFCOM's jurisdiction; (2) the aggregate capacity of the three companies participating in the transaction on the Europe-Asia route amounted to 47%, which significantly enhanced their control over the relevant market; (3) the transaction resulted in a material change of in the relevant market structure, eliminating competition between the three shipping companies, with an HHI index increase from 890 to 2240 with an increment of 1350;(4) the transaction further increased the entry barriers into the international container liner shipping services market; (5) by integrating the routes and international transportation capacity, the transaction may squeeze the development space of competitors, placing them into a further disadvantageous position in the competition. [565]

357. An international scholar commented that '[i]t was absolutely correct for MOFCOM to issue a prohibition order against the P3 network because this is what the antitrust authorities in the US and the EU would do in the same circumstances, that is, it is entitled to protect itself from the negative effects on competition in its domestic market when such competition is adversely affected by outside competition'. [566]

358. Non-competition considerations. Industrial policy and other non-competition considerations may play a role in the AML merger control regime. First, the AML provides that, as a general principle, the State shall protect the legitimate operation of industries dominated by the State-owned economy that are vital to the national economy and national security.[567] The AML also provides that, as a general principle, undertakings may implement concentrations through fair competition and voluntary combination in accordance with the law to expand business scale and increase market competitiveness.[568] These provisions reflect China's industrial policy that emphasises the role of SOEs and encourages the consolidation of domestic companies.

359. In addition to the 'restriction of competition' test, the AML merger control regime provides a public interest test that allows a concentration with competition concerns to be otherwise cleared if the parties can prove that the concentration is in public interest.[569] The AML also requires that the MOFCOM consider the impact of

565. Shang Ming, Comprehensively Summarize Law Enforcement Experience to Continuously Improve the Efficiency of Law Enforcement Actions, *see* China Competition Law and Policy Research Report 2014, compiled by China World Trade Organization Research Association Competition Policy and Legal Committee, Law Press, 2014, pp. 7–8.

566. Franz Jürgen Säcker: Chinesisches Aus für eine Reederei-Allianz, WuW vom 07.11.2014, Heft 11, Seite 1031.

567. AML, Art. 7.

568. *Ibid.*. Art. 5.

569. AML, Art. 28.

a proposed concentration on the national economy.[570] There are examples for merger and acquisition cases in this regard, such as the merger between CSR and CNR in 2015 [571]and the merger between Baosteel and WISCO in 2016.[572] The latter resulted in China's largest and world's second largest iron and steel enterprise.

360. Furthermore, the Information Requirement Guidance issued by the MOFCOM provides that specific explanations should be given in the notification materials if the concentration is related to national security, industrial policy, State-owned assets or well-known brands.[573] The Review Measures further provide that, during the review process, the MOFCOM may solicit opinions on the proposed concentration from the relevant government agencies.[574]

361. National security review. It should be noted that the AML provides that, if mergers and acquisitions of domestic enterprises by foreign investors or other forms of concentrations involving foreign investors' concern national security, apart from the AML review, the transactions shall be examined in accordance with the relevant provisions of the State for national security review.[575] The AML does not clarify what the relevant provisions of the State are and does not provide further guidance on the implementation of the national security review.

362. In addition, the national security provisions of the M&A Rules require a notification to the MOFCOM where a transaction will result in a foreign investor obtaining a controlling equity interest in a domestic Chinese enterprise and the transaction involves a key industry, factors which may impact on State economic security or the possession of a well-known trademark or historical Chinese brand.[576]

363. On 3 February 2011, the General Office of the State Council promulgated the *Circular on Establishing a Mechanism of Security Review of Mergers and Acquisitions of Domestic Enterprises by Foreign Investors 2011* (hereinafter 'Circular on National Security Review'), which took effect on 6 March 2011.[577] The Circular on National Security Review sets out the scope, content, review mechanism, and procedures of the national security review. An Inter-Ministerial Joint Committee (hereinafter 'Joint Committee') is established under the State Council to be responsible for the national security review, and led by the NDRC and the MOFCOM.[578] The Circular on National Security Review establishes China's first formal process for evaluating national security issues arising from foreign takeovers and clarifies how Article 31 of the AML will be applied. Following the issue of the Circular on National Security Review, the MOFCOM has stated that the Department of Foreign Investment Administration under the

570. *Ibid.*, Art. 27(5).

571. *See* http://news.xinhuanet.com/fortune/2015-05/21/c_127825899.htm.

572. *See* http://news.xinhuanet.com/fortune/2016-09/22/c_1119608696.htm.

573. Information Requirement Guidance, Art. 18.

574. Review Measures, Art. 6.

575. AML, Art. 31.

576. M&A Rules, Art. 12.

577. Official Chinese text of the Circular on National Security Review is available at www.gov.cn/zwgk/2011-02/12/content_1802467.htm; English translation is available at www.fdi. gov. cn/pub/FDI_EN/Laws/law_en_info.jsp?docid=130963.

578. Circular on National Security Review, s. III.

MOFCOM has been drafting operational rules and procedures to increase the effectiveness and the transparency of the national security review system:[579]

(1) *Scope of the review.*[580] The national security review system covers foreign takeovers through which foreign investors may gain actual control over domestic enterprises in the following sectors: military (including enterprises located near key and sensitive military facilities and other units concerning national defence and security), key agricultural products, key energy and resources, important infrastructure and transport services, key technologies, and equipment manufacturing concerning national security. Actual control is defined as: (1) a foreign investor (including its parent company and controlled subsidiary) acquiring 50% or more of the equity of the target enterprise; (2) more than one foreign investor acquiring 50% or more of the equity of the target enterprise; (3) acquiring less than 50% of the equity of the target enterprise, but through those voting rights significantly affecting the resolutions of the shareholders' meeting or the board; or (4) other circumstances where effective control over business strategies, finance, personnel and/or technology of the domestic enterprise is being transferred to the foreign investor.

(2) *Content of the review.*[581] The national security review will consider the impact of the reviewable transaction on national defence and security, economic stability, social order, and China's ability to research and develop key technologies concerning national defence.

(3) *Review procedures.*[582] Foreign investors are required to notify reviewable transactions to MOFCOM pursuant to the Circular. The MOFCOM is required to submit a reviewable transaction to the Joint Committee within five working days of its receipt of the notification. The Joint Committee will conduct a general review of the reviewable transaction and, within five working days of its commencement, will solicit written comments from the relevant departments. Written comments are required to be submitted to the Joint Committee within twenty working days of the receipt of the request. The Joint Committee will close the general review within five working days after it receives all written comments if no department considers that the notified transaction will impact national security. If any relevant department considers that the notified transaction will impact national security, a special review will begin within five working days after the Joint Committee receives such written comments. The Joint Committee will close the special review within sixty working days after its commencement or submit the transaction to the State Council for a decision if no consensus is reached within the Joint Committee within those sixty working days. The MOFCOM will issue a written decision of the national security review to the notifying parties. The Joint Committee shall require that the MOFCOM, in cooperation with other relevant departments, terminate those transactions that have impacted or may

579. *See* MOFCOM monthly press conference on 17 Feb. 2011; video clip and script of the press conference are available at http://video.mofcom.gov.cn/topics/2011/0218/2620.html.

580. Circular on National Security Review, s. I.

581. Circular on National Security Review, s. II.

582. Circular on National Security Review, s. IV.

significantly impact national security, through divestiture or implementation of other measures in order to eliminate the impact of the transactions on national security.

364. To implement the Circular on National Security Review, the MOFCOM published the *Interim Measures on the Relevant Matters Concerning the Implementation of Security Review of Mergers and Acquisitions of Domestic Enterprises by Foreign Investors* (hereinafter 'Interim Measures on National Security Review') on 4 March 2011.[583] The Interim Measures on National Security Review were effective from 5 March 2011 to 31 August 2011 and interested parties were invited to submit comments by 10 April 2011. MOFCOM improved the relevant rules based on the assessment of the implementation of the public comments. The Interim Measures on National Security Review provided clarifications on several key procedural issues of the national security system introduced by the Circular on National Security Review, including the documents to be submitted with the security review notification, pre-submission consultation, and the MOFCOM's timeline for reviewing a security review notification. The Interim Measures on National Security Review stipulated that a reviewable transaction will not be approved by a relevant local foreign investment authority and cannot be implemented before a security review notification is submitted to the MOFCOM and the Joint Committee grants clearance.[584]

365. On 25 August 2011, the MOFCOM published the *Measures on the Implementation of Security Review of Mergers and Acquisitions of Domestic Enterprises by Foreign Investors* (hereinafter 'Measures on National Security Review'). The Measures are effective on 1 September 2011 and replace the Interim Measures on National Security Review. The Measures on National Security Review contain twelve articles that provide the key procedures of the national security system, including the documents to be submitted with the security review notification, pre-submission consultation with the MOFCOM, and the MOFCOM's timeline for reviewing a security review notification and submitting the notification to the Inter-Ministerial Joint Committee. Compared with the Interim Measures on National Security Review, the most noteworthy development is the addition of a new Article 9. According to Article 9, whether a merger or acquisition of a domestic enterprise by a foreign investor is subject to the security review system will be assessed on the substantive content and real impact of the transaction. Foreign investors are prohibited from avoiding national security review through any means, including but not limited to stock escrow, trust, multilayer reinvestment, leasing, loans, control agreements, and offshore transactions.[585]

366. *Merger efficiencies.* The AML allows the MOFCOM to clear a concentration that has or may have the effect of eliminating or restricting competition if the parties can prove that the positive effects of the proposed concentration on competition

583. Official Chinese text of the Interim Measures on National Security Review is available at www.mofcom.gov.cn/aarticle/b/c/201103/20110307432771.html.

584. *See* Interim Measures on National Security Review, Arts 3–7.

585. Official Chinese text of the Measures on the Implementation of Security Review of Mergers and Acquisitions of Domestic Enterprises by Foreign Investors is available at www.mofcom.gov.cn/aarticle/b/c/201108/20110807713530.html.

significantly outweigh its negative effects on competition.[586] Pursuant to the Information Requirement Guidance, parties are required to provide information and analyse whether possible efficiencies may arise out of a concentration, including how the efficiencies are to be achieved, the time required to achieve the efficiencies, the quantification of the efficiencies, the level of the resulting benefit to consumers and whether such efficiencies can be achieved in the absence of the concentration.[587] According to the Merger Assessment Measures, the MOFCOM shall consider the impact of the proposed concentration on economic efficiency, in a comprehensive way, together with the impact of the concentration on public interest, whether the concentration involves failing companies, and the existence of countervailing buying power.[588] These rules suggest that merger efficiencies will be considered in the review process.

§1. Horizontal Mergers

367. The Coca-Cola/Huiyuan Decision.[589] The MOFCOM issued its decision to prohibit the proposed USD 2.4 billion acquisition of China Huiyuan Juice Group Limited (hereinafter 'Huiyuan') by The Coca-Cola Company (hereinafter 'Coca-Cola') in March 2009. The proposed transaction concerned two non-alcoholic beverage producers. The *Coca-Cola/Huiyuan* decision was the first time that the MOFCOM had blocked a transaction under the AML merger control regime, and it shed some light on the MOFCOM's approach to the horizontal and conglomerate aspects of merger analysis. Three types of competition concerns were raised about the proposed acquisition. First, the MOFCOM asserted that Coca-Cola might be able to leverage its dominant position in the market for carbonated soft drinks into the market for fruit juice. Second, the MOFCOM held that branding was a key factor for competition in the beverage market. The addition of the famous 'Huiyuan' brand to Coca-Cola's 'Minute Maid' brand could increase entry barriers for potential competitors in the fruit juice market. Third, the MOFCOM was concerned that the proposed transaction could negatively affect the ability of domestic small and medium-sized enterprises to compete in the fruit juice market.

368. During the review of the *Coca-Cola/Huiyuan* notification, the MOFCOM conducted its investigation through written enquiries, verification workshops, seminars, hearings, on-site checks, entrusted investigations, and interviews with stakeholders. During the investigation, the MOFCOM solicited views from the relevant government agencies and industry associations, fruit juice beverage producers, upstream providers of concentrated fruit juice, downstream distributors, the parties to the transaction, the business partners of Coca-Cola, and relevant legal, economic, and agricultural experts. Furthermore, during the review process, the MOFCOM considered an acquisition prohibited by the Australian Competition and Consumer Commission (ACCC) in 2003 involving Coca-Cola Amatil Limited (hereinafter 'CCA') and Berri Ltd (hereinafter 'Berri'), an Australian juice producer. The ACCC considered that the CCA could exert

586. AML, Art. 28.

587. Information Requirement Guidance, Art. 9.

588. Merger Assessment Measures, Art. 12.

589. *See* the *Coca-Cola/Huiyuan* Decision, para. 354 above, n. 1.

its market power to link sales of Berri fruit juice products to its dominant Coca-Cola soft drink product. As retailers would themselves also have commercial incentives to bundle Berri's fruit juice products with CCA's leading portfolio of beverages, the ACCC's investigation strongly suggested that the Berri acquisition would have had the likely effect of reducing consumer choice and, ultimately, higher prices for consumers.[590]

369. In a question and answer session conducted by the MOFCOM regarding the Coca-Cola/Huiyuan notification (the 'MOFCOM Q&A session'),[591] the MOFCOM spokesman indicated that the MOFCOM had paid substantial attention to economic analysis and focused on product substitutability. The MOFCOM noted that, in addition to a share of 60.6% in the market for carbonated drinks in China, Coca-Cola also held other competitive advantages in terms of capital, brands, management, and marketing. Although a distinction was made between the market for carbonated drinks and the market for fruit juice, the MOFCOM noted that both markets were closely related and fell within the wider market of non-alcoholic drinks. Coca-Cola had entered the market for fruit juice, and was eager to extend its market share. Huiyuan, however, was China's largest fruit juice producer and had a market share of 46% for pure juice, 39.8% for juice drinks with 26%–99% juice content, and 10.3% for juice drinks with less than 25% juice content. Moreover, according to the data produced by AC Nielsen in 2007, the largest four producers in the Chinese fruit juice beverage market included United President, Coca-Cola, Master Kong, and Huiyuan. The four producers each held a market share of 21%, 20%, 16%, and 15% respectively in 2007, which meant that Coca-Cola's post-transaction market share in the fruit juice market would have increased to 35%. Such market position and additional competitive advantages would have enabled Coca Cola to leverage its dominance in the carbonated drinks market to the juice market through tying, bundling or other exclusive practices. Moreover, the MOFCOM noted that Coca-Cola would be reasonably expected to further its competitive strength and influence in the juice market following the transaction, thereby leading to significant synergy effects.

370. However, the brevity of the Coca-Cola/Huiyuan decision, with around 1,500 Chinese characters, has drawn criticism due to its lack of detail when assessing the alleged leverage effect. In addition, although the MOFCOM spokesperson had stressed that the decision was based solely on competition factors, the MOFCOM had considered factors that were not expressly mentioned in Article 27 of the AML, that is, branding, potential harm to small and medium-sized enterprises, and the healthy development of the Chinese juice drink industry. This has caused great ambiguity.

371. It is also observed that industrial policy goals may have played a role in the Coca-Cola/Huiyuan decision. First, it is noteworthy that domestic ownership of brands is considered to be an important element of China's industrial policy because famous brands of Chinese companies are a strategic goal of government action as

590. For ACCC's press release and assessment of the proposed *CCA/Berri* transaction, *see* www.accc.gov.au/content/index.phtml/itemId/486557/fromItemId/514753.

591. MOFCOM, *MOFCOM Spokesperson Yao Jian Answers Questions by Journalists on the Anti-Monopoly Review Decision regarding Coca-Cola's Acquisition of Huiyuan* (in Chinese), www.mofcom.gov.cn/aarticle/zhengcejd/bj/200903/20090306124140.html, 25 Mar. 2009.

stipulated in the State Council *Outline of the National Intellectual Property Strategy*.[592] Furthermore, before the AML entered into force, the acquisition of Chinese brands had been regulated by the M&A Rules. Thus, it seems clear that China's industrial policy aims to encourage and promote the creation and ownership of well-known brands by Chinese companies. Second, with respect to small and medium-sized enterprises, commentators have noted that the MOFCOM may be accused of seeking to protect domestic competitors instead of protecting the competition process.[593]

372. Because of the lack of detailed reasoning in the Coca-Cola/Huiyuan decision, it would be difficult for the public to assess the merits of the MOFCOM's competition and economic analysis. For example, the MOFCOM considered that the proposed Coca-Cola/Huiyuan transaction would result in a dominant position in the fruit juice market, strengthen Coca-Cola's market power, and impede effective competition. However, the decision did not clearly define the relevant markets on which the MOFCOM conducted its analysis or describe the MOFCOM's assessment of the available market share data. It is unavoidable that commentators may adopt different approaches to define the market, which may lead to different outcomes. The decision also failed to address how the proposed transaction would result in Coca-Cola having market power. Thus, the lack of detail not only limited the merits of the decision, but also accords with some commentators' evaluation that the MOFCOM factored in some political considerations to favour domestic well-known brands and industrial policy.

373. As illustrated by the *Coca-Cola/Huiyuan* decision, in order to ensure the objective and neutral application of the AML procedural and substantial rules, address ambiguity, and improve accountability, for future decisions, the AMEAs need to ensure that there is sufficient transparency in the review process and provide detailed reasoning of the review decisions.

374. The InBev/Anheuser-Busch Decision.[594] In November 2008, the MOFCOM published its decision to clear InBev's proposed USD 52 billion acquisition of Anheuser-Bush, subject to conditions. The InBev/Anheuser-Busch decision was the first published merger review decision under the AML, and it did not provide any detailed analysis of the transaction. The MOFCOM found that the transaction would not eliminate or restrict competition in China's beer market. However, the MOFCOM decided that, given the size of the acquisition and the large market share and strong market position of the combined entity, restrictive conditions should be imposed to minimise the potential adverse effect of the transaction on China's beer market. The imposed conditions included that: (1) Anheuser-Busch's existing 27% stake in Tsingdao Brewery not be increased; (2) InBev notify the MOFCOM in a timely manner if there are any changes in its controlling shareholders or the shareholders of such controlling

592. The *Outline of the National Intellectual Property Strategy* was promulgated by the State Council on 5 Jun. 2008, official Chinese text available at www.gov.cn/zwgk/2008-06/10/content_1012269.htm, English translation available at www.gov.cn/english/2008-06/21/content_1023471.htm.

593. Hannah C. L. Ha, John M. Hickin & Gerry P. O'Brien, *China's Anti-Monopoly Law Merger Control Regime – 10 Key Questions Answered (Part I)*, www.mondaq.com, 11 Mar. 2010.

594. *See* MOFCOM Announcement [2008] No. 95 Regarding Conditional Clearance of InBev's Acquisition of Anheuser Busch, official Chinese text available at http://fldj.mofcom.gov.cn/aarticle/ztxx/200811/20081105899216.html.

shareholders; (3) InBev not increase its existing 28.56% stake in Zhujiang Brewery; and (4) InBev not hold any stake in two other major breweries in China. Furthermore, InBev was required to notify and obtain prior approval from the MOFCOM before seeking to take any such steps.

375. The Mitsubishi Rayon/Lucite Decision.[595] The MOFCOM published its decision to conditionally clear the USD 1.6 billion acquisition by Mitsubishi Rayon of the Lucite International (hereinafter 'Lucite'), a British chemical producer. The MOFCOM found that Mitsubishi Rayon and Lucite overlapped in a number of product markets, including a significant overlap in the market for MMA, a chemical substance. To a lesser extent, the parties also overlapped in the markets of the related products of SpMA, PMMA pellets, and PMMA boards. The geographic market was found to be China. The MOFCOM decide that, because the parties' combined market share was 64% in the MMA market in China and was much higher than the number two and three players in the MMA market, the combined entity would have a controlling position in the MMA market, leading to the possibility that Mitsubishi Rayon could, post-transaction, eliminate and restrict competitors in the MMA market. Furthermore, as Mitsubishi Rayon was active both in MMA as well as a downstream product market, it would have the ability, post-transaction, to foreclose downstream competitors due to its dominance in the MMA market. The MOFCOM accepted a remedies package from Mitsubishi Rayon where it disposed of at least a part of Lucite's business. However, the MOFCOM allowed Mitsubishi Rayon a degree of flexibility in how to achieve this.

376. Separation packages. The parties agreed to implement one of the two remedies packages: (1) 'capacity separation', whereby Lucite's Chinese entity would sell, in a single transaction, 50% of its annual MMA output to one or more independent third-party buyers for a period of five years at cost (with such cost figures to be verified by an independent auditor); or (2) 'complete separation', whereby if within six months after the completion of the merger (such period extendable by the MOFCOM by another six months) the merged entity was unable to sell 50% of its annual MMA output to the independent third parties, the parties agreed that the MOFCOM may appoint an independent trustee to oversee the sale of 100% equity interest of a specified Lucite Chinese entity.

377. Operational restrictions until completion of the separation. In the period between the completion of the merger and the completion of a separation remedy, Lucite China and Mitsubishi Rayon agreed to operate independently, with separate management teams and boards of directors (hereinafter 'independent operation period'). During the independent operation period, parties would continue to compete with one another in the sale of MMA in China, and they were prohibited from exchanging information relating to prices in China, customer information and other competitively sensitive information. Material infringement of any of the remedies provisions during the independent operation period will result in penalties between CNY 250,000–CNY 500,000.

595. *See* the *Mitsubishi Rayon/Lucite* Decision, para. 354 above, n. 2; also *see* Freshfields Bruckhaus Deringer LLP, 'MOFCOM Intervenes for a Third Time', www.freshfields.com/publications/pdfs/2009/apr09/25743.pdf, April 2009.

378. Restrictions on merged entity in the next five years. The merged entity agreed that, in the five years following completion of the transaction, it would not, without the prior approval of the MOFCOM, acquire a manufacturer in China of MMA, PMMA, and related products or establish facilities to manufacture MMA, PMMA, and related products in China.

379. Compared to its previous merger decisions, in which the MOFCOM provided very little detail about the evidence relied upon, the Mitsubishi/Lucite decision provided a relatively significant amount of detail about the conditions to which the parties agreed. The decision was the first time that a partial divestiture remedy was imposed by the MOFCOM and demonstrated the MOFCOM's increasing sophistication with merger remedies. The MOFCOM had allowed some flexibility in achieving this by allowing the sale of capacity by Mitsubishi Rayon, rather than a full business disposal. In addition, the parties were allowed to complete the transaction before finding a buyer. However, apart from the limited market share information above, very little evidence or explanation of the basis of the MOFCOM's conclusions was included in the decision.

380. The Pfizer/Wyeth Decision.[596] On 29 September 2009, the MOFCOM cleared US pharmaceutical company Pfizer's proposed USD 68 billion acquisition of its competitor Wyeth. According to MOFCOM's decision, Pfizer and Wyeth overlapped in a number of product markets, including a significant overlap in the market for Swine Mycoplasma Pneumonia Vaccine (SMPV). The MOFCOM concluded that the proposed acquisition would result in material changes to the structure of the SMPV market that would result in the elimination or the restriction of competition post-merger. In particular, the MOFCOM found that the combined market share of the parties would be 49.4%, which was significantly higher than the market share of its competitors. Intervet, the second-largest competitor in the market, had a market share of 18.35% and other competitors' market shares were below 10%. The MOFCOM was concerned that the merged entity would be able to expand its market share by leveraging its scale and control the price of SMPV post-merger. Furthermore, the MOFCOM was concerned about the high concentration in the market for SMPV, as the HHI post-merger would be 2,182 with an increase of 336, indicating a very concentrated market. Another area for concern was the perceived high barriers to entry into pharmaceutical products, because research and development for pharmaceuticals is characterised by high costs and long cycles. According to the decision, a market survey had shown that the technical barriers to entering the SMPV market were even higher.

381. To address its concerns, the MOFCOM imposed the following conditions on this acquisition: (1) Pfizer must divest specified SMPV businesses in China (excluding Hong Kong, Macau, and Taiwan) and the businesses to be divested shall include both tangible and intangible assets required for their viability and competitiveness; (2) Pfizer must, within six months of the MOFCOM's approval, through a trustee find a buyer for the businesses to be divested and enter into a sale and purchase agreement with the buyer; the buyer must be independent from Pfizer and Wyeth and meet predetermined standards as to its qualifications and be approved by the MOFCOM; and during this six-month period, Pfizer shall appoint a manager to manage the businesses to be divested in the interim; (3) if Pfizer fails to find a purchaser within

596. *See* the *Pfizer/Wyeth* Decision, para. 354 above, n. 5.

the six-month period following the decision, the MOFCOM will appoint a new trustee to dispose of the businesses to be divested without setting a minimum selling price; and (4) Pfizer shall, within three years of the divesture, at the purchaser's request, provide reasonable technical assistance to the purchaser, assist it in the procurement of raw materials, and provide technical training and advice to the relevant personnel of the purchaser.

382. The Panasonic/Sanyo Decision.[597] On 30 October 2009, the MOFCOM issued its decision to conditionally clear the proposed acquisition of Sanyo Electric Co., Ltd. (hereinafter 'Sanyo') by Panasonic Corporation (hereinafter 'Panasonic'). Sanyo and Panasonic are two well-known consumer appliances and electronic products companies in Japan. The MOFCOM's investigation identified competition concerns in the following three battery markets: (1) rechargeable button lithium batteries; (2) nickel-metal hydride batteries for consumers; and (3) nickel-metal hydride batteries for vehicles. The MOFCOM found that the merged entity would have significant market shares in these markets, which would result in substantial changes in the market structures.

383. To remedy the identified competition concerns, the parties were required to implement the following measures: (1) Sanyo shall completely divest the rechargeable button lithium batteries business of one of its plants in Japan to an independent third party; (2) Sanyo shall divest either: (a) its consumer nickel-metal hydride battery business in Japan to an independent third party and supply its Sub-CD type batteries produced in China to such purchaser; or (b) its consumer nickel-metal hydride battery business in China to an independent third party; (3) Panasonic shall divest its nickel-metal hydride batteries business in Japan to an independent third party; and (4) Panasonic shall, with respect to Panasonic Ev Energy Co. Ltd., a joint venture between Panasonic and Toyota, reduce its capital contribution percentage from 40%–19.5%, and relinquish its voting rights, right to appoint directors, and veto rights relating to the vehicle nickel-metal hydride battery business, and Panasonic Ev Energy Co. Ltd. shall change its name to exclude 'Panasonic'.

384. The Panasonic/Sanyo decision highlights the active role that the MOFCOM is willing to play in international transactions where there appears to be a competition concern in China. The MOFCOM demonstrated that it had conducted thorough investigations before reaching its decision. The decision also demonstrates that the MOFCOM will require remedies to be applied outside of China in order to mitigate the adverse effect on competition in China.

385. The Novartis/Alcon Decision.[598] On 13 August 2010, the MOFCOM announced that it had approved the proposed acquisition of Alcon by Novartis, both global pharmaceutical companies headquartered in Switzerland. The approval was conditional on the fulfilment of Novartis' commitments with respect to ophthalmological pharmaceuticals and contact lens care products in China.

386. During the review, the MOFCOM found that competition concerns arose in the markets for ophthalmological anti-inflammatory/anti-infective combinations and contact lens care products in China because of the parties' high combined market shares and the position of the parties' close competitors in those markets. The parties

597. *See* the *Panasonic/Sanyo* Decision, para. 354 above, n. 3.

598. *See* the *Novartis/Alcon* Decision, para. 354 above, n. 4.

would have a combined global market share of over 60% for ophthalmological anti-infection products. In the market for contact lens care products in China, the parties' combined market share would reach 20% and the merged entity would become the number two player in the market.

387. To address the identified competition concerns, Novartis was required to: (1) completely cease its sales of 'Infectoflam', Novartis' branded ophthalmological anti-inflammatory/anti-infective combinations product, in China by the end of 2010; (2) not relaunch Infectoflam products or similar products with a new brand in the Chinese market within five years of the effective date of the MOFCOM's decision; (3) not sell ophthalmic anti-inflammatory/anti-infection combination products it owns before the completion of the transaction or sell such products from other countries into China; and (4) report, on a yearly basis, the performance of these undertakings to the MOFCOM within such five-year period.

388. Furthermore, within twelve months of the effective date of the MOFCOM's decision, Novartis was required to terminate an exclusive distribution agreement between Shanghai Ciba Vision, Novartis' wholly owned subsidiary, and Hydron Contact Lens Co., Ltd. (hereinafter 'Hydron'), the top contact lens care product manufacturer in China which holds over 30% of the market, and Shanghai Ciba Vision's sole distributor in China. The MOFCOM's concern was that the distribution agreement might enable coordination between the merged entity and Hydron in terms of price, production volume and sales regions, thereby eliminating or restricting competition. Novartis was required to provide the MOFCOM with reports on its performance of the undertakings within one week of the termination of the distribution agreement. Novartis was also required to entrust a trustee to supervise its performance of the imposed conditions in accordance with the MOFCOM's Divestiture Measures.

389. The Seagate/Samsung Decision.[599] On 12 December 2011, the MOFCOM published its conditional clearance decision on the acquisition of the hard disk drive (HDD) business of Samsung by Seagate Technology (hereinafter 'Seagate'). The MOFCOM defined the relevant product market as the HDD market and the relevant geographic market as global. It conducted market investigations and undertook competition analysis, examining issues such as market conditions, procurement patterns, capacity utilisation, product innovation, buyer power, market entry, prior transactions in the HDD market, price changes during specific time periods, and the impact of the transaction on consumers and competition in the HDD market.

390. The MOFCOM found that the HDD market is highly concentrated and that the level of concentration has increased over the past two decades. The five HDD manufacturers (Seagate, Western Digital, Hitachi Storage, Toshiba, and Samsung) held 33%, 29%, 18%, 10%, and 10% share in the global HDD market, respectively, and held similar market shares in the Chinese market. MOFCOM also found that HDD are homogeneous products and that the HDD market is highly transparent. The key customers of HDD products are large personal computer (PC) manufacturers and it is easy and not costly for PC manufacturers to switch suppliers. The MOFCOM also found that large PC manufacturers use closed bids to procure HDD products and

599. *See* MOFCOM Announcement [2011] No. 90 Regarding Conditional Clearance of Seagate's Acquisition of Samsung Hard Disk Drive Business, official Chinese text available at http://fldj.mofcom.gov.cn/article/ztxx/201112/20111207874274.shtml.

negotiate bilaterally with multiple HDD manufacturers on a quarterly basis to obtain and maintain competitive prices. To ensure a continuous and steady supply, large PC manufacturers allocate their demand among two to four HDD manufacturers based on prices and other factors. Thus, the MOFCOM considered that it is important to continue the existing procurement patterns in order to maintain competition in the HDD market.

391. Furthermore, the MOFCOM found that innovation plays a key role in the HDD market and IPRs and know-how are important for HDD manufacturers. Non-IP intellectual assets and economies of scale create barriers to entry and there have been no new entries in the last ten years. The HDD market has a high capacity utilisation rate. When facing a general price increase, large PC manufacturers have no incentives to exercise their countervailing power because they are able to pass on the price increase to end users through raising the prices of PC products. However, smaller HDD distributors and fragmented end users have no bargaining power to counter such price increases. Overall, the MOFCOM concluded that the transaction would eliminate or restrict competition in the HDD market as it will eliminate an important competitor in the HDD market, resulting in adverse effects on Chinese consumers. Given the procurement patterns of large PC manufacturers, the transaction will make it easier for the remaining HDD manufacturers to secure orders simultaneously and thereby weaken the competitive constraints imposed by the procurement model. Thus, the transaction will also give rise to coordinated effects due to the highly transparent nature of the HDD market.

392. Based on the competitive assessment and consultations with the parties, the MOFCOM imposed six conditions. First, Seagate must take measures as specified by the MOFCOM to keep Samsung's brand as an independent competitor. Second, Seagate must fulfil its commitments to maintain and expand Samsung's production capacity within six months following the MOFCOM's clearance decision, and thereafter reasonably determine the production capacity and volume of Samsung's products by taking into account the demand and supply conditions of the market. After implementing the MOFCOM's clearance decision for twelve months, Seagate may apply to MOFCOM to release it from the first and second obligations, subject to the MOFCOM's approval. Third, post the transaction, Seagate must not significantly change its current business pattern or force customers to purchase HDD products exclusively from Seagate or entities controlled by Seagate. Fourth, post the transaction, Seagate must not force TDK (China) Investment Co., Ltd. to supply HDD magnetic heads exclusively to Seagate or its controlled entities or restrict the supply of TDK's HDD magnetic heads to other HDD manufacturers. Fifth, Seagate must, for three years after the clearance decision, invest a minimum of USD 800 million per year in research and development. Finally, Seagate must appoint an independent supervisory trustee to supervise its performance of the relevant obligations and must, within one week after such appointment, provide the MOFCOM with a detailed plan regarding the performance of the relevant obligations.

393. The Western Digital/Hitachi Decision.[600] On 2 March 2012, the MOFCOM published its conditional clearance decision on the acquisition of the HDD business of Hitachi by Western Digital. In contrast to its EU, US, Japanese, and Korean counterparts, the MOFCOM is the only competition authority that imposed both structural and behavioural remedies on the transaction. The MOFCOM's approach to market definition and competitive assessment of the transaction were similar to those in its *Seagate/Samsung* Decision made in December 2011. The relevant market was defined as the global HDD market. The MOFCOM concluded that Western Digital's proposed acquisition of Viviti, a wholly owned subsidiary of Hitachi that directly controls Hitachi Global Storage Technologies Netherlands B.V. and indirectly controls Hitachi Global Storage Technologies Singapore Pte. Ltd., would eliminate or restrict competition in the HDD market. The MOFCOM requested that Western Digital divest the 3.5-inch HDD assets of Hitachi to an independent third party within six months after the clearance decision. In addition, the parties are required to keep their businesses separate for at least twenty-four months, including but not limited to research and development, production, purchasing, marketing, after-sales services, administration, finance, investment, and personnel appointment.

394. AB InBev's Acquisition of SABMiller.[601] In this case, the acquirer, AB InBev, was founded in Brussels in 1977. AB InBev entered into the Chinese market in 1984, and its main products include beers with brands such as Budweiser, Harbin Beer, and Sedrin. The target, SABMiller, was founded in Surrey County, England in 1895. It entered into the Chinese market through the establishment of a joint venture, China Resources Snow Breweries ('CR Snow'), with China Resources Beer (Holdings) Company Limited ('CR Beer') in 1994. Before the transaction, SABMiller held 49% shares in CR Snow. On 11 November 2015, AB InBev and SABMiller entered into the Acquisition Agreement, according to which AB InBev would acquire all the shares in SABMiller. On 8 December 2015, AB InBev engaged in pre-notification discussions with MOFCOM, and MOFCOM expressed high attention to this case. On 8 March 2016, MOFCOM received the merger notification in this case, and required the notification party to submit supplementary materials. On 29 March, MOFCOM confirmed the acceptance of the case on file, and commenced its initial review. On 27 April, MOFCOM decided to enter the in-depth further review stage. During the extended in-depth period of further review, MOFCOM made a decision on 29 July to indicate it though the acquisition would have the effect of eliminating and restricting competition but nonetheless accepted the final commitment proposal submitted by AB InBev. The proposed amendment to the Acquisition Agreement concluded by AB InBev and SABMiller might remove the anticompetitive effect potentially arising from this acquisition. In accordance with Article 27 of the AML, taking into consideration the degree of market concentration in the relevant markets, the market shares of the business

600. *See* MOFCOM Announcement [2012] No. 9 Regarding Conditional Clearance of Western Digital's Acquisition of Hitachi Storage, official Chinese text available at http://fldj.mofcom.gov.cn/article/ztxx/201203/20120307993758.shtml.

601. MOFCOM 2016 No.38 Announcement on the Anti-Monopoly Review Decision to Approve, with Restrictive Conditions, the Concentration of Business Operators in respect of AB InBev's Acquisition of Shares of SABMiller http://fldj.mofcom.gov.cn/article/ztxx/201607/20160701369044.shtml.

operators involved in the concentration and their ability to control the markets, the degree of difficulty for market access, the impact on consumers and other related business operators, etc., MOFCOM made an in-depth analysis of the transaction's impact on market competition:

(1) The transaction would enhance AB InBev's ability to control the market. According to the investigation, in the Chinese mass beer market in 2014, CR Snow and AB InBev were the top one and top three brands, with an aggregate market share of 41%. In seven provinces and cities, including Tianjin and some provinces and cities in Northeastern China, the aggregate market share even accounted for over 70%. In the Chinese mid- and high-end beer market in 2014, AB InBev and CR Snow respectively ranked 1st and 2nd, with an aggregate market share of over 52%, and accounting for over 70% in five provinces and cities including Tianjin City and Anhui Province.
(2) The transaction would reduce competition between the two leading competitors in the Chinese beer market. According to the MOFCOM investigation, AB InBev and CR Snow were close competitors with similar customer groups and sales channels in the mass beer and the mid- and high-end beer markets. The two companies were found to be in intense competition in aspects such as brands, distributors, and customers.
(3) The transaction would increase market access barriers. That means, after completion of the transaction, AB InBev, and CR Beer would have both the incentive and the ability to integrate both parties' sales channels in the Chinese beer market, thereby making it more difficult for other business operators to access the market.
(4) The transaction would harm the interests of downstream distributors. After completion, due to the elimination of competition between AB InBev and CR Snow, distributors would be in a weaker position in the negotiations and possibly get reduced sales incentives, thereby causing the distributors' interests to be harmed.

395. In conclusion, MOFCOM held that the transaction at hand had the effect of eliminating and restricting competition in the Chinese beer market, ultimately harming the interests of Chinese consumers.

396. Since the transaction had anticompetitive effects in the relevant market, and in light of the final commitment proposal submitted by AB InBev and SABMiller, MOFCOM decided to approve the transaction subject to restrictive conditions. In essence, MOFCOM required AB InBev and SABMiller to perform the following obligations: (1) divest 49% shares held by SABMiller in CR Snow; (2) sell to CR Beer 49% shares held by SABMiller in CR Snow strictly in accordance with the remodeled Acquisition Agreement submitted by AB InBev to MOFCOM; (3) the divesture must be completed within twenty-four hours upon completion of AB InBev's acquisition of the shares of SABMiller, and it shall ensure the existence, competiveness, and marketability after divesture.

397. The decision also pointed out that, MOFCOM has the right to inspect the performance by AB InBev and SABMiller of its obligations by means of supervision by a trustee or by itself. If AB InBev and SABMiller were to fail to comply with their obligations, MOFCOM announced it would deal with it in accordance with the relevant provisions of the AML.

398. Abbott Laboratories' Acquisition of St. Jude Medical.[602] This is the decision on conditional approval of the concentration of undertakings recently made by MOFCOM. The acquiring party Abbott Laboratories ('Abbott'), an international medical and healthcare company incorporated in 1990 and headquartered in Illinois, the United States, engages in businesses of drug, nourishment, medical equipment, and diagnosing services. The acquired party St. Jude Medical ('St.Jude'), a global medical equipment company incorporated in 1976 and headquartered in Minnesota, the United States, engages in businesses of vascular medical devices. On 27 April 2016, Abbott and St. Jude signed an M&A agreement, which prescribes that St. Jude would become a wholly owned subsidiary of Abbott after completion of the transaction. On 6 September 2016, MOFCOM accepted the filing of this concentration of undertakings and started a preliminary review. On 6 October, MOFCOM started a further review.

399. During the review, MOCFOM found that the only product with horizontal overlaps on the market of China between Abbot and St.Jude are the vascular closure devices, which are the disposable medical devices for closing vasculars. Therefore, the relevant product market of the case are the vascular closure devices and the relevant geographic market is China. According to Article 27 of the AML, MOCFOM analysed deeply the effects of the concentration of undertakings on the market competition from the perspectives of the concentration degree of the relevant market, the markets shares of parties participating in the concentration, the market power, and the degree of difficulty of the market entry: (1) The proposed transaction would further enhance Abbott's market power in the relevant market. In 2015, Abbott and St. Jude had a 71.3% and 23.9% shares in the relevant market, respectively, the combined market shares was more than 95%; the pre-merger HHI is 5,678, the post-merger HHI is 9,086, and the delta (ΔHHI) between the pre-merger and post-merger HHI is 3,408. This reflects that the relevant market before the transaction was a highly concentrated market and the transaction would further increase the concentrate degree and the market power of Abbott would enhanced as well. (2) In terms of the fierce competition and the counterbalance between both companies due to the similar nature of products, the similar consumer groups and the similar distribution channels, the proposed transaction would eliminate the competition between the two leading companies in the relevant market. (3) As the vascular closure devices have high technology requirements and the market entry needs an entrance permit granted by the supervising departments, competent entrants can hardly appear in the market of China in a short period and therefore the concerns for restricting competition resulting from the concentration are hard to be resolved. (4) After closing the deal, as Abbott would gain stronger market power, it would have the incentive and capability of increasing the price or deferring the price reduction of related products, or reducing the service quality, which would detriments the customers' welfare.

602. MOFCOM, MOFCOM Announcement No. 88 of 2016 on Decisions from Anti-Monopoly Review of the Concentration of Undertakings on Conditional Approval of Proposed Acquisition of Equity in St. Jude Medical by Abbott, http://fldj.mofcom.gov.cn/article/ztxx/201612/20161202440204.shtml, 14 Jul. 2017.

400. On 30 December 2016, MOFCOM released its decision on this concentration, which on the one hand determined that the concentration has the effect of excluding or restricting competition in the vascular closure devices market and on the other hand, in accordance to the final proposal on restrictive conditions delivered by Abbott to MOFCOM, determined that the *Purchasing Agreement* to divesting business signed by Abbott, St. Jude's and Japan's Terumo Corporation on 6 December 2016 can reduce adverse effects on competition resulting from the concentration of undertakings and approved the concentration on conditions accordingly. This approval decision imposed the following obligations on Abbott and St. Jude's: (1) divesting St. Jude's vascular closure business; (2) selling the divestiture to Terumo and providing transition services in strict compliance with the *Purchasing Agreement*; (3) completing the divestiture within twenty days of Abbot's acquisition of St.Jude and confirming the sustainability, competitiveness, and marketability of the divestiture; (4) submitting a written report of the divestiture to MOFCOM within ten days of the divestiture, and submitting a written report of the transition services, every half a year, to MOFCOM. The above obligations of Abbot and St.Jude will be relieved since the day of the conclusion of the transition period.

§2. Vertical Mergers

401. At the time of writing, there are no clear rules regarding vertical mergers. However, the *Mitsubishi Rayon/Lucite* decision discussed above at paragraphs 354 and 375 and the *GM/Delphi* and *Google/Motorola Mobility* decisions discussed below revealed some important insights on the MOFCOM's substantive appraisal on vertical mergers.

402. The GM/Delphi Decision.[603] On 28 September 2009, the MOFCOM conditionally approved the acquisition by General Motors (GM) of Delphi, an auto parts supplier. In its decision, the MOFCOM acknowledged that there was no horizontal overlap between the parties' activities and that they were only vertically related in upstream and downstream markets. On this basis, the MOFCOM concluded that the relevant product markets were the passenger vehicles and the commercial vehicles markets on GM's side and the auto parts markets on Delphi's side. The relevant geographic markets for all the relevant product markets were China. The MOFCOM concluded that, due to GM's and Delphi's leading position in both the global and Chinese automotive and auto parts markets respectively and the state of competition in these markets in China, the transaction could potentially eliminate or restrict competition. In particular, the MOFCOM identified the following areas of concern: (1) as Delphi was the exclusive supplier of auto parts for various Chinese car manufacturers, the proposed acquisition might have an adverse effect on the reliability, price, and quality of the supply of Delphi's auto parts to these Chinese car manufacturers; (2) the proposed transaction might give GM access to certain competitively sensitive information of Chinese car manufacturers such as research and development, technology

603. *See* MOFCOM Announcement [2009] No. 76 Regarding Conditional Clearance of GM's Acquisition of Delphi, official Chinese text available at http://fldj.mofcom.gov.cn/aarticle/ztxx/200909/20090906540211.html.

and vehicle types, given GM's future representation on Delphi's board; (3) given the close relationship between GM and Delphi post-merger, if Chinese car manufacturers wished to switch to other suppliers for auto parts in future, Delphi might adopt a strategy of delaying or refusing to cooperate, for example, by raising the cost of switching suppliers; and (4) GM might increase its procurement of auto parts from Delphi, thereby making it harder for other Chinese auto parts suppliers to enter GM's procurement channels.

403. The MOFCOM imposed the following remedies on the GM/Delphi acquisition to address the identified concerns: (1) the merged entity must commit that Delphi and its affiliates will continue to supply Chinese car manufacturers on a non-discriminatory basis and ensure the timeliness and the reliability of the supply, the quality of the Delphi auto parts, and that no unreasonable conditions will be imposed in relation to the price and quantity; (2) GM and Delphi must not exchange or communicate confidential information about Chinese car manufacturers; (3) the merged entity must commit that Delphi and its affiliates will, at the reasonable request of their customers, cooperate with them to ensure a smooth transition in switching suppliers, and not raise the cost of switching by intentionally delaying their handling of such request or imposing restrictive conditions; and (4) GM must continue to source from various auto parts suppliers, not impose discriminatory conditions in its procurement of auto parts, and not unreasonably favour Delphi.

404. It was reported by Chinese media that, in a closed-door hearing on 18 September 2009, representatives from Chery, one of Delphi's biggest customers in China, and the China Automobile Dealers Association had expressed their concerns about the proposed acquisition.[604] It appeared that some of their concerns were identified as areas of concern in the MOFCOM's decision. This might encourage Chinese competitors and customers to express their concerns more actively in future cases, knowing that the MOFCOM is likely to attach considerable weight to their views in the merger review process.

405. The Google/Motorola Mobility Decision.[605] On 19 May 2012, the MOFCOM announced that it had conditionally approved Google's acquisition of Motorola Mobility and became the only antitrust authority that imposed remedies when approving the transaction. MOFCOM defined the relevant product markets as smart mobile devices and smart mobile device operating systems (OSs), which vertically related with each other. The MOFCOM focused its review on the Chinese market, but noted that the geographic scope of the markets for smart mobile devices and smart mobile device OSs is worldwide. It found that the competitive conditions of the smart mobile devices and the smart mobile device OSs markets are significantly different. The market for smart mobile devices is fragmented, highly competitive, innovative, and fast changing. In contrast, the market for smart mobile device OSs is highly concentrated with high entry barriers. The MOFCOM also found that Google's Android OS holds a dominant position in the market for smart mobile device OSs because of its high market share,

604. Twenty-first Century Business Herald, *GM's Buy Back of Delphi under MOFCOM's Review* (in Chinese), http://epaper.21cbh.com/html/2009-09/23/content_106632.htm, 23 Sep. 2009.

605. *See* MOFCOM Announcement [2012] No. 25 Regarding Conditional Clearance of Google's Acquisition of Motorola Mobility, official Chinese text available at http://fldj.mofcom.gov.cn/article/ztxx/201205/20120508134324.shtml.

the dependence of original equipment manufacturers (OEMs) on it, Google's strong financing and R&D capacities, and significant entry barriers.

406. The MOFCOM considered issues related to Android's free and open-source strategy, Google's fair treatment of OEMs, as well as Motorola Mobility's patent licensing practices. It found that, post-transaction, whether Android will continue to be free and open-source would be important for the relevant parties' reasonable expectations and interests. Furthermore, Google would have incentives and abilities to favour Motorola Mobility through imposing unreasonable patent licensing terms and conditions on other OEMs, impeding competition, and eventually harming the consumer interest.

407. The MOFCOM imposed three obligations on the parties. First, Google must continue its current business practice of keeping the Android platform free of charge and open-source for five years. Second, Google must treat all OEMs in a non-discriminatory manner for five years. Third, Google must honour Motorola Mobility's existing commitment to license its patents on fair, reasonable and non-discriminatory terms. An independent monitoring trustee was required to be appointed to supervise Google's performance of the obligations. Google must report to the MOFCOM and the monitoring trustee every six months regarding its performance of the obligations in the next five years.

408. The most interesting aspect of the *Google/Motorola Mobility* Decision is that the MOFCOM's analysis focused on Android as a key input of smart mobile devices and whether Google would, post-transaction, keep the Android platform free of charge and open to OEMs in a non-discriminatory manner in the Chinese market. In contrast, the EU, US, and Korean agencies' analysis focused on SEPs as inputs for smart mobile devices and whether Google would use those SEPs in a way that was significantly different to Motorola's current practices. It is unclear how MOFCOM reached the conclusion that Google would have incentives to favour Motorola Mobility at the cost of damaging Google's relationship with other Android OEMs and jeopardising Google's mobile search and advertising revenues. However, one should not ignore the fact that the competitive and regulatory landscapes of the Chinese market are significantly different from those in the EU and the US.

409. It is noteworthy that the European Commission said in its *Google/Motorola Mobility* Decision that any real foreclosure effect of the transaction would likely only affect small players in the downstream market.[606] Chinese smart device manufacturers such as Huawei, ZTE, Lenovo, and MIUI are currently active in the middle and low-end segments while international brands such Motorola, Samsung, Sony Ericsson, and LG are active in the high-end product portfolios. Chinese manufacturers are less competitive in terms of innovation, production, distribution, and aftermarket services. Thus Chinese smart device manufacturers may fall into the category of 'small players in the downstream market'. Although the MOFCOM did not disclose the opinions it solicited and received from OEMs during its review, the concerns raised by Chinese manufacturers can be significant and the degree of dependence of Chinese manufacturers on Android is arguably much higher than that of international brands.

410. The MOFCOM's *Google/Motorola Mobility* decision indicates that one should not take it for granted that the approaches and the outcomes of the MOFCOM's

606. *See* Google/Motorola Mobility, Case No COMP/M.6381, para. 98.

merger analysis will be convergent with those taken by the EU and the US authorities. China is a nascent antitrust jurisdiction. The MOFCOM is facing enforcement capacity constraints and pressures on balancing the objectives of the AML to protect competition, on the one hand, and to promote the healthy development of the socialist market economy, on the other hand. Drawing the fine line between efficiencies and China's policy to promote indigenous innovations and protect domestic industries tests the MOFCOM's wisdom and courage.

411. Microsoft's Acquisition of Nokia.[607] The acquiring party Microsoft Corporation ('Microsoft') incorporated in Washington, the United States, in 1975, engages in business of developing, manufacturing, licensing, supporting, and selling computer software, and consumer electronic products. In 1992, Microsoft established a representative office in Beijing and so far has eighteen branch companies and offices in China. The seller Nokia incorporated in Helsinki, Finland, in 1865, whose main products are feature phones, smartphones, network infrastructure, free digital map, and navigation businesses. Nokia manufactures and sells feature phones and smartphones in China, with five related entities within the territory of China. On 2 September 2013, Microsoft and Nokia signed the *Security and Asset Purchase Agreement*. Hereby, Microsoft would acquire all the equipment and the service businesses of Nokia, and Nokia would reserve all of its patents relating to communication and smartphones. MOFCOM received the filling from the parties on 13 September 2013, and decided to carry out a further review on 8 November, and decided to extend the period of further review on 8 February 2014, and made the decision of approval on conditions on 8 April 2014.

412. In its review, MOCFOM focused on the analysis of the 'vertical relationship' between Microsoft 's operating systems for smart mobile terminals, patents for smart mobile terminals, and Nokia's smartphone business, and, in addition, assessed the potential impact on the smartphone market in China which may result in abuse of the mobile communication SEPs held by Nokia.

413. Firstly, MOCFOM believed that the 'vertical relationship' between Microsoft 's operating systems for smart mobile terminals and Nokia's smartphones would not give rise to concerns of restricting or excluding competition. According to statics in 2012, the market shares of Microsoft 's operating systems for smart mobile terminals globally and in China are 2.42% and 1.2% respectively, and the market shares of Nokia's smartphones globally and in China are 4.85% and 3.7% respectively, thus neither Microsoft in the upstream market for operating systems for smart mobile terminals nor Nokia in the downstream market for smartphones has a market dominant position.

414. MOCFOM Further analysed the 'vertical relationship' between Microsoft 's patents for smart mobile terminals and Nokia's smartphones, and drew a conclusion that Microsoft was likely to exclude and restrict competition in China's smartphone market via its licensing program for Android smartphones. The reason is that patents (including SEPs and non-SEPs) under Microsoft's Android licensing program are a

607. MOFCOM, MOFCOM Announcement No. 24 of 2014 on Decisions from Anti-Monopoly Review of the Concentration of Undertakings on Conditional Approval of Proposed Acquisition of Equity in Nokia by Microsoft, http://fldj.mofcom.gov.cn/article/ztxx/201404/20140400542415.shtml , 14 Jul. 2017.

'must-have' technical component to realise the important functions of the Android operating system and Android phones and they are indispensable for producing and manufacturing Android phones, thus Microsoft has the ability to restrict competition in the downstream smartphone market through its Android licensing program. In addition, after the closing of this concentration, Microsoft will enter the area of mobile terminal manufacturing and realise the integration of its operating systems and the production of smartphones, thus Microsoft will have the incentive to exclude or restrict competition in the downstream smartphone market by, for instance, increasing its competitors' costs through raising the royalties paid by other smart terminal manufacturers.

415. In addition, MOCFOM analysed Nokia's possible abuse of SEPs due to the concentration. After the concentration, Nokia will withdraw from the phone production market, but will reserve all the relevant patents for communication and smartphones. Since this concentration will lead to a change of Nokia's business model, Nokia will have an incentive to exclude or restrict competition in China via its SEPs licence, and finally damage customers' welfare.

416. The decision points out that China is a country with both a huge mobile phone manufacturing sector and a large mobile phone consumption market, with a sales volume in China's smartphone market accounting for 34% of the global market in 2013. Given the significance of patents of Microsoft and Nokia to production of smartphones, any refusal to license their patents will substantially prevent competitors from entering the relevant market, distort, eliminate or restrict competition in China's smartphone market. According to the commitments of Nokia and Microsoft, therefore, MOCFOM decided to approve this concentration of undertakings on restrictive conditions.

417. The conditions based on Microsoft's commitments are: (1) Microsoft will not seek an injunction or exclusion order on the basis of those SEPs against smartphones made by smartphone manufacturers in China; (2) Microsoft will offer non-exclusive licences for Android smartphones at royalty rates for Microsoft's programme no greater than royalty rates before this concentration; (3) Microsoft will only seek injunctions on non-SEPs after having concluded that a potential licensee is not negotiating in good faith for a licence; (4) The above commitments for SEPs would be effective permanently; and the commitments for non-SEPs would be effective for a term of eight years.

418. The conditions based on Nokia's commitments are: (1) the licence of SEPs shall follow the Fair, Reasonable, and Non-discriminatory principles and shall not seek licence conditions not in compliance with the FRAND principles; (2) Nokia shall not seek injunctions against licensees in good faith to prevent the implementation of SEPs; (3) no tying for the licence of SEPs; (4) the transferees of Nokia's SEPs shall adhere to the obligations under the commitments and the obligations under the FRAND doctrine; (5) the loyalties will not deviate from the FRAND loyalties calculated at present but may be adjusted properly according to the factors having been considered in the commitments; (6) the above commitments shall be effective permanently.[608]

608. Souhu Finance, MOFCOM Held the 'Anti-Monopoly Practice' Press Conference, http://business.sohu.com/20140408/n397903239.shtml, 28 Apr. 2014.

§3. Market/Product Extension Mergers

419. At the time of writing, there are no clear rules under the AML on market/ product extension mergers.

§4. Pure Conglomerate Mergers

420. At the time of writing, there are no clear rules on pure conglomerate mergers. However, the *Coca-Cola/Huiyuan* decision, as discussed in paragraphs 367–373 above, provides information on the MOFCOM's approach to the conglomerate aspect of merger analysis.

§5. Joint Ventures

421. Only transactions that constitute concentrations of undertakings are potentially subject to the AML merger notification requirement. The AML and its implementing rules are silent on whether joint ventures are subject to the AML merger notification requirement. The MOFCOM, in its Draft Notification Measures, stated that the creation of full-function joint ventures would be subject to AML merger control and thus notifiable provided that the other criteria, such as the change of control and the notification thresholds, were satisfied. However, the final Notification Measures did not include this provision on the notifiability of joint ventures.[609] However, it should be noted that the Notification Form 2012 lists joint ventures, regardless of whether they are full-function or not, as a type of notifiable transactions. To date, the MOFCOM has cleared the transactions conditionally in five cases involving the setting up of joint ventures, including GE/Shenhua, Henkel/Tiande, ARM/Giesecke & Devrient/Gemalto, Keliyuan/ TMCI/ PEVE/Xinzhongyuan/Toyota Tsusho, and Maersk/MSC/CMA CGM.[610]

422. The ARM/Giesecke & Devrient/Gemalto Decision.[611] On 6 December 2012, the MOFCOM announced that it had conditionally approved the proposed joint venture between ARM Holdings (ARM), Giesecke & Devrient (G&D), and Gemalto. ARM is a semiconductor intellectual property supplier based in the UK. G&D, headquartered in Germany, is active in banknote production and processing, security documents, and identification systems security solutions. Gemalto is a provider of digital security solutions headquartered in the Netherlands.

423. The relevant market was defined as 'trusted execution environment' (TEE), a type of security solution that protects trusted sources and data through setting up an

609. Also *see* discussion on joint ventures at paras 142–143 above.

610. Official Chinese text of the relevant decisions are available at http://fldj.mofcom.gov.cn/article/ztxx/.

611. *See* MOFCOM Announcement [2012] No. 87 Regarding Conditional Clearance of the Establishment of a Joint Venture between ARM Holdings, Giesecke & Devrient and Gemalto, official Chinese text available at http://fldj.mofcom.gov.cn/article/ztxx/201205/20120508134324.shtml.

independent execution environment surrounding the operation system. The joint venture will research, develop, and market TEE. The MOFCOM found that ARM's application processors for household electronic products business is vertically related to the joint venture's proposed activities. As a leading licensor of IPRs of application processors for household electronic products, ARM holds a strong market position. The joint venture's activity in the downstream market of researching, developing, and integrating TEE depends on ARM's TrustZone technology, which is part of ARM's IPRs of application processors for household electronic products. Post-transaction, ARM could exercise its market power in the IPRs of application processors for household electronic products market to discriminate against other TEE developers or lower the performance of other TEE by specifically designing its IPRs to do so. The MOFCOM also found that it would be very difficult to enter the market for application processors because potential entrants need to have significant capability and experience in research and development and possess the relevant IPRs. Thus, the MOFCOM considered that the proposed joint venture is likely to have the effect of eliminating or restricting competition in the market for TEE.

424. In order to address the identified competition concerns, the MOFCOM imposed two conditions on ARM. First, post-transaction, ARM shall provide, on a non-discriminatory basis, security monitoring codes and other relevant information about TrustZone that is necessary for the development of TEE based on the TrustZone technology. Second, ARM shall not design its IPRs in a way that would lower the performance of competing TEE. The commitments remain in force for eight years.

425. The Maersk/MSC/CMA CGM Decision.[612] The No. 46 announcement of MOFCOM in 2014 on the antitrust review decision of prohibiting Maersk A/S ('Maersk'), MSC Mediterranean Shipping Company S.A. ('MSC'),and CMA CGM S.A. ('CMA CGM') from establishing a network centre points out that the traditional shipping alliances in the international container liner shipping market conducting cooperation based on vessel sharing agreements and accommodation swap agreement and each alliance member operates independently, thus which in nature is a loose-unit cooperation. However, the parties integrated the shipping capacity of the parties in the global East-West shipping routes (the Asia-Europe routes, the trans-Pacific routes, and the transatlantic routes) after the establishment of the network centre, which is substantially different from the traditional shipping alliances in terms of cooperation forms, operational procedures, and cost sharing, etc. Therefore, MOFCOM believed that a tight alliance fundamentally different from the shipping alliances will be established in this case, which shall undergo review of concentration of undertakings.

426. After examination, MOFCOM found that the relevant product market of this concentration case is defined as the international container liner shipping service market and the relevant geographic market is defined as the Asia-Europe routes, the trans-Pacific routes and the transatlantic routes. As the transatlantic routes do not cover any Chinese ports and the Asia-Europe routes and the trans-Pacific routes both cover Chinese major ports, MOFCOM focused the examination on the competitive effects

612. MOFCOM, MOFCOM Announcement No. 46 of 2014 on Decisions from Anti-Monopoly Review of the Concentration of Undertakings on Prohibition of Proposed Establishment of the Network Center by Maersk, MSC and CMA CGM, http://fldj.mofcom.gov.cn/article/ztxx/201406/20140600628586.shtml , 14 Jul. 2017.

of the proposed transaction on the Asia-Europe routes and the trans-Pacific routes. MOFCOM found that this concentration has serious adverse effects on the market competition due to the following reasons: (1) The combined shares of the parties in the relevant market would be up to 46.7%, and their market power would be significantly enhanced. (2) The HHI of the Asia-Europe routes increased from 890 to 2,240 and the HHI delta is 1,350, thus the concentration degree increased significantly. (3) The transaction will raise the entry barriers to the relevant market. (4) The parties may use their enhanced market power against the interests of consignors. As the final proposal for remedies lacks relevant laws and regulations and credible evidences to resolve MOFCOM's competition concerns, MOFCOM decided the block the concentration.

Part III. Administrative Procedure

Chapter 1. Administrative Investigations Before the Antitrust Authority

427. This chapter describes the rules on administrative investigations against monopoly agreements and abuse of dominance pursuant to the AML and other relevant laws and regulations.

§1. Initiative

I. General Sector Inquiries

428. The AML does not explicitly provide the AMEAs with powers to conduct general inquiries into a sector of the economy. It should be noted that, as discussed in paragraph 145 above, the AMC has powers to organise investigations and evaluate the general competitive conditions of a market and produce evaluation reports.[613] It remains to be seen how such powers may be exercised by the AMC and whether such power will be used in the future to conduct sector enquiries.

429. The AUCL and the Price Law also do not explicitly provide enforcement agencies with powers to conduct general sector enquires. However, as the NDRC is a price regulator in conjunction with its role as a competition authority, the NDRC and its price bureaus above county levels are required to establish a price monitoring system to monitor changes in prices of essential goods and services.[614]

II. Ex Officio Investigations

430. An administrative proceeding under the AML, the AUCL, the Price Law, and the Bidding Law can be initiated by the enforcement agencies on their own initiative.[615] The relevant AML implementing regulations provide that administrative

613. AML, Art. 9(2).
614. Price Law, Art. 28.
615. AML, Art. 38; AUCL, Art. 16; Price Law, Art. 33; Bidding Law, Art. 7.

proceedings can be initiated by enforcement agencies upon referral from other authorities or delegation by higher authorities.[616]

III. Complaints

431. An administrative proceeding under the AML, the AUCL, the Price Law, and the Bidding Law can also be initiated upon receiving complaints.[617] For instance, relevant information reveals that in the Qualcomm case announced by NDRC on February 2015, NDRC's investigation against Qualcomm started in 2009 upon the complaints from two American companies against Qualcomm. On November 2013, NDRC initiated its formal proceeding against Qualcomm, hereafter, another American company provided NDRC with evidence of this case, while NDRC did not disclose the name of this company in accordance with the practice. [618]

432. Under the AML, any organisation or individual is entitled to report suspected monopoly conduct to the AMEAs, and the AMEAs must keep the identity of the complainant confidential. If a complaint is submitted to an AMEA, in writing with the relevant facts and evidence, the AMEA is obliged to open an investigation.[619] The Procedural Measures on Monopoly Agreements and Abuse of Dominance Cases provide rules on the contents of the written complaints and the process under which the SAIC and its local bureaus will verify the complaints and initiate formal investigations.[620] An early draft of the Procedural Measures on Price Monopoly Cases contained similar rules on complaints but the final version only provides a general provision on the scope of investigation in relation to a complaint.[621] This includes: (1) whether the complainant reports the same subject matter to other administrative organs or brings a suit on the same subject matter to the court; (2) basic information about the respondent; (3) the relevant facts and evidence provided by the complainant; and (4) any other matters that may be required to be investigated.[622]

433. Price restriction rules for book distributors rectified after the NDRC received complaints. Three trade associations in the book industry, including the Publishers Association of China, the Books and Periodicals Distribution Association of China, and China Xinhua Bookstore Associations, published the revised *Rules on Trading in the Book Business* on 30 August 2010, which set a series of disciplinary rules for book publishers and distributors in China. The revised rules removed several provisions that prohibited book retailers from selling newly published books at a

616. Procedural Measures on Monopoly Agreements and Abuse of Dominance Cases, Art. 4; Procedural Measures on Price Monopoly Cases, Arts 3–4.

617. AML, Art. 38; AUCL, Art. 4; Price Law, Art. 38; Bidding Law, Art. 65.

618. TechWeb, NDRC fined Qualcomm 6 billion; Detailed Information Disclosure: The Investigation Originated From 3 American Enterprises' Compliant, http://www.techweb.com.cn/it/2015-02-10/2123393.shtml, 10 Feb. 2010.

619. AML, Art. 38.

620. Procedural Measures on Monopoly Agreements and Abuse of Dominance Cases, Arts 5–8.

621. Draft Procedural Measures on Price Monopoly Cases (June 2009 version) (copy on file with the authors), Arts 5–11.

622. Procedural Measures on Price Monopoly Cases, Art. 5.

discount for one year after the publication date and online book retailers from selling newly published books for less than 85% of the original price. The previous rules were issued in January 2010 and had attracted public criticism. The Beijing Consumer Association and a group of lawyers complained to the NDRC and requested that it conduct an investigation into the book distribution sector pursuant to the AML. According to the complainants, the rules restricted retailers' rights to independently set prices, thereby impeding competition and harming consumers. After receiving the complaint, the NDRC required that the trade associations revise their rules. The revisions made the current rules consistent with the AML.[623] As illustrated by this case, complaints can be an effective way to trigger investigations into suspected monopoly conduct.

§2. Powers

I. Requests for Information

434. Under the AML, the AMEAs are authorised to interview undertakings under investigation, interested parties or other relevant individuals and entities and request that they explain the relevant facts and circumstances.[624] Enforcement officials are under confidentiality obligations regarding business secrets that they become aware of during the investigations.[625] Those being investigated are required to cooperate with the AMEAs and not refuse or hinder the investigation.[626] The AUCL and the Price Law prescribe similar powers to the enforcement agencies and obligations of the undertakings and the persons being investigated.[627]

435. Under the AML, those individuals or entities that obstruct investigations by refusing to provide information, providing false information or destroying or concealing evidence are subject to fines (up to CNY 100,000 for individuals and up to CNY 1 million for entities) or criminal penalties if the obstruction constitutes a crime.[628] The relevant AML implementing regulations provide that the AMEAs may request that the undertakings under investigation, interested parties or other relevant individuals or entities submit a range of written documents within a prescribed period of time. The requested information may include: (1) basic information about the undertakings under investigation, such as legal form, contact information, copies of business licences or registration certificates, as well as production and operation information, such as turnover, tax paid, business transactions and agreements, for the past three years; (2) copies of identity cards and contact information of the relevant individuals under investigation; (3) the articles of association of any trade associations

623. China News Service, *Book Trading Rules Revised; Restrictions on Discount Repealed* (in Chinese), available at http://news.xinhuanet.com/2010-09/02/c_12508923.htm, 2 Sep. 2010.
624. AML, Art. 39(2).
625. *Ibid.*, Art. 41.
626. *Ibid.*, Art. 42.
627. AUCL, Arts 17(1)–(2) & 19; Price Law, Arts 34 (1)–(2), 35 & 36.
628. AML, Art. 52.

under investigation, as well as the relevant industry policies and meetings and activities relating to the suspected monopoly conduct; and (4) other information that the AMEAs deem necessary.[629]

II. Investigating and Search Powers

436. The AMEAs are authorised with substantial powers to investigate monopoly conduct, including: (1) inspecting business premises or any relevant places of the undertakings under investigation; (2) interviewing the undertakings under investigation or other relevant individuals or undertakings; (3) inspecting and copying relevant documents and materials such as agreements, accounting records, business correspondence, and electronic data; (4) seizing and retaining relevant evidence; (5) and inquiring into the bank accounts of the undertakings under investigation.[630]

437. The investigation should be carried out by at least two enforcement officials who are requested to present enforcement credentials. The officials must keep a written record of the inspection, which should be signed by the undertakings or individuals being investigated. The AMEAs and their officials are required to maintain the confidentiality of any business secrets obtained during the investigation and the identities of the informants.[631] Details of the investigative powers of the SAIC and the NDRC are further stipulated in the Procedural Measures on Monopoly Agreements and the Abuse of Dominance Cases and the Procedural Measures on Price Monopoly Cases.

438. However, a significant body of procedural and technical details remains missing from the AML and the relevant AML implementing regulations. For example, it is unclear whether the undertakings or the individuals under investigation have the right to require the inspectors to wait until the arrival of external counsel. There are no clear limitations to the power of the inspectors during a dawn raid. In addition, it should be noted that the concept of 'legal professional privilege' does not exist under the Chinese law. This means that confidential communications between external lawyers and clients are not protected and the inspectors are able to retain any documents or records that contain such communications.

439. Sanctions for the obstruction of investigation. Under the AML, fines up to CNY 20,000 may be imposed on individuals and fines up to CNY 200,000 may be imposed on entities for obstruction of investigations, such as refusing to provide information, providing false information, or destroying or concealing evidence. If the circumstances are serious, fines between CNY 20,000 and CNY 100,000 may be imposed on the responsible individuals and fines between CNY 200,000 and CNY 1,000,000 may be imposed on the responsible entities. If the obstruction constitutes a criminal offence, the responsible individuals or entities may be prosecuted pursuant to the Criminal Law.[632] To date, there are no reported cases where sanctions for the obstruction of investigations have been imposed pursuant to the AML.

629. Procedural Measures on Monopoly Agreements and Abuse of Dominance Cases, Art. 12; Procedural Measures on Price Monopoly Cases, Art. 14.
630. AML, Art. 39.
631. AML, Arts 40–41 & 38, para. 2.
632. AML, Art. 52.

440. On 7 December 2016, NDRC announced that it has made an administrative penalty decision on *Medtronic (Shanghai) Management ('Medtronic')* 's price-related monopolistic conduct with a fine of RMB 118.5 million. This is NDRC's first antitrust enforcement case in the medical devices industry. Medtronic is the largest medical device company in the world, which entered into China's market in 1996, providing numerous advanced products and treatments including cardiac pacemaker, insulin pump, and other devices for the cardiac surgery and otorhinolaryngology. The enforcement authority confirmed that Medtronic, at least from 2014, had entered into a monopoly agreement with the platform providers and the first-level distributors to restrict the resale price, the bidding price and the minimum sales price of relevant medical device products, and these conducts in violation of the AML cannot be subject to the conditions for exemptions. It is reported that the anti-monopoly law enforcement officials have conducted surprise inspections against Medtronic (Shanghai) Management. However, more than forty officials were locked in Medtronic's headquarter for more than six hours, and the investigated company has been resistant to the inspection and refused to cooperate from 9:30 am to 4:00 pm. Later, after more than a dozen communication between Medtronic's management and its headquarter in the United States, the company finally chose to cooperate with the investigation. [633]

441. Investigative powers under other relevant laws and regulations. Among other competition-related laws and regulations, the AUCL, and the Price Law specify the enforcement agencies' investigative powers. Under the AUCL, the SAIC, and its local bureaus above the county level have the following powers when investigating unfair competition practices: (1) interrogating companies, interested parties, and witnesses and requiring them to supply evidence or other documents related to the alleged unfair practices; (2) examining and taking copies of agreements, accounting records, documents, records, faxes or letters and other materials related to the alleged unfair practices; and (3) examining property connected with the suspected infringements and, where necessary, ordering the companies under investigation to suspend sales and to provide details on the source and quantity of products obtained. Pending examination, such property cannot be removed, concealed or destroyed by the company.[634]

442. The Price Law provides similar investigative powers to the NDRC and its local price bureaus above the county level.[635] In addition, if any evidence may be destroyed or difficult to obtain later on, the enforcement agencies may register and preserve the evidence and such evidence cannot be removed, concealed or destroyed.[636]

III. Cooperation with Other State Institutions

443. The Procedural Measures on Monopoly Agreements and Abuse of Dominance Cases require that the SAIC and its local bureaus strengthen information exchange and enforcement coordination with other AMEAs and relevant government departments

633. Sohu News, NDRC's Officers Were Locked 6 hours by 40 People during the Investigation into Medtronic, http://news.sohu.com/20161209/n475347475.shtml 9 Dec. 2016.

634. AUCL, Art. 17.

635. Price Law, Art. 34(1)–(3).

636. *Ibid.*, Art. 34(4).

when conducting the AML enforcement work.[637] An early draft of the Procedural Measures on Price Monopoly Cases contained a provision imposing similar cooperation duties on the NDRC and its local price bureaus.[638] However, this provision was removed from the final Procedural Measures on Price Monopoly Cases. All the announcements of conditionally approving or prohibiting the concentration of undertakings released by the Anti-Monopoly Bureau ('AMB') of MOCFOM have content of describing the work for review, which usually includes soliciting opinions from related governmental departments and industry associations.

§3. Right of Defence

444. The AML, the AML implementing regulations, and other competition-related laws afford limited procedural guarantees for those accused of wrongdoing. The AML provides that undertakings under investigation have the right to state their opinions. The AMEAs are required to verify the facts, justifications, and evidence presented by the undertakings and the AMEA and its officials are required to keep commercial secrets obtained during investigations as confidential.[639] Except for rules on confidentiality and the right to make a statement, the AML is silent on other procedural rights for undertakings under investigation.

445. However, it is important to note that the Procedural Measures on Price Monopoly Cases and the Procedural Measures on Monopoly Agreements and Abuse of Dominance Cases stipulate that any issues concerning the investigation, hearing, and penalty procedures that are not covered in those regulations shall be handled pursuant to the relevant provisions of the *Administrative Penalty Law 1996* (amended 2009) (hereinafter 'Administrative Penalty Law').[640] This means that the AML enforcement activities of the SAIC, the NDRC, and their respective local bureaus should follow the rules set out in the Administrative Penalty Law.[641] For example, pursuant to the Administrative Penalty Law, the enforcement agency shall fully hear the party's opinions, re-examine the facts and evidence put forward by that party, and accept those facts and evidence should they be established.[642] The enforcement agency shall not impose heavier penalties on the party because of the party's self-defence.[643]

446. The AML, the AML implementing regulations, other competition-related laws, and the Administrative Penalty Law do not expressly provide rules on the right to appoint external lawyers. However, the Administrative Penalty Law does allow the

637. Procedural Measures on Monopoly Agreements and Abuse of Dominance Cases, Art. 28.
638. Draft Procedural Measures on Price Monopoly Cases (June 2009 version) (copy on file with the authors), Art. 35.
639. AML, Arts 41 & 43.
640. The Administrative Penalty Law was promulgated by the NPC on 17 Mar. 1996 and effective on 1 Oct. 1996 (with minor amendment made in 2009), English translation available at www.npc.gov.cn/englishnpc/Law/2007-12/11/content_1383613.htm.
641. *See* Administrative Penalty Law, Arts 30–32, 41.
642. *Ibid.*, Arts 30–32.
643. *Ibid.*, Art. 32, para. 2.

party to entrust agencies (up to two persons) to attend the hearing.[644] It is uncertain whether external lawyers are able to involve at the beginning of the proceeding. In addition, as discussed at paragraph 438 above, the concept of legal privilege does not exist under the current Chinese law.

I. Content and Notification of Opening Decisions

447. The AML, the AML implementing regulations, other competition-related laws, and the Administrative Penalty Law do not expressly provide rules on the content and the notification of opening decisions for monopoly agreements and abuse of dominance cases. However, after more than eight years' practice, the antitrust enforcement decisions become more detailed and the enforcement procedures become more transparent. For instance, in the prohibited Coca-Cola's acquisition of Huiyuan Case in March 2009, the announcement only ran to a length of 1400 words.[645] In the conditionally approved Microsoft's acquisition of Nokia Case in April 2014, the announcement ran to a length of 10,000 words. [646]The administrative penalty decision of SAIC on Tetra Pak's abuse of market dominant position In November 2016 ran to a length of nearly 30,000 words, the legal and economic analysis of which is full and accurate and received high comments from the antitrust academia and the business circles. [647]

II. The Proceedings: Hearings, Access to Files, Briefs

448. The AML, the AML implementing regulations, and other competition-related laws do not expressly provide rules on hearings and access to files and briefs for monopoly agreements and abuse of dominance cases.[648]

449. Pursuant to the Administrative Penalty Law, before making a decision to impose certain types of administrative penalties, including orders for the suspension of production or business, revocation of a business permit or a licence or imposition of a comparatively large amount of fine, enforcement agencies are required to notify the parties of their rights to request hearings.[649] If a party makes such a request, the enforcement agencies are obliged to arrange a hearing and the party shall not bear the expenses for the hearing. The Administrative Penalty Law further provides basic rules on hearing procedures, including time limits for hearing requests and notification of a hearing, the eligible chairperson of a hearing (who should be a person other than the

644. Administrative Penalty Law, Art. 42.

645. *See* http://fldj.mofcom.gov.cn/article/ztxx/200903/20090306108494.shtml

646. *See* http://fldj.mofcom.gov.cn/article/ztxx/201404/20140400542415.shtml

647. *See* SAIC Competition Enforcement Decision No. 10 2016, available at http://www.saic.gov.cn/zwgk/gggs/jzzf/cfjd/201611/P020161116513025279743.pdf.

648. The AML merger control implementing regulations provide detailed rules on hearings. *See* a discussion at para. 419 below.

649. Administrative Penalty Law, Art. 42.

investigator of the case), the party's right to entrust agencies, confidentiality, defence, cross-examination of facts and evidence, and written records of the hearing.[650]

III. Statement of Objections

450. As regards monopoly agreements and abuse of dominance, the AML, the AML implementing regulations, other competition-related laws, and the Administrative Penalty Law do not expressly provide rules on statement of objections. However, the enforcement authorities will analyse whether the involved merger transactions, monopoly agreements or conducts of abusing the market dominant position exclude or restrict competition and whether they are in violation of certain provisions of the AML.

IV. Final Hearing and Decision

451. Under the AML, the AMEAs are required to render decisions if, after investigation and verification, they consider that the suspected conduct constitutes monopoly conduct.[651] The AML, the AML implementing regulations, and other competition-related laws and regulations do not provide detailed rules regarding final hearings and decisions in relation to restrictive agreements and abuse of dominance cases. However, the AMEAs should comply with the rules on hearing procedure and final decisions stipulated by the Administrative Penalty Law.[652]

452. Pursuant to the Administrative Penalty Law, enforcement agencies are required to ascertain the facts establishing the alleged violation and not impose any penalties if the facts are unclear. Before deciding to impose an administrative penalty, the enforcement agency is required to notify the party of the facts, grounds and basis upon which the administrative penalty is based, and the party's legitimate right to state the case and self-defend.

453. Pursuant to the Administrative Penalty Law, enforcement agencies are required to deliver decisions if administrative penalties are imposed. A decision should include the following information: (1) the name, title, and address of the party; (2) the facts and evidence of the violation of laws, regulations or rules; (3) the types of the administrative penalty imposed and their legal basis; (4) the time limit for the enforcement of the administrative penalty; (5) the venue and time limit for applying for administrative reconsideration or the bringing of an administrative lawsuit if the party is dissatisfied about the decision; and (6) the identity of the enforcement agency that made the decision and the date on which the decision was made.[653] Before making a decision on an administrative penalty, if the enforcement agency fails to notify the party of the facts of the violation and the grounds and the basis upon which the administrative penalty is imposed, or refuses to hear the party's statement and defence, the administrative penalty decision shall be invalid, except that the party relinquishes the right to make

650. *Ibid.*,
651. AML, Art. 44.
652. Administrative Penalty Law, Arts 42–43.
653. Administrative Penalty Law, Art. 39.

a statement or to defend itself.[654] The Administrative Penalty Law also stipulates that administrative penalty that is not imposed in accordance with law or in compliance with legal procedures is invalid.[655] Those who have suffered damages due to administrative penalty imposed in violation of law shall have the right to claim compensation.[656]

654. *Ibid.*, Arts 31, 32 & 41.
655. *Ibid.*, Art. 3.
656. *Ibid.*, Art. 6, para. 2.

Chapter 2. Voluntary Notification and Clearance Decisions: Merger Control

454. Please refer to paragraphs 91–98 and 351–426 above for review of main provisions and the application of the AML merger control regime.

455. Notifiable materials. Pursuant to the AML and the Notification Measures, the filing materials and the documents to be submitted include the following: (1) a notification form, containing the names of the parties, registered business addresses, scope of business as well as the date on which the concentration will take place; (2) explanations on the influence of the concentration on the competition situation in the relevant market; (3) the transaction agreement and other relevant documents; (4) the financial and the accounting reports for the previous accounting year of the participating undertakings, audited by public accountants; and (5) other documents and materials as may be required by the authority.

456. A standard notification form, currently the Notification Form 2012, is provided by the MOFCOM for the parties' reference. Many sections of the standard notification form are similar to the European Commission's Form CO, although the MOFCOM imposes more extensive additional information requirements on the parties. For example, the notifying party is required to provide opinions of relevant parties, including but not limited to sector regulators, local government, trade associations, media, and the general public for an assessment of the concentration's potential social effect. Experience suggests that the MOFCOM requires filings to be relatively detailed before they will be accepted as complete.

457. On 11 February 2014, MOFCOM issued the *Provisional Regulation on Simple Cases*,[657] which prescribes that the following circumstances of concentrations of undertakings can be treated as a simple case: (1) all of the undertakings participating in the concentration account for an aggregate market share of less than 15% in the same relevant market; (2) the undertakings participating in the concentration have upstream-downstream relationship and they account for less than 25% market share in the upstream and downstream markets; (3) the undertakings participating in the concentration are not in the same relevant market and have no upstream-downstream relationship and they account for less than 25% market share in each of the markets related to the transaction; (4) the undertakings participating in the concentration have set up a joint venture outside China and such joint venture does not engage in any economic activity inside China; (5) the undertakings participating in the concentration have acquired equity interests or assets of an enterprise outside China and such enterprise does not engage in any economic activity inside China; or (6) a joint venture jointly controlled by two or more undertakings comes under the control of one or more of the undertakings after the concentration.

458. Comparing with the notification of non-simple cases, the procedures for the notification of simple cases does not have a significant difference, while the contents

657. Provisional Regulation on the Standards Applicable to Simple Cases of Concentrations between Business Operators were promulgated by the MOFCOM on 18 Apr. 2014, official Chinese text available at http://fldj.mofcom.gov.cn/article/c/201409/20140900743277.shtml.

of the notification are simplified. In other words, even though the parties participating in the concentration still need to fill in the notification form, submit the concentration agreement, provide the financial accounting reports in the previous fiscal year of each of the undertakings participating in the concentration, etc., they should also illustrate the impacts of the concentration on competition in the relevant market, which includes the introduction to the concentration, the definition of the relevant market, the market shares of the participants in the relevant market, main rivals and their market shares, assessment of the impact of the concentration on the relevant market and its references, etc. However, the notifying party does not need to illustrate, in accordance with the *Notification Measures* released in 2009, the market power of undertakings participating in the concentration, the degree of market concentration, market entry, the current development status of the industry, and the impacts of the concentration on the competition structure, development of the industry, progress of technology, development of the national economy, consumers and other undertakings. Once the simple case is accepted by MOFCOM, the Public Statement filled by the notifying party will be displayed for ten days on the website of the AMB of MOFCOM. The introduction of the simple case notification procedure not only significantly reduces the information for notification by parties participating in the concentration, but also eases undertakings' burden for notification. In addition, a decision can usually be made on the notification of a simple case within thirty days after the acceptance,[658] which greatly speeds up the case review.

§1. PRELIMINARY FILING OBLIGATIONS

I. Criteria and Thresholds

459. Filing is mandatory and suspensory. Under the AML, a concentration must not be implemented until clearance has been obtained from the MOFCOM. The MOFCOM has the power to block a concentration or impose remedies before clearing the concentration.

460. Mergers, acquisitions or other types of transactions that are characterised as concentrations of undertakings are caught by the AML merger filing obligations if they meet the notification thresholds set out in the Notification Thresholds Rules.[659] A mandatory notification obligation will be triggered if any of the following thresholds are met:[660]

(1) the total worldwide turnover of all undertakings participating in the concentration is more than CNY 10 billion in the preceding accounting year and the China-wide

658. The Provisional Regulation on Simple Cases does not make clear the review procedures of simple cases. For example, how long can the concentration be cleared; whether other agencies' opinions are required in simple case procedures as that in the general procedure.

659. AML, Art. 21; Notification Thresholds Rules, Art. 3.

660. Notification Thresholds Rules, Art. 3.

turnover of each of at least two undertakings participating in the concentrations is more than CNY 400 million in such year; or

(2) the total China-wide turnover of all undertakings participating in the concentration is more than CNY 2 billion in the preceding accounting year and the China-wide turnover of each of at least two of the undertakings participating in the concentrations is more than CNY 400 million in such year.

461. Voluntary notification. It should be borne in mind that the MOFCOM has the discretion to review a concentration that does not meet any of the notification thresholds, if, based on the facts and the evidence gathered pursuant to the prescribed procedures, the MOFCOM considers that the concentration has or may have the effect of eliminating or restricting competition.[661] *Notification Thresholds Rules* adopted on 1 August 2008, Article 4 Where a concentration of undertakings does not reach any of the thresholds specified in Article 3 of these Provisions, but facts and evidence collected in accordance with the prescribed procedures establish that such concentration effects, or is likely to effect, the elimination or restriction of competition, the competent commerce department of the State Council shall initiate an investigation in accordance with law. [662] This means that the MOFCOM has the ability to review a non-notifiable concentration and impose remedies if it finds that there is the effect of eliminating or restricting competition. Under the MOFCOM's Draft Measures on Non-notifiable Concentrations, such discretionary review may be initiated in the event of complaints from customers and competitors.[663] In addition, the Notification Measures provide that, in cases where a concentration does not meet the notification thresholds, the undertakings participating in the concentration may nevertheless voluntarily notify such a concentration.[664] This means that, in practice, parties may choose to file on a voluntary basis in circumstances where the transaction may raise competition concerns.

462. Exceptions to notification. The AML provides that a notifiable concentration should not be implemented without a prior notification. The following are the two exceptions to the notification obligation: (1) an undertaking concerned already holds more than half of the voting rights or assets of all other undertakings involved in the concentration; or (2) an undertaking not involved in the concentration holds more than half of the voting rights or assets of all other undertakings involved in the concentration.[665]

II. Turnover Calculation

463. The Notification Measures set out rules for the calculation of turnover, which generally follow prevailing international practices. The following principles apply when determining whether a notification obligation is triggered:

661. Notification Thresholds Rules, Art. 4.
662. . Notification Thresholds Rules, Art. 4.
663. Draft Measures on Non-notifiable Concentrations, Art. 3.
664. Notification Measures, Art. 16.
665. AML, Art. 23.

(1) *Measuring turnover.* Turnover should reflect the sales of products and the provision of services for the whole of the preceding accounting year after deducting the relevant taxes and surcharges.[666]

(2) *Allocation of turnover.* Turnover within China means turnover derived from transactions in which the purchaser of products or services provided by the undertaking is located in China. That means that turnover should be allocated according to the place where the customer is located.[667] An early draft of the Notification Measures provided that 'for the purpose of these measures, turnover from Hong Kong Special Administration Region, Macao Special Administration Region, and Taiwan is not regarded as turnover generated within China'.[668] However, the final version removes this rule and does not expressly state that turnover generated from these jurisdictions should be regarded as turnover within China. This may cause uncertainty on the notifiability of borderline cases where the inclusion of Hong Kong or Taiwan turnover may meet the China-wide turnover threshold.

(3) *Aggregation of group turnover.* Turnover is calculated on a group basis but intra-group sales should be excluded. The turnover of an undertaking participating in a concentration should include the turnover of the undertaking, the undertaking's directly or indirectly controlled subsidiaries, the undertaking's ultimate parents (described as entities directly or indirectly controlling the undertaking), the ultimate parents' other directly or indirectly controlled subsidiaries, and other entities jointly controlled by two or more aforementioned entities.[669]

(4) *Focusing on the turnover of the target instead of the seller.* When a concentration consists of an acquisition of parts of one or more undertakings, only the turnover relating to the subject of the concentration shall be included in the calculation of turnover for the seller.[670]

464. Staggered operations or follow-up deals. Two or more concentrations that take place within a two-year period between the same undertakings shall be treated as the one and the same concentration arising on the date of the last transaction, provided that the notification thresholds are met for all of the transactions taken cumulatively.[671]

465. Turnover calculation rules for financial institutions. The Notification Threshold Rules state that specific measures will be formulated in calculating the turnover of undertakings in the banking, insurance, securities, and futures industries by taking into account the actual circumstances of these special sectors. In July 2009, the Turnover Calculation Measures for Financial Institutions were issued.[672] These measures essentially set a higher notification threshold for transactions undertaken by

666. Notification Measures, Art. 4, para. 1.
667. *Ibid.*, Art. 4, para. 2.
668. Draft Notification Measures (March 2009 version), Art. 4.
669. Notification Measures, Art. 5.
670. *Ibid.*, Art. 7(1).
671. Notification Measures, Art. 7(2).
672. Official Chinese text of the Turnover Calculation Measures for Financial Institutions is available at http://fldj.mofcom.gov.cn/aarticle/c/200907/20090706411691.html.

financial institutions by stipulating that only 10% of the turnover (after the deduction of business taxes and surcharges) will be counted for the purpose of calculating turnover for financial institutions. In addition, a list of items that should be included when calculating turnover for financial institutions is provided. The turnover of banking institutions shall include net interest earnings, handling fees and net commission earnings, income from changes in fair market value, income from currency exchange, and other operating income.[673] The turnover of securities trading companies includes handling fees and net commission earnings (including earnings from brokerage, asset management, underwriting and sponsoring, and financial advisory), net interest earnings, investment income, income from currency exchange, and other operating income.[674] The turnover of futures companies shall include handling fees and net commission earnings and net interest earnings from bank deposits.[675] The turnover of fund management companies shall include earnings from management fees and handling fee earnings.[676] The turnover of insurance companies shall include insurance premiums of the original insurance contracts plus reinsurance premiums received less ceded premiums.[677]

III. Market Share Calculation

466. The AML merger control regime does not apply a market share test to determine notifiability. The current notification thresholds, based on objective turnover criteria, are purely monetary.

IV. Other Relevant Notions

467. Definition of control or decisive influence. The AML and the AML implementing regulations to date do not provide a definition of control or decisive influence. Therefore, whether there is an acquisition of control or an ability to exercise decisive influence will be assessed on a case-by-case basis.

468. An early draft of the Notification Measures provided some help in determining when minority investments could give rise to control. The basic rules were that, in the absence of an acquisition of over 50% of the voting rights or assets of another undertaking, if the acquirer obtains the ability to decide the appointment of one or more board members and key management members, budgets, operations and sales, pricing, substantial investments or other important management and operational strategies, an acquisition of control exists that can be caught by the notification requirements.[678] However, these rules were removed from the final version of Notification Measures, and there is no longer any definition of control relating to minority stake acquisitions. Accordingly, the issue of whether an acquisition of minority equity or

673. Turnover Calculation Measures for Financial Institutions, Art. 3.
674. *Ibid.*, Art. 4.
675. *Ibid.*, Art. 5.
676. *Ibid.*, Art. 6.
677. *Ibid.*, Art. 8.
678. Draft Notification Measures (March 2009 version), Art. 3(2).

assets leads to an acquisition of control or decisive influence by one undertaking over another undertaking will need to be determined on a case-by-case basis and in consultation with the MOFCOM during the pre-notification consultation process. Practitioners have indicated that the MOFCOM tends to follow the European approach and often deems a transaction resulting in a joint control or a negative control as a concentration of undertakings.[679]

469. Joint ventures. The AML does not specifically address the circumstances in which joint ventures should be analysed as concentrations as opposed to potential monopoly agreements. An early draft of the Notification Measures provided that 'the establishment of a new continuously and independently operating enterprise by two or more undertakings fall into the scope of concentrations of undertakings as provided in Article 20 of the AML'.[680] This provision was deleted from the final Notification Measures, which no longer address the treatment of joint ventures. However, as noted in paragraphs 142–143 above, joint ventures, regardless of whether they are full-function or not, are deemed as a type of notifiable transactions under the AML merger control regime. In the prohibited P3 case in 2014, MOFCOM have considered that P3 is a tight joint operation instead of a traditional loose-knit shipping alliance in the international container liner shipping market. [681]However, in the case of MOFCOM's conditionally approval of a proposed Chinese joint venture among Corun, Toyota China, PEVE, Xinzhongyuan, and Toyota Tsusho in 2014, MOFCOM directly regarded the establishment of the joint venture as a concentration and reviewed it accordingly. [682]

470. The notifying party and filing fee. Pursuant to the Notification Measures, the notification of a concentration effected by way of merger shall be made by all undertakings involved in the merger. For a concentration effected by other means, the undertaking acquiring control or exert decisive influence shall make the notification, with the assistance of the other undertakings to the concentration.[683] In practice, a target company may be involved as a joint filing party. Filing fees have not been introduced at the time of writing.

679. Nicholas French & Michael Han, *China*, in *Getting the Deal Through: Merger Control 2011*, 93 (Global Competition Review ed., London: Law Business Research, 2010).

680. Draft Notification Measures (March 2009 version), Art. 3, para. 2.

681. MOFCOM, MOFCOM Announcement No. 46 of 2014 on Decisions from Anti-Monopoly Review of the Concentration of Undertakings on Prohibition of Proposed Establishment of the Network Center by Maersk, MSC and CMA CGM, http://fldj.mofcom.gov.cn/article/ztxx/201406/20140600628586.shtml , 14 Jul. 2017.

682. MOFCOM, MOFCOM Announcement No. 24 of 2014 on Decisions from Anti-Monopoly Review of the Concentration of Undertakings on Conditional Approval of Proposed Joint Venture among Corun, Toyota China, PEVE and Xinzhongyuan and Toyota Tsusho, http://fldj.mofcom.gov.cn/article/ztxx/201407/20140700648291.shtml.14 Jul. 2017.

683. Notification Measures, Art. 9.

§2. Structure of Proceedings

I. Preliminary Assessment and Full Investigation

471. The AML contemplates a two-phase review process of merger control. The Notification Measures and the Review Measures detail a number of key procedural issues regarding the hearing and the issuance of a statement of objections.

472. Investigations. The MOFCOM may investigate a notified concentration by requesting information and documents from the parties, customers, suppliers, competitors, and other relevant entities or government agencies.[684] The MOFCOM's recent practice indicates that the MOFCOM has actively solicited the views of trade associations, market participants, and government authorities and conducted on-site investigations when it deems necessary.[685]

473. Hearing. The Review Measures provide that the MOFCOM may convene a hearing upon its own initiative or at the request of the relevant parties. The MOFCOM may invite a broad range of interested parties and experts, including the undertakings participating in the concentration, competitors, upstream and downstream enterprises, trade associations, government departments, and consumers to participate at the hearing by delivering written or oral statements.[686] Hearing procedures also exist in the examination of antitrust cases by NDRC and SAIC, while the initiation of which requires the application of related parties. For instance, in the penalty decision against Tetra Pak's abuse of market dominant position, SAIC pointed that, on 15 September 2016, SAIC delivered the Notice of Hearing on Administrative Penalty Decision to the party and informed it about the facts, reasons, basis and contents of the administrative penalty, and informed the party that it has the right of statement, defence and applying for a hearing, while the party neither makes a statement nor apply for a hearing within the statutory period.[687]

II. Time Framework

474. Deadlines for filing. The AML does not provide for any deadlines for filing; however notifiable concentrations cannot be closed without being notified to and cleared by the MOFCOM.[688]

475. Initial review and further review. The initial review period (Phase I) is thirty days, commencing on the date that the MOFCOM accepts the filing as complete. At the end of the initial review period, the MOFCOM must issue either a written decision to clear the transaction or a written notice of further review.[689] Upon the

684. Notification Measures, Art. 13; Review Measures, Arts 4–5.

685. *See* a discussion on the *Coca-Cola/Huiyuan* Decision at paras 367–373 above.

686. Review Measures, Art. 7.

687. *See* SAIC Competition Enforcement Decision No. 10 2016, available at http://www.saic.gov.cn/zwgk/gggs/jzzf/cfjd/201611/P020161116513025279743.pdf.

688. AML, Art. 21; Notification Threshold Rules, Art. 3.

689. AML, Art. 25, para. 1.

expiration of the initial review period, if the filing party does not receive any written notice of further review, the transaction is deemed to have been cleared and the parties are free to implement the concentration.[690] If the filing party receives a written notice of further review, a further review period of ninety days (Phase II) commences.[691] Under certain circumstances, the further review period may be extended by a maximum of sixty days. The extension may be granted where: (1) the parties agree; (2) the documents or materials submitted are inaccurate or need further verification; or (3) the relevant circumstances have significantly changed following the notification.[692] The AML and the Review Measures are silent on whether the time framework can be suspended by the MOFCOM.

476. Previously, it was unclear to the parties involved and their counsel as to when a review phase began and ended. The Notification Measures and the Review Measures filled in the gap by requiring that the MOFCOM notify the parties in writing when the notification is deemed complete and when the initial and further review periods begin.[693]

477. Expedited review. No formal expedited review process is available at present. However, the MOFCOM has shown that it is willing to be flexible in certain procedural issues. For example, it is reported that, in the *Fiat/Chrysler* transaction, the parties cited financial exigencies as the reason for expedited review and the MOFCOM considered the request and cleared the transaction in a significantly reduced time frame. Normally, at least a month would have been spent on pre-notification consultations with a further month required for the Phase I review. However, in the *Fiat/Chrysler* notification, the parties were able to have the entire review process (including pre-notification consultations) completed within three weeks.[694] On 11 February 2014, MOFCOM issued the *Provisional Regulation on Simple Case,*[695] which prescribes certain circumstances of concentrations of undertakings can be treated as a simple case.

III. Right of Defence

478. Statement of objections. The AML provides that an undertaking under investigation has the right to state its opinions. The AMEAs are required to verify the facts, justifications, and evidence presented by the undertaking.[696] However, the AML does not expressly provide that the MOFCOM will, before issuing a final decision, issue a statement of objections to the notifying parties, setting out its findings and giving the undertakings the opportunity to respond in writing or at an oral hearing.

690. *Ibid.*, Art. 25, para. 2.
691. *Ibid.*, Art. 26, para. 1.
692. *Ibid.*, Art. 26, para. 2.
693. Notification Measures, Art. 14; Review Measures, Art. 9.
694. Michael Han, Alvaro Iza & Bruce McCulloch, *Introduction*, in *Getting the Deal Through: Merger Control 2010*, 4 (Global Competition Review ed., London: Law Business Research, 2009).
695. *See* http://fldj.mofcom.gov.cn/article/c/201409/20140900743277.shtml.
696. AML, Art. 43.

The Review Measures remedy the uncertainty by expressly requiring that the MOFCOM issue the notifying parties with a statement of objection if the MOFCOM finds that the proposed concentration has or may have the effect of eliminating or restricting competition, and to set a reasonable time limit for the undertakings to submit a written defence.[697] The parties' written defence should present relevant facts and analysis and be supported by evidence. Failure to submit a timely written defence may be construed as conceding to the objections.[698] The right of defence is a fundamental right in the process of the antitrust examination. According to the information from NDRC, during the process of examination of the Qualcomm case, Derek Aberle, the CEO of Qualcomm, led a delegation to visit NDRC for at least seven times and exchanged opinions with, Xu Kunlin, the former Deputy Director-General of the Price Supervision Anti-Monopoly Bureau ('PSAMB') on the investigation and the final resolution of this case. [699]

479. Publicity and confidentiality. The AML does not require that the MOFCOM make the pre-merger notifications that it receives public, nor does the AML require that the MOFCOM publish its decision where it decides to unconditionally clear a concentration. The MOFCOM is only required to publish its decision when it blocks a concentration or imposes remedies on the parties.[700] In the case of unconditional clearances, the MOFCOM provides the parties with a written confirmation of approval.[701] To improve transparency, the MOFCOM started to publish information of unconditional merger clearance in November 2012. Since then, the MOFCOM releases updated information on unconditional merger decisions on a quarterly basis.[702]

480. With respect to the issue of confidentiality, the AML provides that the AMEAs and its staff must keep confidential any commercial secrets obtained during an investigation.[703] In addition, under the Notification Measures, if the filing party does not wish for the information provided by it to be published or disclosed, it must mark the content that is to be kept confidential. A non-confidential version of the filing materials must be provided at the same time.[704] The Review Measures also impose confidentiality obligations on other organisations and individuals if they become aware of any business secrets or other confidential information during the review process.[705] Detailed implementing rules on the protection of confidential information have yet to be promulgated.

---

697. Review Measures, Art. 10, para. 1.
698. *Ibid.*, Art. 10, para. 2.
699. NDRC, The Deputy Director General of the Anti-Monopoly Bureau of NDRC Exchanged Views with Qualcomm Regarding the Final Resolution, http://jjs.ndrc.gov.cn/gzdt/201412/t20141226_658119.html , 14 Jul. 2017.
700. AML, Art. 30.
701. Review Measures, Art. 9.
702. Information on MOFCOM's unconditional merger decisions (in Chinese) are available at http://fldj.mofcom.gov.cn/article/zcfb/.
703. AML, Art. 41.
704. Notification Measures, Art. 12, para. 3.
705. Review Measures, Art. 16.

§3. Clearance and Conditional Clearance

481. Sanctions for closing before clearance. The AML provides for various legal sanctions for non-compliance with AML merger control. Undertakings that fail to notify a notifiable transaction to MOFCOM may be subject to various penalties. The MOFCOM may order that the undertakings cease the implementation of the concentration, dispose of shares or assets, transfer certain businesses within a given time limit or adopt any other necessary measures to restore the market to its state before the implementation of the concentration. The MOFCOM may also impose a fine of a maximum of CNY 500,000.[706] No sanctions have been applied so far.

482. Substantive test. Please *see* discussions at paragraphs 108–111 above.

483. Ancillary restrictions. The AML does not provide any provisions concerning ancillary restrictions. It remains to be seen how ancillary restrictions will be assessed and treated under the AML merger control regime.

I. Conditions and Undertakings

A. Content

484. Types of merger remedies. If the MOFCOM has concerns over the competitive effects of a proposed concentration, the MOFCOM may attach remedies to its clearance of such a concentration. According to the *Regulation on Merger Remedies 2014*,[707] MOFCOM may impose the following three measures of remedies: (1) structural conditions such as divestiture of tangible assets, intangible assets (e.g., intellectual property) or relevant interests; (2) behavioural conditions such as opening up of infrastructural facilities (e.g., networks or platforms), licensing of key technologies (including patents, know-hows or other intellectual property), and termination of exclusivity agreements; (3) hybrid conditions which are combinations of both structural and behavioural conditions. Examples of the three types of remedies exist in practice.

485. Requirements for merger remedies. Pursuant to the AML, the MOFCOM may conditionally approve a concentration in order to reduce its negative effect on competition.[708] According to the Review Measures, remedies proposed by undertakings should be able to remove or reduce the anticompetitive effects of the concentration and shall be practically enforceable. Written versions of the remedies should be clear and precise to allow their effectiveness and practicability to be properly evaluated.[709]

486. MOFCOM's practice as regards merger remedies. In *InBev/Anheuser-Busch*,[710] although the MOFCOM acknowledged that the merger did not appear to

706. AML, Art. 48.

707. Regulation on the Imposition of Restrictive Conditions on Concentrations between Business Operators (for Trial Implementation) were promulgated by the MOFCOM on 4 Dec. 2014, official Chinese text available at http://www.mofcom.gov.cn/article/b/c/201412/20141200835207.shtml.

708. AML, Art. 29.

709. Review Measures, Art. 12.

710. *See* the *InBev/Anheuser Busch* Decision, para. 374 above.

give rise to serious competition issues, the MOFCOM imposed unusual behavioural remedies that seemed to mainly address industrial policy considerations rather than competition concerns. The remedies imposed included limiting the parties' ability to increase their existing stakes in Chinese breweries as well as InBev's ability to acquire stakes in two other major breweries in China.

487. In *Mitsubishi Rayon/Lucite*,[711] the MOFCOM accepted a remedies package that essentially amounted to the disposal of at least a part of Lucite's business but allowed a degree of flexibility on how to achieve this. To address the competition concerns on horizontal and vertical overlaps in the MMA market, the MOFCOM gave the parties six months (extendable by another six months) to find buyers for half of Lucite's production capacity of MMA in China for a period of five years. If the parties failed to do so, a trustee would be appointed to sell the entire stake of the specified Lucite Chinese entity. In addition, the merger entities were requested not to acquire or establish any new manufacturing facilities of the relevant and related products in China for five years without the MOFCOM's consent. In *GM/Delphi*,[712] the MOFCOM imposed behavioural remedies relating to information exchange restrictions and continuity of supply obligations. In *Pfizer/Wyeth*,[713] the MOFCOM imposed structural remedies according to which Pfizer was given six months to divest its relevant business. In *Panasonic/Sanyo*,[714] the MOFCOM required the divestiture of businesses outside of China in a transaction involving two non-Chinese businesses.

488. In *Novartis/Alcon*,[715] the MOFCOM required that Novartis terminate its distribution agreement with its sole Chinese distributor, which was the first time that the MOFCOM had considered the coordinated effects in a published decision. In *Seagate/Samsung* and in *Western Digital/Hitachi*, the MOFCOM identified coordinated effects because the global suppliers of hard disk drives were reduced from five to three post the two transactions. In *Seagate/Samsung*, the MOFCOM was the only competition authority to impose conditions on its clearance of the transaction. The European Commission and the US FTC unconditionally approved the transaction. In *Western Digital/Hitachi*, the MOFCOM required that Western Digital should divest the 3.5-inch HDD assets of Hitachi to an independent third party within six months. In addition, the parties were required to keep their businesses separate for at least twenty-four months, including but not limited to research and development, production, purchasing, marketing, after-sales services, administration, finance, investment, and personnel appointment. In contrast to its EU, US, Japanese, and Korean counterparts, the MOFCOM was the only competition authority that imposed both structural and behavioural remedies on the transaction.[716]

711. *See* the *Mitsubishi Rayon/Lucite* Decision, paras 375–379 above.
712. *See* the *GM/Delphi* Decision, paras 402–404 above.
713. *See* the *Pfizer/Wyeth* Decision, paras 380–381 above.
714. *See* the *Panasonic/Sanyo* Decision, paras 382–384 above.
715. *See* the *Novartis/Alcon* Decision, paras 385–388 above.
716. *See* the *Seagate/Samsung* and *Western Digital/Hitachi* Decisions, paras 389–392 above.

B. Timing

489. The MOFCOM promulgated its Divestiture Measures in accordance with the Review Measures. However, the Divestiture Measures do not clarify when parties may propose remedies to the MOFCOM during the merger review process. It is reported that the MOFCOM has recently sought consultation on the Draft Merger Remedy Measures concerning other procedural and substantive issues associated with merger remedies.[717] To date, the Draft Merger Remedy Measures have not been made publicly available.

490. The Divesture Measures stipulate that an undertaking that is subject to divestiture remedies should find a buyer, enter into a sales agreement and transfer the designated assets or businesses to the buyer within three months from the date on which the sales agreement is entered into. Such deadlines can be extended upon the MOFCOM's approval.[718] Within fifteen days from the date of the MOFCOM's decision on the concentration, a supervisory trustee will be appointed to supervise the agreement between the merging party and the buyer of the designated assets.[719] A divestiture trustee will be appointed to find buyers to sell the assets or businesses on the merging party's behalf if that party fails to sell the designated assets within the prescribed time period.[720] The monitoring and divestiture trustees will report to the MOFCOM during the divestiture proceeding.[721] The Divesture Measures also set out the criteria for eligible trustees and buyers and the obligations of merging entities during the divestiture proceeding.[722]

491. According to Article 6 of the *Regulation on Merger Remedies*, [723]in respect of the effect of eliminating or restricting competition found by MOFCOM, if the notifying party makes a conditions proposal, it shall submit the final proposal prior to twenty days from the expiry date of the further review period; if the notifying party fails to make any conditions proposal during the specified time limit, or the conditions proposal put forward is not sufficient to reduce the adverse effects of the concentration on competition, then MOFCOM shall prohibit such concentration; The notifying party may also make a conditions proposal before MOFCOM brings up its finding that the concentration has or may have the effects of eliminating or restricting competition. According to Article 7, if the notifying party makes a conditions proposal within the specified time limit, MOFCOM shall negotiate with the notifying party and assess the effectiveness, feasibility, and timeliness of the conditions proposal, and inform the notifying party of the assessment result; Where the preferred option of the conditions

717. *See* MOFCOM, 'The Anti-Monopoly Bureau of the MOFCOM Held Legislative Seminar' (in Chinese), http://fldj.mofcom.gov.cn/aarticle/xxfb/201007/20100707045197.html, 27 Jul. 2010.
718. Divesture Measures, Art. 3, para. 2.
719. *Ibid.*, Art. 4, para. 4.
720. *Ibid.*, Art. 3, para. 1.
721. *Ibid.*, Art. 5, para. 2.
722. *Ibid.*, Arts 5, paras 1, 9 & 12.
723. Regulation on the Imposition of Restrictive Conditions on Concentrations between Business Operators (for Trial Implementation) were promulgated by the MOFCOM on 4 Dec. 2014, official Chinese text available at http://www.mofcom.gov.cn/article/b/c/201412/20141200835207.shtml.

proposal put forward by the notifying party has the risk of being unable to be implemented, MOFCOM may, in its review decision, require the notifying party to put forward an alternative option in addition to the preferred option. The alternative option shall have more rigorous conditions than the preferred option, which may consist of different core assets, including tangible assets, intangible assets (e.g., intellectual property) or relevant interests.

492. According to Article 10 of the *Regulation on Merger Remedies*, where a divestiture is imposed as a restrictive condition, it may take the form of self-divestiture or entrusted-divestiture. Self-divestiture refers to a situation that the divestiture obligor, within the time limit specified in the review decision, finds a proper purchaser, enters into a sale agreement, and obtains examination and approval from MOFCOM. Entrusted-divestiture refers to a situation that when the divestiture obligor fails to complete self-divestiture on time, the divestiture trustee, within the time limit specified in the review decision, finds a purchaser, enters into a sale agreement, and obtains examination and approval from MOFCOM. According to Article 11, for self-divestiture, the divestiture obligor shall find a purchaser within the time limit specified in the review decision. The purchaser of the divestiture business shall meet the following requirements: (1) it shall be independent of the undertakings participating in the concentration; (2) it shall possess the necessary resources, ability, and incentive to employ the divestiture business to participate in market competition; (3) it shall obtain the approval from other regulatory authorities; (4) it shall not raise money from undertakings participating in the concentration for purchasing the divestiture business; and (5) any other requirements made by MOFCOM based on the specific circumstances of the case. The factors of production that the purchaser has or is able to obtain by other means shall match with the divestiture business, and the purchaser is entitled to request MOFCOM to make necessary adjustment to the scope of the divestiture business. According to Article 12, the divestiture obligor shall submit the candidates for the purchaser and the sale agreement between itself and the purchaser to MOFCOM within the time limit specified in the review decision. Any agreements between the divestiture obligor and the purchaser, including sale agreement and interim agreement, shall not contain clauses contradicting the review decision. The divestiture obligor shall submit no less than three candidates for the potential purchaser, monitoring trustee and divestiture trustee respectively for MOFCOM's review. Under special circumstances and subject to MOFCOM's consent, the aforesaid candidates can be less than three. MOFCOM shall review the candidates for monitoring trustee, divestiture trustee and purchaser, the mandate, and the proposed sale agreement submitted by the divestiture obligor, so as to ensure that they comply with the requirements of the review decision. The time spent by MOFCOM in the process of the above-mentioned review and approval shall not be counted into the divestiture period. According to Article 13, where the review decision does not specify a period for self-divestiture, the divestiture obligor shall find a proper purchaser and enter into a sale agreement within six months from the date of the review decision. Based on the specific circumstances of the case, and with reasons provided by the divestiture obligor, MOFCOM may extend the self-divestiture period at its discretion, but such extension shall not exceed three months at the maximum. Where the review decision does not specify a period for entrusted-divestiture, the divestiture trustee shall find a proper purchaser and enter into a sale agreement within six months from the commencement date of the entrusted-divestiture. According to Article 14, MOFCOM may require the divestiture obligor to find a purchaser and enter into a sale agreement before the implementation of the concentration if: (1) there is a significant risk that the competitiveness and the marketability of the divestiture business may not be maintained before the divestiture; (2) the identity of the purchaser has a decisive influence on whether the divestiture business can restore market competition; or (3) any third party makes a claim against the divestiture business. According to Article 15, the divestiture obligor shall transfer the divestiture business to the purchaser and complete the related legal procedures such as the assignment of ownership within three months from the date of entering into the sale agreement. Based on the specific circumstances of the case, and following an application made by the divestiture obligor (with reasons), MOFCOM may extend the business transfer period at its discretion. According to Article 16, if the acquisition of the divestiture business by the MOFCOM approved purchaser reaches the threshold for notification of concentrations of undertakings stipulated in the Regulation of the State Council on the Thresholds for Notifications of Concentrations of Undertakings, the purchaser shall file notification with MOFCOM.

§4. Relations with Other Merger Control Authorities

I. Other Authorities Within the Local Jurisdiction

493. The MOFCOM is the sole authority responsible for implementing the AML merger control regime. There are no other authorities within China that have the power to enforce the AML merger control rules.

II. International Coordination

494. To date, China is not a member of the International Competition Network and there are no formal coordination mechanisms between the MOFCOM and merger control authorities of other jurisdictions. However, the MOFCOM has maintained informal cooperation with other jurisdictions. For example, during the process of drafting the AML and the AML implementing regulations, there was extensive cooperation and consultation between the MOFCOM and antitrust authorities in other jurisdictions such as the EU, the US, and Japan.

495. Apart from enforcing the AML merger control rules, the Anti-Monopoly Bureau of the MOFCOM also has the authority to coordinate bilateral and multilateral cooperation in competition policy and coordinate overseas antitrust litigation involving Chinese enterprises.[724] For example, the EU-China Competition Policy Dialogue was signed between the MOFCOM and the European Commission Directorate-General

724. *See* information of duties and authorities of the Anti-Monopoly Bureau of MOFCOM, at: http://fldj.mofcom.gov.cn/aarticle/gywm/200809/20080905756026.html (in Chinese).

for Competition with the aim of establishing a permanent forum for consultation and transparency between China and the EU in the area of competition policy.[725]

725. Also *see* paras 32–39 above for more information on international cooperation.

Chapter 3. Challenging of the Administrative Decisions

496. Decisions made by the AMEAs are binding on the undertakings to which they are addressed. According to the AML, a party who disagrees with a decision on restrictive agreements or abuse of dominance made by the NDRC, the SAIC or a corresponding local bureau can apply for administrative reconsideration. If the party is unsatisfied with the outcome of the administrative reconsideration, it can bring an action before a people's court. The party is also allowed to challenge the decision by directly bringing an action before a people's court.[726] An unsatisfied party who wishes to contest a merger review decision made by the MOFCOM must appeal for administrative reconsideration in the first instance. If the party is still unsatisfied with the outcome of the administrative reconsideration, it can bring an action before a people's court.[727] Therefore, while administrative reconsideration is a prerequisite for challenging the MOFCOM's merger review decisions, it is not a prerequisite for challenging administrative decisions made pursuant to the AML by the NDRC, the SAIC or a corresponding local bureau.

497. Under the AUCL, a party who disagrees with a decision made by the SAIC or its local bureau can, within fifteen days after receipt of the decision, apply for administrative reconsideration to the competent authority at the next higher level. If the party is unsatisfied with the outcome of the administrative reconsideration, it can bring an action before a people's court within fifteen days after receipt of the reconsideration decision. The party is also allowed to challenge the original decision by directly bringing an action before the people's courts within fifteen days after receipt of the original decision.[728] Although the Price Law and the Bidding Law do not expressly prescribe a mechanism for challenging administrative decisions made by the enforcement agencies, a similar mechanism is available to dissatisfied parties pursuant to the *Administrative Reconsideration Law 1999* (amended 2009) (hereinafter 'Administrative Reconsideration Law').[729] However, it should be noted that the time limit for applying for administrative reconsideration is sixty days under the Administrative Reconsideration Law.[730]

498. Although administrative litigation is provided as a statutory remedy for dissatisfied parties to challenge decisions made by the AMEAs, the AML does not provide any further information on matters such as jurisdiction, standing, and time limits. Judges in charge of the Administrative Tribunal of the Supreme People's Court

726. AML, Art. 53, para. 1. 'Administrative reconsideration' refers to individuals, legal persons, and other organisations requesting for administrative organs to reconsider the legality and/or appropriateness of specific administrative actions; *see* Administrative Reconsideration Law, Art. 2.
727. AML, Art. 53, para. 2.
728. AUCL, Art. 29.
729. The Administrative Reconsideration Law was promulgated by the Standing Committee of the NPC on 29 Apr. 1999 and effective on 1 Oct. 1999 (with minor amendment made in 2009), English translation available at www.npc.gov.cn/englishnpc/Law/2007-12/11/content_1383562.htm.
730. *See* para. 503 below.

have confirmed that the general principles set out in the *Administrative Litigation Law 1989* (hereinafter 'Administrative Litigation Law', amended 2014,2017) shall apply to administrative lawsuits challenging the decisions made by the AMEAs.[731] It has also been confirmed that, considering the complex nature of AML cases, the people's courts will study the application of laws and strengthen judicial review.[732]

499. Reviewable actions. Specific administrative actions, which refer to administrative actions that address specific individuals, legal persons or other organisations and affect the counterparties' interests, rights and obligations, are reviewable under Chinese laws. The Administrative Litigation Law lists twelve types of specific administrative actions that are judicially reviewable, and of these twelve types, three types are relevant to the enforcement of the AML and other competition-related laws and regulations. These types are: (1) administrative sanctions, such as detention, fines, the revocation of business licences or permits, orders to suspend production or business and the confiscation of properties; (2) coercive administrative measures, such as the seizure or freezing of properties; and (3) administrative organs abusing their administrative powers to eliminate or restrict competition.[733]

500. Under the AML, decisions imposed by the AMEAs are specific administrative actions and thus are subject to administrative reconsideration and/or administrative litigation. The AML also prohibits administrative organs from abusing their administrative powers to promulgate rules containing provisions that eliminate or restrict competition.[734]

§1. Competent Courts

501. Pursuant to the Administrative Litigation Law, the general principle is that proceedings should be brought to the courts of the defendants' place of domicile, and courts of different levels have jurisdiction to hear cases as the first instance court, depending on the nature and the importance of the dispute.[735] Therefore, the Court of First Instance for an action challenging a decision made by the NDRC, the SAIC or the MOFCOM is the intermediate people's court in Beijing. For an action challenging a decision made by local bureaus of the enforcement agencies, the first instance court will be one of the intermediate people's courts at a municipal level, depending on the place where the local bureaus are located.[736] Although the first instance court can also

731. The Administrative Litigation Law was promulgated by the NPC on 4 Apr. 1989 and effective on 1 Oct. 1990, English translation available at www.fdi.gov.cn/pub/FDI_EN/Laws/law_en_info.jsp?docid=50985.

732. People's Court Daily, *Strengthen Anti-Monopoly Judicial Review and Protecting Fair Competition – an Interview with Judges in Charge of the Administrative Tribunal of the Supreme People's Court* (in Chinese), http://rmfyb.chinacourt.org/public/detail.php?id=123368, 3 Nov. 2008. The interview also covered matters including standing, scope of the review and evidentiary rules.

733. Administrative Litigation Law, Art. 12(1)(2)(8).

734. AML, Art. 37.

735. Administrative Litigation Law, Arts 14–17.

736. *Ibid.*, Art. 15.

be a higher people's court if the case is important and complex;[737] however, according to official statistics, this has rarely happened in previous administrative litigation.[738]

502. The appellate courts are the higher people's court in Beijing or higher people's courts at provincial level for cases started at intermediate people's courts.[739] Litigation in China is subject to one appeal only.

§2. Time Limits

503. Dissatisfied parties may request for administrative reconsideration within sixty days after the decision is delivered, unless otherwise stipulated by law.[740] The time limit for the reviewing institution to deliver its reconsideration decision is sixty days, which may be extended by up to thirty days for complex cases.[741] If the parties are not satisfied with the outcome of the administrative reconsideration, they may bring an administrative action to the courts within fifteen days after the reconsideration decision is delivered or if the reviewing institution fails to make the reconsideration decision within the sixty-day time limit.[742]

504. The time period for the first instance court to deliver a judgment for an administrative lawsuit is six months, and the time period for the appellant court to deliver a final judgment is three months.[743] Given the complexity of competition cases, the time limits may be too tight for courts to deliver judgments. The prescribed time limits can be extended upon approval from a higher people's court or from the Supreme People's Court if a higher people's court acts as the first instance court.[744] The Administrative Litigation Law does not prescribe the maximum time period for the delivery of a judgment. The infinitely extendable time limits may undermine the certainty and the legitimate expectations of the parties involved.

§3. Scope of Judicial Review

505. The Administrative Litigation Law provides six circumstances in which a specific administrative action may be revoked, partially revoked or modified by the people's courts. The courts may also order that the administrative organ perform a new specific administrative action or fulfil its legal responsibilities. These circumstances include situations where the administrative organ has: (1) relied upon inadequate

737. *Ibid.*, Art. 17.
738. Based on the authors' review of various editions of the *Yearbook of Chinese Legal System* (China Year Book Publishing) and the *Yearbook of Chinese Judicial Administration* (China Law Press), from 1989–2006, no reported first trial of administrative litigation started from a higher people's court.
739. Administrative Litigation Law, Art. 85.
740. Administrative Reconsideration Law, Art. 9.
741. *Ibid.*, Art. 31.
742. Administrative Litigation Law, Art. 45.
743. Administrative Litigation Law, Arts 81& 88.
744. *Ibid.*, Arts 81 & 88.

principal evidence; (2) applied the laws incorrectly; (3) failed to follow the legally prescribed procedures; (4) exceeded its powers; (5) abused its powers; (6) apparently inappropriate.[745]

506. To date, there have been no actions brought to challenge the decisions made by the AMEAs. Currently, cases of administrative lawsuits against anti-monopoly administrative decisions have arisen. It is reported that, on November 2015, Shanxi Province decontrolled the charging standard of auto inspection. The price will be determined by the market rather than the government. After the decontrol of the price, the Xian branch of the Shanxi auto inspection association organised thirty-one auto inspection organisations in three regions, i.e., Xian, Shangluo, and Yangling and conspired to increase the charging standard of the inspection. The PSAMB of NDRC conducted an investigation and made a penalty decision jointly with Shanxi Provincial Price Bureau. In April 2016, Shanxi Provincial Price Bureau imposed an administrative penalty on the involved parties for reaching and implementing the price-related monopoly agreement according to law. Some of the involved parties were dissatisfied with the decision and applied for administrative reconsiderations and lodged administrative lawsuits respectively. For example, the involved party Shanxi Western International Auto City Company was dissatisfied with the administrative penalty decision made by Shanxi Provincial Price Bureau and applied for an administrative reconsideration to the People's Government of Shaanxi Province to revoke the administrative penalty decision. On May 2016, the Shanxi Province Government affirmed Shanxi Price Bureau's penalty decision after the hearing. Another involved party is Xian Honglin Industry Company who filed an administrative lawsuit in front of Xian Railroad Transport Court to request the court to revoke the administrative penalty decision of Shaanxi Provincial Price Bureau on September 2016. After the trial, Xian Railroad Transport Court made the first instance judgment on 21 December 2016, which rejected the claims of the plaintiff Xian Honglin Industry Company for the fact on which Shanxi Provincial Price Bureau made the administrative penalty decision is clear, the application of laws and regulations is correct, and the legal procedure is complied with under Article 69 of the *Administrative Procedure Law of the People's Republic of China*. It is reported that it is the first case of judicial review against the price-related monopoly penalty decision with a judgment in China.[746]

745. Administrative Litigation Law, Art. 70.

746. *See* http://jjs.ndrc.gov.cn/fjgld/201612/t20161226_832626.html.

Selected Bibliography

Bush, Nathan. 'The PRC Antimonopoly Law: Unanswered Questions and Challenges Ahead'. *Antitrust Source* (October 2007).

China Society for World Trade Organization Studies (ed.). *Report on Competition Law and Policy of China 2012* (Chinese version). Beijing: Law Press, 2012.

Dabbah, Maher. 'The Development of Sound Competition Law and Policy in China: An (Im)possible Dream?'. *World Competition* 30, no. 2 (2007): 341–363.

Emch, Adrian & David Stallibrass (eds.). *China's Anti-Monopoly Law: The First Five Years*. Alphen aan den Rijn: Kluwer Law International, 2013.

Fels, Allan. 'Administrative Monopoly – A Comparison of China, Australia, the USA and the EU' (Chinese version). In *Issues Surrounding the Enforcement of the Anti-Monopoly Law*, edited by Xiaoye Wang. Beijing: Social Sciences Academic Press, 2010, 308–321.

Fels, Allan, Xiaoye Wang & Jessica Su (eds). *China Competition Bulletin*. August (2010) to July/August (2013) editions.

Fox, Eleanor. 'An Anti-Monopoly Law for China – Scaling the Walls of Government Restraints'. *Antitrust Law Journal* 75 (2008): 173–194.

Furse, Mark. 'Merger Control in China: The First Year of Enforcement'. *European Competition Law Review* 31, no. 3 (2010): 98–105.

Gerber, David. *Global Competition: Law, Markets, and Globalization*. Oxford: Oxford University Press, 2010.

Global Competition Review (ed.). *Getting the Deal Through: Merger Control 2010*. London: Law Business Research, 2009.

Global Competition Review (ed.). *Getting the Deal Through: Merger Control 2011*. London: Law Business Research, 2010.

Ha, Hannah C. L., John M. Hickin & Gerry P. O'Brien. *China's Anti-Monopoly Law Merger Control Regime – 10 Key Questions Answered (Part I)*. www. mondaq. com, 11 March 2010.

Han, Michael & Jessica Su. 'China's Antimonopoly Law: Status Quo and Outlook'. *Global Competition Policy* (August 2008).

Harris, H. Stephen Jr & Rodney J. Ganske. 'The Monopolization and IP Abuse Provisions of China's AML: Concerns and a Proposal'. *Antitrust Law Journal* 75 (2008): 213–229.

He, Zhonglin & Zhu Li. 'Principal Questions of Civil Anti-Monopoly Litigation: Report of the Consultation Meeting of Civil Anti-Monopoly Litigation and Judicial Interpretation' (Chinese version). *People's Court Daily* (6 August 2009): 6.

Huang, Yong. 'Pursuing the Second Best: The History, Momentum, and Remaining Issues of China's Anti-Monopoly Law'. *Antitrust Law Journal* 75 (2008): 126–28.

Kong, Xiangjun & He Zhonglin. 'Establishing China's Anti-Monopoly Civil Litigation Regime'. In *Report on Competition Law and Policy of China 2010* (Chinese version), edited by China Society for World Trade Organization Studies. Beijing: Law Press, 2010.

Lin, Chris X. 'A Quiet Revolution: An Overview of China's Judicial Reform'. *Asian-Pacific Law & Policy Journal* 4, no. 2 (2003): 255–319.

Maddison, Angus. *Chinese Economic Performance in the Long Run*. 2nd edn. Paris: OECD, 2007.

OECD. *OECD Reviews of Regulatory Reform: China – Defining the Boundary between the Market and the State*. Paris: OECD, 2009.

Owen, Bruce M., Su Sun & Wentong Zheng. 'China's Competition Policy Reforms: The Anti-Monopoly Law and Beyond'. *Antitrust Law Journal* 75 (2008): 231–265.

State Administration for Industry and Commerce and Chinese Academy of Social Sciences International Law Research Centre. *Selected Anti-Monopoly Cases and Analysis on China's Anti-Monopoly Enforcement* (Chinese version). Beijing: Law Press, 2007.

Wang, Xiaoye, 'The Prospect of Antimonopoly Legislation in China'. *Washington University Global Studies Law Review* 1 (2002): 201–231.

Wang, Xiaoye, 'Issues Surrounding the Drafting of China's Anti-Monopoly Law'. *Washington University Global Studies Law Review* 3 (2004): 285–296.

Wang, Xiaoye, 'Highlights of China's New Anti-Monopoly Law'. *Antitrust Law Journal* 75 (2008): 133–150.

Wang, Xiaoye. 'The New Chinese Anti-Monopoly Law: A Survey of a Work in Progress'. *The Antitrust Bulletin* 54, no. 3 (2009): 579–619.

Wang, Xiaoye (ed.). *Issues Surrounding the Enforcement of the Anti-Monopoly Law* (Chinese version). Beijing: Social Sciences Academic Press, 2010.

Wang, Kui Hua. *Chinese Commercial Law*. South Melbourne: Oxford University Press, 2000.

Williams, Mark. *Competition Policy and Law in China, Hong Kong, and Taiwan*. Cambridge: Cambridge University Press, 2005.

Selected Bibliography

Wong, Stanley. 'Effectiveness of Technical Assistance in Capacity Building on Competition Law and Policy: The Case of China'. In *China's Anti-Monopoly Law: The First Five Years*, edited by Adrian Emch & David Stallibrass. Alphen aan den Rijn: Kluwer Law International, 2013.

Wu, Zhengguo. 'Perspectives on the Chinese Anti-Monopoly Law'. *Antitrust Law Journal* 75 (2008): 73–116.

Xun, Yang. & Jessica Su. 'Anti-Monopoly Suits Heat Up'. *China Law & Practice* 23, no. 8 (October 2009): 23–25.

Selected Bibliography

Made in the USA
Monee, IL
18 October 2026

66037589R10111